SHORT TAKES

D0012923

EDITED BY JUDITH KITCHEN AND MARY PAUMIER JONES

In Brief: Short Takes on the Personal

In Short: A Collection of Brief Creative Nonfiction

OTHER BOOKS BY JUDITH KITCHEN

ESSAYS

Only the Dance: Essays on Time and Memory

Distance and Direction

NOVEL

The House on Eccles Road

Short Takes

BRIEF ENCOUNTERS
WITH CONTEMPORARY
NONFICTION

EDITED BY JUDITH KITCHEN

W. W. NORTON & COMPANY
NEW YORK   LONDON

Copyright © 2005 by Judith Kitchen

For information about permission to reproduce selections from this book, write to
Permissions, W. W. Norton & Company, Inc., 500 Fifth Avenue, New York, NY 10110

Manufacturing by The Haddon Craftsmen, Inc.
Production manager: Anna Oler

Library of Congress Cataloging-in-Publication Data

Short takes : brief encounters with contemporary nonfiction /
edited by Judith Kitchen.— 1st ed.
p. cm.
ISBN 0-393-32600-4 (pbk.)
1. American essays—20th century. 2. Reportage literature, American.
I. Kitchen, Judith.
PS688.S46 2005
814'.5408—dc22

2005008220

W. W. Norton & Company, Inc., 500 Fifth Avenue, New York, N.Y. 10110
www.wwnorton.com

W. W. Norton & Company Ltd., Castle House, 75/76 Wells Street, London W1T 3QT

5 6 7 8 9 0

For
Anmanda, Simon
Robin, Benjamin, and Ian

I am grateful for help from Mary Paumier Jones, who again gave me the benefit of her prodigious reading and her astute responses. Thanks also to Lia Purpura for steering me in new directions. I am especially indebted to Carol Houck Smith, whose generous support for these anthologies has helped to define the term "shorts." As always, Stan. Finally, thanks to the writers who are gathered here.

CONTENTS

EDITOR'S INTRODUCTION

I n the years since *In Short* (1996) and *In Brief* (1999) were published, readers have come to expect and delight in the quick jab and deft parry of what we now simply call a short. In fact, the short has established itself as a kind of literary subspecies: one online journal—appropriately dubbed *Brevity*—dedicates itself entirely to pieces under a thousand words, and other literary journals—such as the beautifully produced *Water-Stone Review*—have begun to feature the short essay as an integral part of their menus. By dividing their longer pieces into many connected segments, contemporary writers have embraced the short unit as a means of reaching an audience. In the century of the New York minute and the Internet, the short has come into its own.

Short Takes extends this trend, collecting under one cover seventy-seven writers whose wide range of voices and styles invites the reader to savor the manifold ways today's writers of nonfiction look at our changing world. Most of these selections were created to be short: succinct, but not slight. They exhibit a recognizable length/depth ratio. Others have been carved from longer pieces, usually stand-alone segments that have been composed in a "mosaic" style, complete with their own sense of closure. As in the earlier volumes, I have garnered a variety of "forms"—from formal essays to journal entries to lyrics to the patchwork of memoir—that demonstrate the various ways we humans have of telling our stories. In making my selections, I've kept in mind the larger question of the role of "truth" in a nonfictional piece. Since writing is, of necessity, subjective, and memory is, by definition, selective, the "facts" of the essay must be evaluated in a wider context. In very different ways, the pieces by Gerald Stern and Mary Clearman Blew address this issue, and Anne McDuffie explores it openly as she reiterates her grandfather's version of events. Amy Tan shows us how one truth can alter another.

An even more complicated question arises: in this day of mix-and-match genre, of the nonfiction novel and the fabricated documentary, what makes a piece nonfiction? Stephen Dunn's two meditations were taken from a book of poems; Ron Carlson's humorous disclaimer comes from a book of fiction (though his piece was carefully printed on gray paper to differentiate it from the stories it refers to); the selections by Barbara Mallonee and Verlyn Klinkenborg first appeared as newspaper columns; and Luc Sante's "Unknown Soldier" was performed onstage (using forty-five voices). To further complicate matters, S. L. Wisenberg's imagined diary of Anne

Frank's sister might technically be called fiction—but not when we realize it serves as speculation in a memoir examining the lasting effects of the Holocaust. She builds her essay on the facts as we've all come to know them, and she reminds us periodically of what can never be known—and why.

Peggy Shumaker opens the book with the "we" of shared experience, while Albert Goldbarth closes it by noting the singular within the communal. Meanwhile, Sven Birkerts reminds us that essayists "accept that it is their lot to be solitary in the world." As readers, we probe that solitude. We look as much for *how* an author approaches a subject as we do for the subject itself. We participate by paying attention to the attention that is paid. This is nowhere more true than when we encounter the stilled moment of clarified perception that defines a lyric essay.

Each of these short pieces conveys the fundamental mark of an essay—the building of a process of thought through a singular contemplative voice—to show how we see the same world differently. Whether the piece is in first, second, or third person, active or passive voice, past or present tense, anecdotal or speculative, the reader senses the presence of the author—the "I" that perceives, records, shapes, and amplifies.

Short Takes takes the measure of our times. In the years since the two earlier collections, the events of September 11, 2001, have altered our perception of the world, and of ourselves. Paul Zimmer deals with this overtly at the outset while Naomi Shihab Nye alludes to it obliquely in her conclusion, but in some way all the essays reflect that change of mood and can be read against that backdrop. Ideas are reexamined and history is intensified. A sequence on war and its aftereffects feels inevitable. If these essays do not provide an answer, at least they phrase—and rephrase—the troubling questions facing the twenty-first century.

If water (in its myriad guises) provides the central imagery of this collection, then "confluence" is the operative word. With the fluidity of water, these pieces flow through and around each other. With uncanny serendipity, the essays cohere, speaking to each other in fascinating ways. John McPhee excerpts one representative fish from his long treatise on the American shad, and Sandra Swinburne follows with a mini-treatise on McPhee. M. J. Iuppa's "Daylight Savings Time" (with its illicit lost hour) conveys the same disjunction as Pico Iyer's jet lag. Reg Saner spends his morning looking hard at a coyote; Charles Bergman raises the philosophical issue of how animals look at us. Joe Mackall moves toward silence, while Stephen Kuusisto shows us how to listen with the exquisite concentration of the blind.

Short Takes has been arranged so that ideas, impressions, and attitudes overlap; they collide and circle each other, tightening the noose of interconnection. Like mirrors facing mirrors, certain concepts or images replicate themselves: museums, books, mythology, winter, trains, horses, wheat, voile, C-130s, Lascaux, the stars. A single phrase—"catch and release"—repeats itself in separate essays, as do the names of the colors abandoned by the Crayola company. Things connect, oppose, reflect, repeat, accumulate. Opposites attract. As with Sherman Alexie's Sacagawea, contradictions abound. In the end, they define a larger, inclusive whole.

"Themes" emerge: war, family, the endangered environment, urban living, parenthood, assimilation, time, weather, beauty—and that old standby, love, in its many and varied permutations. One motif that recurs frequently is that of the words we've imported from other languages. Thoreau is clearly the patron saint, and Bad French becomes the flavor of the day. Coupled with images of pioneers, the Fourth of July, apple pie, and more than one Chevy, this collection speaks to a self-conscious American identity.

When the essays are read in sequence, the nation emerges as a vast imaginative landscape, built on dream and adversity. If the reader takes a scattershot approach, dipping in at random, the same vision is likely to surface through chance juxtaposition of images. Peter Balakian's memory of his Armenian grandmother watching the Yankees, for instance, resonates with other essays on immigration and assimilation, but it also pairs with Joseph Epstein's meditation on baseball. To reinforce this observation, I challenged poet Marvin Bell to write a series of prose "echoes"—or jazz refrains—that take up several of the already established ideas and turn them into something new.

Finally, *Short Takes* is not so much about being brief (under two thousand words) as it is about its subtitle—discovering the nature of contemporary nonfiction and encountering some of the most exciting writers in present-day America. If

style makes the person, then this American persona is infi-
nitely diverse, invigoratingly complex, full of the inventive
surprise and judicious insight that add up to a powerful state-
ment about what is most on our minds in these early years of
the twenty-first century.

SHORT TAKES

PEGGY SHUMAKER

MOVING WATER, TUCSON

Thunderclouds gathered every afternoon during the monsoons. Warm rain felt good on faces lifted to lick water from the sky. We played outside, having sense enough to go out and revel in the rain. We savored the first cool hours since summer hit.

The arroyo behind our house trickled with moving water. Kids gathered to see what it might bring. Tumbleweed, spears of ocotillo, creosote, a doll's arm, some kid's fort. Broken bottles, a red sweater. Whatever was nailed down, torn loose.

We stood on edges of sand, waiting for brown walls of water. We could hear it, massive water, not far off. The whole desert might come apart at once, might send horny toads and Gila monsters swirling, wet nightmares clawing both banks of the worst they could imagine and then some.

Under sheet lightning cracking the sky, somebody's teenage

brother decided to ride the flash flood. He stood on wood in the bottom of the ditch, straddling the puny stream. "Get out, it's coming," kids yelled. "GET OUT," we yelled. The kid bent his knees, held out his arms.

Land turned liquid, that fast, water yanked our feet, stole our thongs, pulled in the edges of the arroyo, dragged whole trees, root wads and all, along, battering rams thrust down-stream, anything you left there gone, anything you meant to go back and get history, water so high you couldn't touch bot-tom, water so fast you couldn't get out of it, water so huge the earth couldn't take it, water . . . We couldn't step back. We had to be there, to see for ourselves. Water in a place where water's always holy. Water remaking the world.

That kid on plywood, that kid waiting for the flood. He stood and the water lifted him. He stood, his eyes not seeing us. For a moment, we all wanted to be him, to be part of some-thing so wet, so fast, so powerful, so much bigger than our-selves. That kid rode the flash flood inside us, the flash flood outside us. Artist unglued on a scrap of glued wood. For a few drenched seconds, he rode. The water took him, faster than you can believe. He kept his head up. Water you couldn't see through, water half dirt, water whirling hard. Heavy rain weighed down our clothes. We stepped closer to the crumbling shore, saw him downstream smash against the footbridge at the end of the block. Water held him there, rushing on.

LUCIA PERILLO

BRIEF HISTORY OF MY THUMB

I remember how it felt to get into the car. This was the part I liked best, the part when I was a little afraid.

To the driver—who was usually a man alone—my eyes gave just a flicker. Sometimes a woman would stop and I knew what was coming: a lecture about the risk. She was trying to save me, and who knows, she may have. The next car coming along might have belonged to the psychopath who would have killed me long ago.

In the beginning, I climbed in with my high school friends—into the cars' interiors, dark and sweaty, like caves. We girls, and it was always girls, let ourselves be borne to strange towns where we walked around for a while, never too long, then came back home. Just two miles north lay a tangle of freeways and a bridge over the wide spot in the river. But I never traveled across it—that would be like going to a country where the people spoke another language I had been either too stupid or lazy to learn.

What I mean is: to go there would have made me feel guilty. Also, the point was not to go anywhere.

Then what *was* the point? The explanation I delegate to Heraclitus, of whose writing only fragments remain. His aphorisms ponder the nature of reality as flux:

> *The rule that makes*
> *its subject weary*
> *is a sentence*
> *of hard labor.*
>
> *For this reason,*
> *change gives rest.*

Heraclitus is the Greek philosopher who famously said that you can't step into the same river twice. Or more precisely he said that just as the river he stepped into "is not the same, and is, so I am as I am not." A teenager likewise inhabits two states, though I would have scorned anyone who identified me as child and not adult. I thought of my life as analogous to fire, which also obsessed Heraclitus. When I stood by the road, its ditch-wind fed me and made me rise.

Later I moved not too far away from home, but to Quebec, where people did speak a different language. I chose a foreign country to give my acquiescing to this conventional duty— going to college—a varnish of exoticness and escape. I wanted to escape my house where the televisions blared and people screamed. The cars, by contrast, were calm places where I was almost always free to smoke cigarettes.

In Montreal, it seemed everyone smoked and everyone hitchhiked, because of a bus strike that went on for weeks. Beautiful women stood alone in the slush at the side of the road and valiantly stuck out their thumbs. Goodwill pervaded the cold air as if our clouds of frozen breath had all melded into one. The strike's ending made me sad, when the sexy French women in their high-heeled boots suddenly disappeared back to whatever swanky place they'd come from.

In my sophomore year I transferred to the agricultural college, whose buildings squatted in a wind-scoured pasture between two freeways, thirty miles from downtown. To go in and out of the city, I took quivering concrete ramps and roads with flying buttresses. I cut my hair and wore a watch cap and down jacket, so that I looked like a husky boy. Dimly I was aware that I was acting out an archetype from folksongs and legends: that of the wife who goes to war or the pirate whose bound breasts are discovered after his death. When I stood by myself on the elevated highways that roared above the factories, the gusts of semis nearly blew me away.

But in my youth I rode inside a bubble of luck: the worst thing that ever happened was that a man pulled out his penis. I started making up rules: number one was to never look at the driver. He could have his penis out until the cows came home and I would not know, I would not see, and so I cannot tell you now how many times it happened.

Rule number two was not to get into cars that had more than one man in them, because once I rode squashed in a

car full of guys when the one who had his arm across my
shoulder let his hand droop until it touched the side of my
breast. Just the side, just through my shirt. He was daring me
to scream.

Several times while hitchhiking I found myself inappropri-
ately dressed, as in a type of anxiety dream. Somehow my
bra disappeared in the car with the boys, and the shirt's
crinkly green cloth, I realized, had shrunk a bit and puckered
around each button to reveal a glimpse of skin. Early on, I'd
decided that it was a bad idea to call attention to the trans-
gressions of the men, because then they might decide to hurt
you. With these Quebecois guys, half boys, half men, I
announced they'd missed their turn and they believed me,
and let me off, safe, in a muddy strip between the speeding
cars and the concrete barricade.

When I graduated from college I went to live briefly on a
farm in Vermont that was run by women, where one of my
housemates made her living by crocheting vests and taking
them to craft fairs around the country. Lucy did not own a
car; few of the women on the farm had enough money or
would have wanted a machine that was such an ecological
scourge. So she sent her vests by mail and hitchhiked after
them. When I asked whether she was afraid of being raped,
she answered that she had been, recently, and then of course
I wanted to know why she still hitched.

"What I can't bear to give up is the feeling," she said. "Just
me and my thumb all alone on the road." I said I knew exactly
what she was talking about. The immense spaces inside of
which the hitcher becomes tiny. And the sudden diminish-

ment is thrilling: *whoosh*. Small becomes big, and there you are, standing alone with Heraclitus again.

(Yet now I see how clueless I was. Compared to her, I knew nothing, and she resisted my attempts that summer to pry from her the horrid scene.)

These stories come from the late seventies and early eighties, and came to an end when I bought a truck. By then the sentiment of the highway was changing anyway, so that no one of legitimate sanity, it seemed, picked up hitchhikers anymore. For a while I felt obligated to make the reciprocal gesture, until more than one loser scared me when I realized he had nowhere to go and wanted to attach himself to my journey. Then I had to scramble for an excuse to kick him out of my truck.

But some of the ones I've blown by still haunt me, like the Indian woman on crutches way out in the desert. She's wearing a bandanna and she's crying. I think about turning around sometimes, but now it's twenty years too late.

And some of the ones I picked up still haunt me too, like the man-boy in Colorado who was traveling to an uncle who had promised him a job. He did not know exactly where he was headed, and so I tossed him the Rand McNally road atlas. He flipped and flipped, from one cover to the other, until I realized that he couldn't alphabetize, could not read the word "Colorado" where it was printed in the corner of the page. He had the name of the town written on a scrap of paper but could not pronounce the words. "Booey veh . . . " he muttered before finally handing me the scrap, on which I decoded *Buena Vista* spelled in the strange hieroglyphics of someone who hadn't mastered the alphabet.

Now, in the new millennium, we drive and make phone calls at the same time, and the car operates in sympathy with the clock. This is no country for backpacked young women. The road would tell them: *You don't know what kind of river you're stepping into, I may never be the same, but that doesn't mean that I am good.*

I trade stories often enough with women my age, about our lives as hitchers, to know it is not an uncommon history, though it's not a word we use anymore—*hitch*—except in regards to knots. We've experienced middle-aged re-entry and hunker now inside the nose cone that has returned safely (maybe), unraped (no—the other woman often has her rape story to tell, if she will tell it), bobbing in the sea. Heraclitus had nothing good to say about the state of being wet. Better to be a dry thing, he thought, ready to burst into flames.

But some stories can't help being soggy, as on one dusk-time in New Hampshire, when I find myself in my man-boy costume. Lugging skis and a pack, I have just come from Tuckerman's Ravine, a bowl whose walls are famously steep, and I am feeling like an epic hero for having skied down them alone. This time, instead of mysteriously ending up half clothed, I've just as mysteriously ended up on the road with too much stuff for anyone's car. My thumb brings no luck as the darkness keeps thickening.

Finally a semi stops—its headlights bore a tunnel through the swirling globs of wet snow as I climb into its cab. The driver reacts with surprise when he realizes I am a girl, and for a while I try to talk to him in my bad French, though in no time my drivel puts me to sleep. I must have dozed a long time—it is another of those mysteries, how we crossed the border—and I wake slumped against him as if we were lovers. My drool is cold and wets his sleeve, though I can tell he is touched by my trusting him, in the absence of words, to bear me safely through the storm.

My translations come from Brooks Haxton's *Fragments: The Collected Wisdom of Heraclitus,* published by Viking in 2001.

STEPHEN KUUSISTO

NIGHT SONG

My earliest memory of hearing comes from 1958. I'm standing on a dock in Helsinki, Finland. My father holds my hand. It's March and the harbor is dotted with ice. My blindness allows me to see colors and torn geometries. Shards of ice drift before us and my father tells me they look like continents. "There's Australia," he says. "There's Hawaii." I see no distinction between sky and ice. I see only endless plains of gray Baltic light. When a person appears before me he or she resembles nothing more than the black trunk of a tree.

A troupe of women emerges from the mist. They are the walking trees of Dunsinane, black and green. These are the old women of the neighborhood unfurling their carpets on the shore of the frozen sea.

Lordy! Lordy! Then they sing!

The tree women sing and beat carpets in the Baltic wind. My father tells me to listen.

"These are the old songs," he says.

The women croak, chant, breathe and weep.

These women are forest people. Arctic people. They have survived starvation, civil war and then another war, the "Winter War" with the Russians.

They hang their carpets on tall racks that stand along the seashore and beat them with wooden bats.

They sing over and over a song of night. The song unwinds from a spool. I remember its terrible darkness. They were together singing a song that rose from a place deeper than dreams. Even a boy knows what this is.

This is not only my earliest memory of sound—it's also my earliest memory. As I near fifty I realize that sound has been exceptionally important in my blind life. I have also come to realize that I've largely ignored this fact. Although I have lived by listening, I've been inattentive about the role of chance sound in my life.

My parents and I lived in the south harbor of Helsinki, just a short walk from the open-air market where fish peddlers and butchers had their stalls. We walked across the cobbled square and I'd tilt my head in the harbor light and listen to the gulls and ravens. The gulls sounded like mewing cats and the ravens sounded like hinges in need of oil. I walked about listening to the polyphony of hungry birds.

The Russian Orthodox Church had mysterious bells.

And winter wouldn't give up. We traveled into the country and I heard the reindeer bells. Old farm. Runners of a sleigh crossing ice . . . What else?

The woman who sold flowers, singing just for me . . . And her little daughter who played a wooden recorder . . .

Wind poured into the city through the masts of sailboats.

There's an old man who sells potatoes from a dory in the harbor. His voice is like sand. He talks to me every day.

Potatoes from the earth, potatoes from the cellar! You can still taste the summer! You can still taste the summer!

Later I would think of his voice when reading of trolls under bridges.

What else?

Sound of knife blades in the tinsmith's stall . . .

The rumble of streetcars . . .

The clacking of a loom . . . My mother weaving a rug . . .

The sound of my father's typing late in the night.

Sound of a wooden top that whistles like a teakettle as it spins . . . my first toy . . .

A winter tree tapping at the window . . .

My father is a visiting professor at the University of Helsinki and he has time to walk with me and introduce me to the chance music of the city.

One day he takes me to the house of a glassblower. This is my first experience of synesthesia: the strange suffusion of one sense with another . . . The glassblower takes his long-stemmed pipe out of the flames. I can barely make out the red halo of the fire. The glassblower explains how he pushes breath into the molten glass and then I hear him inhale. As he leans into his art there comes a spirited cry from a cuckoo clock on the far wall. Delicacy and irreverence have been forever linked in my mind from that very moment.

On the way home we ride the tram and I listen to the wintry talk of the passengers. I love the sound of Finnish, especially the oddly whispered Finnish of strangers sitting side by side on the tram. The Finns inhale as they speak, a lovely sotto voce confirmation that two minds are in solemn agreement. Whispers and inhalations as twilight covers the city. I talk to the empty seat beside me and speak Finnish to an imaginary friend who I name Matti. I hold my breath and listen to the rocking of the tram. I exhale and speak in a flurry to my little doppelgänger. My father is lost in his newspaper. I'm lost on the heart's road of whispered confidences.

The entire world is green or white. Blindness is veil after veil of forest colors. But what a thrill it is to be a sightless child in a city of sounds.

Our apartment is in the south harbor. My mother is weaving a carpet and listening to the radio. She tells us that the Russian navy is coming, that it's just been announced. And then we hear the booming of the guns from the archipelago of islands that stretches out into the Baltic. The Soviet navy is conducting war games and we stand on our balcony and listen to the guns of the destroyers. A neighbor woman leaning from her balcony tells us this is the sound that made her hair turn white. I worry for days that we will all have white hair. I ask my parents all kinds of questions about growing old. Why

do the Russians want to make people old? I put such great
faith in sound: sound is this tree and that grass; this man; this
dimension of light and shade. Meanwhile the evening wind
arrives and the Russian navy goes away.

April turns to May and the park spins itself into green
smoke; leaves in the trees again; and an old man plays his
accordion in a grove of birches. A little girl whose name I can
no longer recall teaches me to waltz. I'm sure that her parents
have told her I'm blind. She must have been around eight
years old. She sways me back and forth in the light of the
birches. The old man plays slowly and I feel something of the
Zen-body: wherever I am I am there. By the age of four I've
found the intricacies of listening are inexhaustible.

In late 1959 we fly home to the United States. I love the
groan and rumble of the plane's propellers. What a fabulous
sound they make! I rest my head against the cabin wall and
feel the vibration rattle through my bones. I breathe and hum
and let the engines push my own little song. I imitate the Kale-
vala cadences and sorrows of the Finnish carpet ladies and
groan in unison with the straining metal of the airplane.

A blind kid rarely sleeps. Small blind people hear a hundred
sounds and learn early to make analogies.

I hear the trees that surround our New Hampshire house.
A spruce sways in the wind and so I think a door is opening,
a door with rusted hinges and locks.

At sunup while my parents sleep I dress quickly and slip
from the house. I walk through a meadow, blindly following

patterns of light and shade until I reach the university's horse barn. Somewhere in all this cool emptiness a horse is breathing. He sounds like water going down a drain.

I take one step forward into a pyramid of fragrances.

What a thing! To be a young boy smelling hay and leather and turds!

What a thing!

And the horse gurgles like water in the back of a boat.

Mice scurry like beaded curtains disturbed by a hand.

I stand in this magical nowhere and listen to the full range of sounds in a barn.

I am a blind child approaching a horse!

Behind me a cat mews.

Who would guess that horses sometimes hold their breath?

The horse must be eyeing me from his corner.

Now two cats are talking.

Wind pushes forcefully at the high roof.

Somewhere up high a timber creaks.

My horse is still holding his breath.

When will he breathe again?

Come on, boy!

Breathe for me!

Where are you?

I hear him rubbing his flank against a wall.

And now he breathes again with a great deflation!

He sounds like a fat balloon venting in swift circles.

And now I imitate him with my arm pressed to my lips.

I make great flatulent noises by pressing my lips to my forearm.

How do you like that, horse?

He snorts.

I notice the ringing of silence. An insect travels between our bursts of forced air.

Sunlight heats my face because I'm standing in a long sunbeam.

I am in the luminous whereabouts of horse! I am a very small boy and I have wandered about a mile from home. Although I can see colors and shapes in sunlight, in the barn I am completely blind.

But I have made up my mind to touch this horse.

Judging by his breathing, his slow release of air, that sound of a concertina, judging by this, I am nearly beside him. And so I reach out and there is the great wet fruit of his nose, the velvet bone of his enormous face. And we stand there together for a little while, all alive and all alone.

And so at night when I can't sleep I think of this horse. I think of his glory—his fat sound. I think of how he pinches the air around him with his breathing. The house and the trees move in the night wind. The horse is dry wood talking. He's all nerves and nostrils. He tightens and then unwinds like a clock. He groans like the Finnish women who stand beside the ocean waving their sticks. Strophe and antistrophe. Early. I've crossed a threshold. Hearing. Insomnia. Walking the uncertain space that opens before me. Step. Rhythm. Pulse beat. Night songs. Precision.

REBECCA McCLANAHAN

SIGNS AND WONDERS

Artillery sounds wake me: car alarms screeching, honking, beeping—you know the drill—and a jack-hammer breaking open the sidewalk outside our window. No, not our window, I remind myself. The window of the apartment we've been subletting these past four years—and the lease is almost up again. Another two years? My husband's leaving it up to me. He could live anywhere, he's that kind of guy. Easy, adaptable, like the ducks in the park. Things just roll right off his back.

When we first moved to the city, we couldn't believe how cheap the flowers were. "What a city," we said. "We can buy flowers every week, fill the apartment with them, the bath-tub. What a city!" Then we went to the grocery store, and when I saw the prices I started to cry. "How can we possibly afford . . . we'll have to give up . . . Oh my God," I shrieked, "what will we eat?"

"We'll just have to eat flowers," he said.

Last week, I would have signed a hundred-year lease. After all, this *is* the best city in the world, and I was just coming off one of my New York highs, the kind that hits when you least expect it and suddenly it's like first love again, first lust, and you wonder how you could possibly live anywhere else. Then a steam pipe bursts, the couple in the apartment above you straps their steel-toed boots back on, you step in a puddle of urine on the subway platform and some guy with three rings in his nose calls you Bitch and spits on you because—who knows?—you look like his second-grade teacher, or some president's wife, or his mother, and you think, *Live another two years in this jackhammering, siren-screaming, piss-puddling city? In someone else's apartment—because who can afford their own? Someone else's bed, plates, forks, spoons?*

Maybe it's the wrong day to decide. Maybe I need some air. Maybe I need a sign. So I go where I always go when I need a sign—the park, and oh look, a day so beautiful you'd gladly pay the universe if it were charging. The leaves on the gink-gos are falling as I speak, gold coins upon gold coins. And there in the pond are my geese, my ducks, how I admire them. Look, one is passing up bread crumbs to catch a blossom. He's eating flowers.

Along the promenade are the skaters in their T-shirts: *Kickimus Maximus Assimus. Are you talking to* me? *Fun loving criminal.* One guy's skating backwards, a small compact black man so graceful he doesn't need skates, his hip joints are on ball bearings, rolling in one smooth movement. But I know it's harder than it looks, isn't everything? Even for the ducks. If you peek just beneath the surface of the water, you can see their little paddle-wheel feet working, churning. It breaks your heart: little New York ducks have to keep moving all the time.

I stop at a bench beside a ragged guy in a black hat. His shopping cart is plastered with handmade signs. New York is a city of signs: Curb your dog. Curb your dogma. Love your neighbor, your neighbor's dog. His signs are bright red painted on cardboard: *Society of Jesus Christ. Society of Disabled Artists. Call me Ray.*

"So, Ray," I say, "you're an artist?"

He rummages in his cart and pulls out a painting of a bonfire, flames breaking into bloom.

I ask if he's ever seen a flame like that, or is it imagination.

"I like to think about Moses," he says. "I was seeing the burning bush."

My Bible knowledge is rusty, but I'm hungry for a sign. "God spoke to him in the fire, right?"

"That's right."

"In words?" I ask.

"*Through* him. Spirit."

I tell him I used to be in a gospel choir, but I was only a lowly backup singer.

"Never call yourself lowly," he says.

Closer now, I can see his face beneath the hat: almost handsome. But the smell is ripe, and I won't be staying. Anyway, it's his bench; I'm just subletting. A lowly subletter, I think for an instant, then stop myself. But it *is* his bench and I should respect that. I don't like it when people come to my gazebo. It took me months to find it, the most beautiful place in the park. There's even a place to fish. I can lean my back against the wooden slats, put my feet up, watch the geese form their predictable patterns. A limited vocabulary can be a good thing: that V, I mean. It's a comfort knowing you can always count on the geese. They won't slip into some ragged U or split into individual I's. It's good to have something to count on, like the gondola that glides through about this time of day, sliding under the bow bridge, the gondolier always singing badly *O sole mio*, which is the perfect song for New York, right? *O sole mio*, oh my sun, my ducks, my forks, oh my anything. Crazy, isn't it? When so much of New York is about we: *O sole wio*.

Still, it's a beautiful spot, my gazebo, and I'd tell you where it is, but what if word got out? A few weeks ago, on my birthday, no less, I couldn't even get a seat. It hadn't been a good week, the odometer of my life was clicking too fast, too many zeros stacking up. Birthdays can do that to you, especially in the city. Especially when you do what we did—wait until middle age to move here. "Like, isn't that backwards?" my niece had said. "I mean, like, don't most people go to New York when they're young?"

So I really needed my gazebo that day, but some homeless guy was stretched out the whole length of it, beside a grocery cart with a handmade sign sticking out of the top: *I'm at the peak of my life.* I wondered if the sign was meant for me, if it was trying to tell me something. Because the homeless guy seemed fine with his life, more than fine, actually, lying there in my gazebo, one hand on top of the blanket, the other beneath, and, well, how do I put this delicately? Pleasuring himself. While looking directly into my eyes. Later, walking home, I had to laugh. Maybe at my age I should take it as a compliment, that I could inspire such . . . peaks. How much longer do I have on that meter? A few more clicks, and I'll look like those two ancient women over there, sharing a bag of peanuts like an old married couple.

Ah, the partners we make, the families we create in this city of strangers. Like that big guy on Ninth Avenue—big as a truck, I know you've seen him, he rides that little bike everywhere, with the little basket on the front. In it is one of those Cabbage Patch dolls that were popular a decade or so ago. He dresses her for the weather, secures her in with a seat belt, places a helmet on her head. Such care. And yesterday, beside the carousel, a teenage boy was strapped into a wheelchair, his head lolling, large brown eyes rolling up to the sky, his mouth opening, like a bird's, on a spoon lifted by a large, dark Hispanic woman. Caretakers, they call these women, or caregivers: give, take. You see them all over the city. The two were facing each other—he in his wheelchair, she on the green bench, their knees touching. Steam was rising from the thermos of soup. First she dipped the spoon in the thermos, blowing on it to cool it. Then she put it to her mouth and tested to be sure the soup was safe, that it wouldn't burn him.

When you see things like that you just want to break into lullaby. Sing someone to sleep in this town that never sleeps. Adopt an artist, a duck, a whole Cabbage Patch family. Look,

here's a family now, spilling out of my gazebo, with their fishing poles, their buckets and bait, their beautiful children—
black eyes, black hair, dimpled hands—the kind of children
you want to touch but you can't of course, especially in New
York. The little boy is wrestling a bright red carp the color of
the fire in Ray's painting, and now his sister is catching the
carp in a net. Don't they know it's against the rules posted all
over the park? *Catch and release.* Yes, that's it. Catch and
release. Look but don't touch. Enjoy for the moment, then let
it go—the fiery carp, the brilliant day, the black-eyed children
with the dimpled hands, the coins on the ginkgo trees swirling
down, down. Our lives are sublets anyway, and too quickly
gone at that. And what better place to live out our leases.
Curb your dog, your dogma, love your neighbor, your neighbor's dog. We're at the peak of our lives. *O sole wio.* Catch
and release.

RICHARD RODRIGUEZ

FROM "MEXICO'S CHILDREN"

When I was a boy it was still possible for Mexican farmworkers in California to commute between the past and the future.

The past returned every October. The white sky clarified to blue and fog opened white fissures in the landscape.

After the tomatoes and the melons and the grapes had been picked, it was time for Mexicans to load up their cars and head back into Mexico for the winter.

The schoolteacher said aloud to my mother what a shame it was the Mexicans did that—took their children out of school.

Like wandering Jews, Mexicans had no true home but the tabernacle of memory.

The schoolteacher was scandalized by what she took as the Mexicans' disregard of their children's future. The children failed their tests. They made no friends. What did it matter? Come November, they would be gone to some bright world that smelled like the cafeteria on Thursdays—Bean Days. Next spring they would be enrolled in some other school, in some other Valley town.

The schoolroom myth of America described an ocean— immigrants leaving behind several time zones and all the names for things.

Mexican-American memory described proximity. There are large Mexican-American populations in Seattle and Chicago and Kansas City, but the majority of Mexican Americans live, where most have always lived, in the Southwestern United States, one or two hours from Mexico, which is within the possibility of recourse to Mexico or within the sound of her voice.

My father knew men in Sacramento who had walked up from Mexico.

There is a confluence of earth. The cut of the land or its fold, the bleaching sky, the swath of the wind, the length of shadows—all these suggested Mexico. Mitigated was the sense of dislocation otherwise familiar to immigrant experience.

By November the fog would thicken, the roads would be dangerous. Better to be off by late October. Families in old trucks and cars headed south down two-land highways, past browning fields. Rolls of toilet paper streaming from rolled-down windows. After submitting themselves to the vegetable cycle of California for a season, these Mexicans were free. They were Mexicans! And what better thing to be?

HAIIII-EEE. HAI. HAI. HAI.

There is confluence of history.

Cities, rivers, mountains retain Spanish names. California was once Mexico.

The fog closes in, condenses, and drips day and night from the bare limbs of trees. And my mother looks out the kitchen window and cannot see the neighbor's house.

Amnesia fixes the American regard of the past. I remember a graduate student at Columbia University during the Vietnam years; she might have been an ingenue out of Henry James. "After Vietnam, I'll never again believe that America is the good and pure country I once thought it to be," the young woman said.

Whereas Mexican Americans have paid a price for the clarity of their past.

Consider my father: when he decided to apply for American citizenship, my father told no one, none of his friends, those men with whom he had come to this country looking for work. American citizenship would have seemed a betrayal of Mexico, a sin against memory. One afternoon, like a man with something to hide, my father slipped away. He went downtown to the Federal Building in Sacramento and disappeared into America.

MARY CLEARMAN BLEW

TENINO

W est of the spectacular scenery of the Cascade Mountains, but still a long way from the ocean, inland Washington State spreads into serene meadows in the shelter of low hills. Subdivisions sprawling down from Olympia have taken over many of these meadows, and auto repair shops and fertilizer dealerships in brightly colored aluminum siding are open for business along the two-lane highway that angles northeast from Interstate 5, and yet there are moments when the June sunlight on ripening grass, the cattle sleeping amid the white faces of daisies, and the soft shape of firs along the surrounding hills suggest to me that this is a road my aunt may have driven toward a new teaching job in 1942.

In her later years my aunt had a habit of beginning sentences with, "When I lived in Tenino—" and, in part because

I cannot remember how she ended those sentences, I have turned off I-5 this morning to follow this highway through pastures and meadows toward a town where I have never been. All roads lead somewhere, but I am beginning to wonder if this one really leads to Tenino. I have seen no markers since I turned off the interstate, and when I pass a roadside grocery offering beer and ice and propane, I tell myself that I should have stopped and asked. But my own lifetime habit has been to press on, around just one more bend in the road, over one more hill to see what lies beyond. It is a habit which has too often led me miles in the wrong direction.

From her early twenties until she was eighty, my aunt kept a record of her life in leatherbound five-year diaries, writing just two or three sentences a day on pages that allowed her to glance back at what she had written the years before, and ending only when senile dementia destroyed her ability to hold a thought. After her death I began reading her diaries, trying to learn something about my own life from the way she had lived hers. I had the idea of writing a book based on her entries during World War II, which had been a time of great transition for her, and I got as far as a first draft. But the book has resisted me, as though it does not want to be written, and now I'm driving miles out of my way to Tenino, Washington, where my aunt taught school during most of the war, to get a sense of the place and what it may reveal.

Much of what I know about Tenino comes from the photograph of its main street, probably taken in the late 1930s, on a postcard that my aunt kept. According to my road atlas, the present population of the town is about 1,300, and I sus-

pect that during World War II its population was around
1,000. Perhaps it was more of a market center then than now,
when its residents can take I-5 to shop in Olympia or even
Seattle in a fraction of the time it would have taken in those
days of bumpy roads and gas rationing.

*Went to Olympia to shop for birthdays. Swore it is the last
time for me*, writes my aunt in November of 1944. *The bus
was crowded. I had to stand both ways.*

In the postcard photograph, Tenino's main street looks self-
contained and unhurried. Only the faint shadow of firs at the
far end of the street reveals that this is the Pacific Northwest
and not any small farm town, anywhere, with its unshaded
pavement and sidewalks and overhead power lines and single
streetlight. Anything you really needed you could find along
these two or three business blocks of single-story buildings of
brick facades over dressed sandstone. A Model A truck is
parked beside the Tenino Feed Store, a few more cars beside
Puget Sound Power & Light and the barbershop and the drugstore and Campbell & Campbell, which offers dry goods,
shoes, and hardware. There's a fire hydrant on the corner,
and a fellow in a dark suit, white shirt and tie (no hat, so he's
probably just stepped out of his office for a breath of air, or
perhaps to watch the photographer) leaning on the pillar outside the real estate office. Farther down the street I can make
out a Café sign, but not whether it's the Jiffy, where my aunt
often ate dinner or met friends.

She mentions the war very little in her diaries, however,
which is one of the reasons why I've had difficulty writing the
book I originally envisioned. After an initial outburst—*I say*

little about the war. It shadows every day—she seems concerned mainly with scarcities or inconveniences. *Out of cigarettes. Damn it. Ordered some Sat. but they never got in.* Or, *Was able to get a box of marshmallows, the first in a year, thot they would make a nice treat for the Bluebirds.* She is saddened by the combat death of a local boy—*Dix Moser was killed. I feel so sorry for his mother*—and she occasionally notes a really dramatic event: on the road home to Montana with one of her sisters on June 6, 1944, she writes, *D-Day—invasion—we got in on the middle of a broadcast,* but then adds, *Had a fairly good day. Made Cheney. Paid $3 for a cabin.*

For her in 1943 and 1944, the war just is. It goes on and on, it sometimes seems as though it never will be over, but meanwhile she goes about her life, teaching and gossiping and shopping for treats for her bluebird troop and dealing with her own small crises. Reading her diaries, I feel as though I'm living within a memory like my own, which after all occupies no space, but lives in its small realm of bone and brain and worries, not about some plotted "past" which somehow exists "behind" it, but about the frayed edges of a dimensionless map whose markings of roads and rivers and events are overlaid, like a series of transparencies, upon the shifting present.

At this moment the highway ahead suddenly looks more promising; from the 35 mph sign, I must be nearing a town, and yes, there's another sign, I'm entering Tenino, and next to that sign, the Lions Club emblem, and I remember fleetingly my aunt's notation—*The Lions Club gave a dinner & reception for the teachers. It was the nicest reception I was ever at*—and I have time to wonder if the Lions still hold their

receptions for the local teachers every fall, and then the highway slows into a street which bends and suddenly I'm looking down the main street of Tenino, the same main street in
the postcard photograph that I've studied for so long, and I
catch my breath, because it's like driving through a veil into
the past.

Of course the street is not the same. The businesses have
changed. There's a café, but it's not the Jiffy, and there's an
espresso bar, and a couple of antique shops, and a quilting
shop, all very contemporary. What is unchanged is the street
itself, the sunny pavement and the sandstone buildings just as
they were, and yes, carved into one long facade is Campbell
& Campbell, the name of the department store, long closed,
but where, fifty years ago, my aunt mentioned in her diary
that sheets could be had on sale for $2.50.

I should park my car and walk up and down this street, taking my time; but time is what I don't have, I'm due in Portland,
Oregon, this afternoon, and I still have to locate the Tenino
branch of the Timberland Regional Library and look through
what they've got of local history, and so I drive around the corner past the old sandstone city hall and wait for a crocodile of
preschoolers between two teachers to cross the street, spot the
library immediately, and turn into the parking lot.

Through these modern glass doors is no haunted past, but
lots of ordinary light falling through enormous windows on
the clean surfaces of pale tables and chairs, the circulation,
and the tidy freestanding shelves of plastic-jacketed fiction
and nonfiction. The helpful woman at the circulation desk
knows just where to find the material I need; she pulls out a

slim paperback local history written in the 1970s, together with a few pamphlets and a couple of yearbooks, and I thank her and settle with my notepad at one of the tables.

The town of Tenino began as an accidental outcome of a dispute in the state capitol over the placement of a railroad line. A rail spur ran out to the sandstone quarry—and yes, of course there would be a quarry, all those sandstone buildings on the main street that I'd noted in the postcard photograph, and my aunt's diary notation for September 19, 1943—*Dorothy [and I] went to the quarry & picked blackberries. It's a good swimming hole*—the quarry dates from 1888 and supplied much of the building materials not only for Tenino but for the state capitol. Quarrying operations ceased in 1926, and a natural spring eventually filled the old pit, making it a natural swimming pool. *Dorothy & I went swimming [again] in the old quarry 90 ft. deep*, my aunt records on September 24, 1943, and adds, *So hot this afternoon.*

I come across more trivia as I read. From March 23 to April 2, 1944, the Tenino schools were closed to help stop a scarlet fever epidemic.

March 21, 1944: Nurse was out late tonight—they may close school for 2 weeks—how I hope—what a vacation. I could get caught up with everything.

March 23, 1944: Hot dog! School out till April 3. Ten whole days of vacation. Isn't it wonderful.

Trivia is what has caused problems for me with the book I've been writing. Who cares, I have asked myself, about a stone quarry used as a swimming hole in southwest Washington State, or about a scarlet fever epidemic in 1944 that a young schoolteacher welcomed so fervently because it gave her a ten-day vacation from classes. And yet, when I look up from the book of local history I've been reading and see the room around me filled with light, the preschoolers in their corner listening to their story being read aloud, I feel a curious elation, as though I've discovered details that matter. For just this moment, in this spinning light, I feel buoyant enough to float.

Is this sensation a testament to the power of close reading, or is it a testament to the habit of writing, however mundane, that not only connects the dots of local history but transcends history? It seems to me that, if only for the length of a sentence, I have been freed from the inexorability of past tense. I can open one of my aunt's diaries at any page and experience her simultaneity of past and present; and in a kind of dramatic irony, I often can draw upon my memory and research to foretell her future. Each of us, even the preschoolers, live in the present and contain the past, and we cannot describe the future until it, too, becomes the past. All else is illusory, no matter how hard I try to see around the next bend in the road or over the next hill. Small wonder, then, that I have had trouble writing this book when what has always mattered most to me has been the precious trivia.

MARK SPRAGG

IN WYOMING

FROM "WIND"

Tis place is violent, and it is raw. Wyoming is not a land that lends itself to nakedness, or leniency. There is an edge here, living is accomplished on that edge. Most birds migrate. Hibernation is viewed as necessary, not stolid. The crippled, old, the inattentive perish. And there is the wind.

The wind blows through most every day unchoreographed with the spontaneous inelegance of a brawl. There are tracts where the currents draw so relentlessly that the trees that surround a home, or line an irrigation ditch, all lean east, grown permanently east, as though mere columns of submissive filings bowed toward some fickle pole. Little is decorative. There are few orchards. Fruit enters by interstate, truck-ripened, not tree-ripened. Wyoming boasts coal, oil, gas, uranium, widely scattered herds of sheep and cattle, and once,

several million bison. The winds have worked the bison skeletons pink, white, finally to dust. The carboniferous forests
rose up and fell and moldered under the winds, layer upon
layer, pressed finally into coal. The winds predate the coal.
The winds wail a hymn of transience.

On the windward sides of homes, trees are planted in a
descending weave of cottonwood, spruce, Russian olive, finished with something thorny, stiff, and fast-growing—a hem of
caragana: a windbreak; utilitarian first, ornamental by accident. Shade is a random luxury. There is nearly always at least
a breeze. Like death and taxes, it can be counted on. Almost
one hundred thousand square miles and a half million residents; there aren't that many homes. Towns grip the banks of
watercourses, tenaciously. Ghost towns list, finally tumbling to
the east. Gone the way of the buffalo bones. To dust.

There are precious few songbirds. Raptors ride the
updrafts. The hares, voles, mice, skunks, squirrels, rats,
shrews, and rabbits exist squinting into the sun and wind, their
eyes water, their hearts spike in terror when swept by the
inevitable shadow of predators. The meadowlark is the state's
bird, but I think of them as hors d'oeuvres, their song a dinner bell. Eagle, falcon, hawk, owl live here year-round. The true
residents. The natives. The gourmands. Their land-bound relatives work the middle ground. Lynx, lion, fox circle the table.
Coyotes make their living where they can: as gypsies do.

Much of the landscape is classified as subarctic steppe. In
Laramie a winter's evening entertainment consists of watching the gauges on the local weather channel. Thirty-below-
zero, sixty-mile-an-hour winds, are standard fare. From early

fall to late spring Wyoming's odor is that of a whetted stone; the tang of mineral slipping endlessly against mineral. There is no tulip festival in Wyoming. The smell of sap risen in cottonwood and pine is remembered, and cherished.

And then the winds quit. It happens on five or six days every season, more often in the summer and autumn. The sky settles as the dome of a perfect bell settles—blue, uninterrupted, moistureless. It is nothing in Wyoming to look twenty miles in every direction, the horizons scribbled in sharp contrast at the peripheries. "No wind," we shout in wonder. We speak too loudly. We are accustomed to screaming over the yowl of air. We quiet to a whisper. "No wind," we whisper. We smile and slump. Think of the slouch that survivors effect at the end of crisis. That is our posture.

We emerge from our shelters. If it is summer we expose our soft bellies to the sun, gaining confidence, we breathe deeply, glut ourselves with the scent of sage, a stimulating and narcotic perfume. We tend our yards. Paint our homes. Wash cars. My neighbor burns back overgrowths of dried weed, heaps of tumbleweed. He mends his fence. "Nice day," he says. I've heard him say as much when it is thirteen degrees above zero. What he means is that the wind is not blowing.

The foolish become bold. They start construction projects that will require more than forty-eight hours to complete. The rest of us work tentatively. We remember we are serfs. We know the lord is only absent, not dethroned. I pass through bouts of giddiness; I cannot help myself, but like the mice and voles, I remain alert. In Wyoming the price of innocence is high. There is a big wind out there, on its way home to our high plains.

ANN DAUM

THOSE WHO STAY AND
THOSE WHO GO

The winds that blow prairie grasses flat from the root push hard against the people and buildings of Murdo, South Dakota, too. Some days, the sun itself seems to blow right outside the horizon, and clouds move so fast you can't catch their shadow with a stepped-up Chevy.

Women learn to hold their skirts between their knees and children grow up leaning. Years later, those who end up staying walk down Main Street on calm days leaning from the waist, facing an imaginary wind.

There are four paved streets in Murdo. One blinking traffic light. Not much to tempt high school graduates to stay.

Kids can work at the truck stop, waiting tables, pumping gas, or washing dishes, through high school and beyond. There are four other gas stations in town. There is the SuperValu market. The Tee-Pee and Star restaurants. The Pioneer Auto

Museum and Hallmark gift shop. There is a feed store attached to the grain elevator. The soil conservation building, post office, West River Electric Company, a telephone repair service, one plumber. The Silver Grill café, the high school and grade school, a public library open only on Thursday afternoons. The Blue Bison bar and four hotels. There is hourly work driving tractors and bucking hay bales every summer, sometimes a job watching pregnant heifers all night long during spring calving.

A lot of kids move off to Sioux Falls or Rapid City, where there are jobs. Some go as far as Omaha or Minneapolis, others go farther. These are the ones who leave, and they are recognized as such early on.

Don't ask me how people know. I knew. I could run a finger down the pictures in the high school yearbook, picking who would stay and who would go.

We hear about the ones who go in bits and pieces. They're mentioned now and then in Bernice Baughman's newspaper, the *Coyote*. There's a scholarship announcement here, a birth announcement there. But these kids who leave drift from people's thoughts and fade away, until they return for a visit, and people stare low and long and hard, as if trying to make out a particularly grainy picture. No one's sure what to say. These kids have stepped over an invisible line, and are never seen quite the same way.

For those who stay, the nights start getting long. There's no question about having children. Everyone does if they can, if for no other reason than to break the silence of those winter nights. There is joy as well, though not the kind most people expect. Joy comes in small, daily pleasures. The incredible colors of the sunsets here. Watching your son win a buckle at a 4-H rodeo. Neighbors helping your husband harvest wheat when he's laid up for a week with kidney stones. I could go on.

I've mentioned the jobs people who stay might have. There are other things to do. Church twice on Sundays, Wednesday nights, more days if you can think of reasons. Study groups. Men's prayer breakfasts. Ladies' aid.

There are spring banquets, father and son dinners, Book-and-Thimble club readings, the Lions Club raffles. The grade school Christmas concert. Gideon meetings, where men hand out stacks of Bibles, hold hands in a circle to pray. There are pool tables, and enough bottles of beer to make you forget your day, your week, maybe even a whole year, at the Blue Bison bar.

In between, though, are days stretching longer than an empty country road. Those who stay learn early: this is a flat and sparsely peopled land. There will be few travelers and fewer friends. Loneliness is just another disease here. Its symptoms are sicknesses, too. Depression. Alcoholism. Parochialism. Suicide.

Some winter nights people crowd in to watch high school basketball in the sweltering auditorium. Everyone comes to watch, sweat, and munch burned popcorn, whether they have a boy playing or not. Down vests and waterproof parkas spill out of the coatroom, where they're nestled three to a hanger. School kids sit at the west end of the bleachers, girls lean back between the boys' legs. Fat girls, and girls with pimples, sit alone. Outside, stars glitter like holes punched in the blackest cloth. The cold is still and burning.

I'm a somewhere-in-between. I've been gone so much, most people consider me a leaver. But I run a business from our family ranch and haven't missed a summer's worth of ranch work since I could walk and shinny up a horse. It's true I've spent most of the last three winters in Colorado, finishing graduate school, and five winters before that working on my undergraduate degree. But all along I was building up my broodmare herd, waiting for the day I would come back home. I have built my business and my life around a four-thousand-acre square of prairie, and no matter how far I travel, that will always be my home.

Even so, I don't really belong. After eight years of college, I am a stranger in my hometown. Jackie Schwartz, who was one grade ahead of me in school, looks at my shoes whenever I walk into the hardware store where she works.

I remember sitting with her in the attic of the auditorium, where the band stores its tubas and bass drums and music stands. Jackie and I watched the basketball games from up there, leaning over a flimsy balcony rail, occasionally daring our stomachs to settle in our shoes by leaning just a bit too far.

It seemed we knew before anybody in the stands whether the ball would sink through the basket, whether the compli-cated zone defense was working. We giggled at our view of couples in the student section of the stands—whose hands were where, under whose sweater. And we both felt safe telling our secrets there.

"I feel like God up here," Jackie told me once. "It's the only place I can look down on everyone else, but no one's watching me. No one can get at me here."

I knew Jackie sometimes came to school with purple bruises behind her freckles, but I never asked her why. That wasn't something we talked about when I was growing up. No one in Murdo did.

After Jackie said that, the basketball game still went on below, but it seemed silly somehow. As if we could see the pattern of it all, how the game would turn out, just by watching from this height. From where we stood, the plays really did look like the arrows and semicircles and curving lines we'd seen on Coach Wheeler's board. It was all so simple. When the smell of sweat and popcorn finally reached us, at the end of the second half, it was time to go home.

Now we're both adults, and she observes me carefully, from a distance of two arm's lengths, as she's writing up my ticket. Her hair is pulled back in a ponytail with bangs, just the way she wore it in school. She has two boys of her own now, both blond and bucktoothed and freckled like their mother. I've seen them at the Dairy Freeze on summer nights, along with her redheaded husband, Jerry Smith. He was a senior back in our days of balcony watching. One of those boys who always had a freshman or sophomore girl leaning back into his lap, his hands always hidden in the woolen folds of her jacket.

"How's it going?" I ask. "Had any rain out your way?"

She looks up at me, face freckled from the sun. "Nope. Been dry." She looks back down. I think I see bruising under her eyes, fragile, the color of the sky.

I nod and take my receipt, not knowing what to say. We are strangers now, seeing the world from our different places.

In other towns I am also a stranger. I stop along a busy street, somewhere far from South Dakota, to search the sky for dark clouds piling on the horizon, wonder at the chance for rain. My fleeting thoughts: Are the horses in? Ranch trucks protected from the hail? Tomatoes covered?

It's more than this. Somehow I don't belong anywhere but inside myself, and sometimes even there I'm restless. What keeps me in South Dakota?

Horses looking up from their graze as I walk by. Clouds moving across the sun. The grass that holds the prairie dirt. Thirsty roots sunk deep.

PAMELA MICHAEL

THE KHAN MEN OF AGRA

One good thing about monsoons: they sure keep the dust down, I thought to myself, peering out the milky window of the Taj Express. I surveyed the approaching station from my uncertain perch between two lurching cars, ready to grab my bag and disembark purposefully. Despite the early hour, the platform slowly scrolling past me was packed with people.

Of the dozen or so bony hands struggling to wrench my suitcase from my grip as I stepped off the train at Agra, perhaps two were porters, four or five were rickshaw drivers, three or four were taxi drivers, and maybe a couple were thieves. The sudden rush of mostly barefoot men in states of undress ranging from rags to britches brought me face to face with the difficulty of "reading" a person's demeanor or intentions in an unfamiliar culture. What to do?

I already knew from my few days in New Delhi that I would have to choose one of these men—not because I didn't want to carry my own bag, but because I would be hounded mercilessly until I paid someone to do it for me. It's a defensive necessity, and an effective hedge for women traveling alone who must rely on their own wits and the unreliable kindness of strangers—the taxi-*wallah* as protector and guide. In Delhi, though, the competitive tourist market is based more on ingenuity and charm than intimidation. Many of the drivers had developed very engaging come-ons, my favorite being the rickshaw driver who purred, "And which part of the world is suffering in your absence, Madam?"

My reluctance to hire anyone apparently was being interpreted as a bargaining ploy. Several men had begun to yell at each other and gesture toward me, ired by the low rates to which their competitors were sinking for the privilege of snagging a greenhorn tourist fresh off the train. Not wanting to see the end result of such a bidding war, I handed over my bag to the oldest, most decrepit-looking of the bunch, deciding I might be able to outrun (or overtake?) him if I had to and also because he had an engaging (if toothless) smile.

Triumphant, he hoisted my bag on top of his turban and beckoned me to follow as he set out across the tracks. For the first few minutes the old man had to fend off a persistent few rival drivers who thought they could convince me to change my mind by casting aspersions on the character, safety record, and vehicle of the man I had chosen, whose name, he told me, was Khan, Kallu Khan.

Halfway through the station, in a particularly crowded

spot, Kallu handed my bag to another (much younger and, I theorized, more fleet-footed) man.

"Hey, wait a minute!" I protested.

"My cousin Iki," Kallu assured me.

"So, what's he doing with my bag?" I asked.

"Helper," I was told.

I went into red alert and quickened my pace to keep up with Iki and my luggage. As we reached the street it began to rain again, part of the deluge/blue sky monsoon cycle to which I had become accustomed. Over my objections, Iki put my bag in the trunk of their car, a battered Hindustan Ambassador that was unmarked except by mind, no reassuring "Agra Taxi Company" emblazoned on the door.

"Thief might steal suitcase in backseat, Madam," Kallu explained. I acquiesced—the dry shelter of the "taxi" looked inviting and I was worn down by the ceaseless demands on my ability to communicate, decipher, make decisions, find, respond, protect, etc., that travel entails, even in a four-star situation, which the Agra train station was decidedly not.

Once under way, my relief at having escaped the crowd and rain was somewhat dampened by my realization that I was on a rather deserted road with two men who were probably making the same kind of un- and misinformed assumptions about me that I was making about them. I peered out the rain-streaked window to my right to get my bearings and to take in some of the sights I had come to India to see. I was also tentatively toying with escape options. All I could see was a blur of red, towering overhead and as far into the distance as I could make out. The Red Fort, of course, I had done my homework, so I knew the walls were seventy feet high, surrounded by a moat. On my left was a long stretch of sparse forest, separated from the roadway by a crumbling low iron fence.

Suddenly, Iki pulled the car over on the left and stopped alongside a broken place in the fence. Kallu got out of the passenger side and opened my door, saying, "Now I show you something no tourist ever see, Madam."

"That's all right," I said, "let's just get to the hotel. Tomorrow is better," I demurred.

"Please, Madam," he insisted, and, sensing my concern about my suitcase, he added, "Don't worry, Iki stay here with your bag."

I was already chastising myself for being so naive and trying to decide how much real danger I was in when I looked— really looked—into Kallu's eyes for the first time. They were kind; kind and bloodshot, but kind. In an instant I made the sort of decision that every traveler has to make from time to time: you decide to take a risk, trust a stranger, enter a cave, explore a trail, act on intuition, and experience something new. It is this giving oneself over to a strange culture or environment that often reaps the most reward, that makes travel so worthwhile and exhilarating.

As if to affirm my decision, the rain stopped. "OK, Mr. Khan, you show me," I said. We walked down a muddy path through a stand of stilted trees, leaving Iki behind, smoking a *bidi*. My courage faltered a couple of times, when I caught a glimpse of a spectral, loinclothed man through the leaves, but I said nothing and slogged on, hoping for the best.

It came quickly and totally unexpectedly: an enormous mauve river, its banks aflutter with river-washed tattered clothes hanging from piles and vines—work in progress of dhobi-*wallahs*, the laundrymen. Directly across the river, luminescent in a moisture-laden haze, was the Taj Mahal, seen from an angle that, to be sure, few tourists ever see and shared with affection by a man who clearly derived great pride from its grandeur. The monument's splendor was all the more striking, its manifest extravagance even more flamboyant in contrast to the faded homespun garments flapping rhythmically in the humid monsoon breeze. We could only stand there and beam at each other on the shores of the mighty Yamuna, the Khan man and I. I like to think it was a sweet kind of victory for us both.

SALMAN RUSHDIE

WATER'S EDGE

FROM "STEP ACROSS THIS LINE"

The first frontier was the water's edge, and there was a first moment, because how could there not have been such a moment, when a living thing came up from the ocean, crossed that boundary, and found that it could breathe. Before that first creature drew that first breath there would have been other moments when other creatures made the same attempt and fell fainting back into the waves, or else suffocated, flopping fishily from side to side, on the same seashore and another, and another. There were perhaps millions of these unrecorded retreats, these anonymous deaths, before the first successful step across the waterline. As we imagine the scene of that triumphant crossing—our volcanic young planet, the smoky, sulfurous air, the hot sea, the red glow in the sky, the exhausted entity gasping on the unfamiliar, inhospitable shore—we can't help wondering about those proto-creatures. What motivated them? Why did the sea so thoroughly lose its appeal that they risked everything to migrate from the old into the new? What urge was born in them that overpowered even the survival instinct? How did they intuit that air could be breathed—and how, living underwater as they did, could they begin to grow the lungs that allowed them to breathe it?

But our extremely pre-human ancestors did not have "motives" in the sense that we understand the term, the scientist in the room protests. The sea neither appealed to them, nor did it disappoint. They had no intuitions, but were driven by the imperatives hidden in their uncracked genetic codes. There was no daring here, no heroism, no adventurous, transgressive spirit. These beach-crawlers did not travel from water to air because they were curious, or in search of jobs. They neither chose nor willed their deeds. Random mutation and natural selection were their mighty, impersonal driving forces. They were just fish who by chance learned how to crawl.

But so, in a way, are we. Our own births mirror that first crossing of the frontier between the elements. As we emerge from amniotic fluid, from the liquid universe of the womb, we, too, discover that we can breathe; we, too, leave behind a kind of waterworld to become denizens of earth and air. Unsurprisingly, then, imagination defies a science and sees that first, ancient, successful half-and-halfer as our spiritual ancestor, ascribing to that strange metamorph the will to change its world. In its victorious transition we recognize and celebrate the prototype of our own literal, moral, and metaphorical frontier crossings, applauding the same drive that made Columbus's ships head for the edge of the world, or the pioneers take to their covered wagons. The image of Neil Armstrong taking his first moonwalk echoes the first movements of life on earth. In our deepest natures, we are frontier-crossing beings. We know this by the stories we tell ourselves; for we are storytelling animals, too. There is a story about a mermaid, a half-and-half creature, who gave up her fishy half for the love of a man. Was that it, then, we allow ourselves to wonder. Was that the primal urge? Did we come questing out of the waters for love?

NAOMI SHIHAB NYE

SOMEONE I LOVE

Someone I love so much cut down my primrose patch. It looked like an oval of overgrown weeds to him, in the front yard, beyond the stones of the flowerbeds, near the black mailbox on the post. He did not know that for weeks I had been carefully tending and watering it, as a few primroses floated their pink heads above the green mass, unfurled their delicate bonnets. With dozens of buds waiting to shine, we were on the brink, everything popping open, despite the headlines, all sweet flower beings from under the ground remembering what they were supposed to do.

He mowed it down with the old push lawn mower. I was out of town—he didn't ask his father, who knew how precious it was to me—his father was in the back while this was happening and didn't see—there wasn't a second thought—why would we have such a tall patch in the yard—what does my mother do when she comes out here with the old shovel and the bucket and the mysterious sacks of rose food and mulch, poking around in the earth, trimming, the clippers in her pocket, bending to the wild tangle of jasmine on the fence, the Dutchman's-pipe, the happy oregano, the funny cacti crowding together in complicated profusion like a family, the miniature chiles—what does she do, why is this here?

He just cut it down. It wasn't easy.

He must have pushed really hard to get it to go.

When I stood outside in my nightie the next dreamy-sweet morning at dawn after returning home on the midnight plane, watering my bluebonnets snapdragons butterfly bush lantana, wanting to feel tied to the earth again, as I always do when I get home, rooted in soil and stone and old caliche and bamboo and trees, a hundred years of memory in their trunks and bushes we didn't plant, and the healthy esperanza never losing her hope, and the banana palms poking out their fine and gracious greenery, when I suddenly saw what was gone, what wasn't there, not there, impossible, I was so shocked I let the hose run all over my bare feet. The cold stun of fury filled me, sorrow rising and pouring into questions: who could do this, why, why, how could anyone? I thought of the time my daddy came home to find every head cut off his giant sunflowers right after they had opened their faces to the sky, and only the empty stalks remaining, heads slashed to the ground, his disbelieving sorrow as he went to his room and lay down on the bed and closed his eyes, and I thought, I will not mention this, I am too sad to mention it, this is the pain of people everywhere, this is the pain this year deserves.

But at breakfast I went a little strange like the lady down the street who shows up at people's doors with a snarling dog and a hammer in her pocket, I went wild and furious and he swore they just looked like weeds to him, why hadn't I warned him, why did I only tell Dad?

I pointed them out to you weeks ago, I said.

He said, I don't remember flower things like that.

And it was the season of blooming and understanding. It was the season of pulling weeds in other corners, hiding from headlines, wondering what it would do if the whole house had been erased or just the books and paintings or what about the whole reckless garden or (then it gets unthinkable but we make ourselves think it now and then to stay human) the child's arms or legs, what would I do? If I did not love him, who would I become?

JOE MACKALL

WORDS OF MY YOUTH

I.

I stand at the edge of my suburban driveway on Fairlawn Drive, sunned and safe. My friend Mick and I play Wiffle ball. Each swing of the bat sends the ball flying into the mystery grip of physics and aerodynamic wonder. The ball appears headed straight up before some hidden hand of wind and speed and serrated plastic jerks it over to the lawn of the widow next door. Mrs. Worth's boxer drools the day away, watching from the backyard in its own state of ignorant awe. We take turns "smacking the shit" out of the plastic ball. I don't notice, not right away, an older kid—a man really—walking down the other side of the street, his eyes straight ahead. Not from around here. As the kid-man gets closer, I focus more intently on the game, as if this focus will protect me from what's about to happen. I chase the ball as if catching it matters more than anything, more than my first kiss or my last day of school. I make careful throws, keeping my eye on the ball, trying to anticipate the direction of its flight and fall.

I fear—as I so often fear—that something I have done has found its way back to me. And now I'll pay. Five or six houses away now, the kid-man crosses the street. He's not from around here, but I recognize him from somewhere. There's something in the way the kid-man never looks around, as if his entire world centers on a horizon only he can see. He's smoking. Not a good sign. I pick the ball up off the boxer's drool-wet lawn, wipe the drool on my jeans, and toss it a few feet in the air. When I look up I see the kid-man—black hair greased and straight, a broken mustache, patches of dirt and beard—punch Mick in the nose. Mick bends over and covers his nose with cupped hands in one motion. Blood oozes through his summer-stained fingers and drips onto the hot cement. Although the kid-man—eighteen, nineteen, probably—has just punched Mick in the face, I'm stunned stupid when the kid-man walks over to me and slams me in the nose. We run to the porch.

"My girlfriend's not a dyke," the kid-man says, as he lights a new cigarette from the old and walks off.

It's true. We have called the man's girlfriend a dyke. Often and repeatedly. But still, standing behind the harsh-sounding, cool-sounding word with blood dripping from my nose, I, who only a minute ago was playing Wiffle ball on a summer afternoon, realize I cannot define nor do I understand the word we all so love to use.

II.

Again on the Wiffle ball driveway, also summer, also my twelfth year, I call one of my Gentile friends a dumb Jew. Soon all of us revel in the discovery of this new slur. This new way of degrading each other catches on quickly. Not one of the Catholic boys schooled in the Judeo-Christian tradition is sure why calling somebody a dumb Jew is derogatory. But we celebrate this new slur anyway. But wait. Wasn't Jesus a Jew? Isn't Bill Rosenberg a Jew? We all love Bill. This must be something else. It sounds different. It sounds like it shouldn't be said. So we say it and love saying it, we boys without weapons.

The screen door slams. My mother has caught the sound of the slur. She motions for me to come inside. "Tell your friends to go home," she says.

I do not have to. They're gone. This is 1971, and the suburbs. Somebody's parent is everybody's parent. Parents stick together. They know who the real enemy is.

She grabs my hair and pulls me into the house. Inside my head I'm screaming.

I do not say a word.

"What did you say out there? What were you saying?"

I understand that my mother knows the answer to her questions. I realize I had better not repeat what I said outside, not even in answer to her questions. I know she never wants to hear that again. Not ever. Not from me. Not from anybody.

"Where did you ever hear a thing like that? That kind of talk?" she asks.

An excellent question. I honestly do not know. I have no idea. The slur just seems to have been out there, there and somehow not there, like incense, like the way a Wiffle ball whips and dips, the way adults laugh at things kids don't understand, the way background noise from a baseball game leaks out of transistor radios, the way bits of gravel bounce out of pickup truck beds, the way factory fires flirt with the night sky, the way sonic booms burst the lie of silence.

LAWRENCE SUTIN

SIX POSTCARDS

"Jeune Mère"

I was born to a strong and tender and frightened woman. My mother lost her parents and her sisters in the Holocaust. She was gang-raped by Russian partisans in the Polish woods after escaping from the Nazi ghetto established in her hometown of Stolpce. In marrying my father—a Jewish partisan leader who gave her shelter in an underground bunker—she was staking her soul on creating a new family. Her first baby, a boy, died shortly after his premature birth in the fall of 1945. Dread brought on that early delivery. My mother had learned of a pogrom carried out by Poles against those surviving Jews trying to return to their homes in the nearby town of Katowice. "Even after the Germans surrendered, the Poles continued to kill us," my mother told me. She told me everything from the time I was old enough to follow the basic sense, at six or so. I was the third child, after my unnamed dead brother and after my sister, who entered life in a displaced persons camp in Germany in 1947. As to bearing children, my mother knew an old Yiddish saying: "Three is two and two is one." My sister and I were both treated as if we were each the only one, the precious one, the one who could be lost at any time. I came out of my mother's womb on time and healthy in October 1951, the first member of the family born in America. But I was not born into an American home. There was herring, butter, and pumpernickel bread on our breakfast table, along with strong sweet tea. We spoke Yiddish a lot. As a young boy, I would ask Mother what we were having for dinner and she would tell me, *"drek mit leber,"* "shit with liver," meaning don't ask what there will be to eat, be thankful there will be something. When I was born, she remembered, I know, the emaciated lost one laid on the windowsill to die by a small-town Polish physician who had no way to treat him. Mother never wanted to give him a name. I never asked why but I knew that naming him would have made it worse. I was named after her father Lazar, in Hebrew Eliezer, in English Larry. I was one, living for two, and my mother was living for me, but fiercely, tending me like a bruise.

"Man and Boy"

Fathers more easily love their daughters. Sons are the continuation of us in an obvious sense, so obvious that it is unbearable. In the case of my father and myself, I had the fullness of his face and his desire to write, which had been abandoned when he came to America with a family to raise. What he wanted to see in me were the practical choices he had made confirmed. At times in my youth he justly found me clumsy, cowardly, callous, and he let it be known. His anger had, then, the finality of a curse. The great task in the life of a son is to realize that his father is right and then to proceed to be wrong. It's your only chance to become someone you haven't already met. My father also let his love be known. Once he cried because he feared I did not love him back. Lay down on his bed fully dressed in the middle of the day and cried. My mother found me and pulled me by my scruff to the doorway of their bedroom to see. She was hating me so I lay down beside him and hugged him. That was hard. He was a middle-aged man who was sobbing and sweaty and his body was heavy and so soft I imagined his ribs giving way like a snowman's on the first warm winter day. I could hear his heart and it sounded as if it was working harder than it could take. I hugged him until he stopped crying. I whispered in his ear that I loved him.

"Frère et Soeur"

Even my mother says that my sister and I have nothing in common. People say that I look like my father and my sister looks like my mother. I think I look like my mother. People say that personality-wise, my sister is like my father and I'm like my mother. To me, my sister is kind and anxious. To her, I am funny and impatient. We share no interests, don't like the same anything. I am a suspicious intellectual and she's so blandly sentimental. Socially, we get along nicely at what you call family occasions but we don't spend much time alone together. But we're bound together by being their children, the survivors of the survivors. We heard the stories as kids and they got into our dreams, storm troopers breaking down the doors of all our hiding places. We are amongst the very few who realize constantly what can happen and how much our children would need us. There is a code connected to that that only we know and can enforce upon each other. I rebel against the code, which embarrasses me as trauma. But in secret I keep it. On my sister it fits like a space suit she knows she'd be crazy ever to get out of. My parents won't fully die until my sister's time comes.

"Summer Girls"

Oh, the summer girls. Oh, the days of trying to pose and use my body like a natural man of the earth so as to draw their eyes. Playing baseball while girls watched was a different kind of baseball altogether. It was as if there were major-league scouts sitting in the stands (the shaded hill behind the back-stop) assessing our genetic skills and sexual hustle. Yes, the summer girls talked amongst themselves, sometimes ignored the play, often wandered off to their own backyard gatherings in which dolls and fleecy pets held sway. Still, they were taking us in with precision and passion, even if that precision was instinct and that passion was scorn.

"Father Holding Baby"

I say to you that I have been a good father. The one and only time I slipped hard came when Sarah was just a few months old. My wife Mab had gone off one evening to a meeting. Did the young suckling baby miss her mama? Yes, she did. Was Daddy confident with baby alone with him in the house? No. Shortly after Mama left, baby cried and Daddy fed her a bottle and some soft, blended apricots from a glass jar. It was quiet for a while and baby played with colored rings on a blanket spread on the living room carpet. Then baby started to cry again and Daddy picked her up and held her and walked with her and cooed to her and kissed her lightly on the top of her head and sang to her in the fleeciest voice he could some Grateful Dead ballads that had always sounded to him like lullabies. He had wanted to be a father someday and had thought he would be a good one because he wanted to be. Baby kept crying. Daddy kept walking and rocking baby in his arms and cooing and singing and trying to keep a smile on his face when it came close to hers. Baby kept crying. Baby kept crying. It was nearly an hour and the crying only stopped when baby sobbed, running out of breath. Sleep, baby. No. Baby kept crying. Crying. The sound of a cry is designed by nature to make you unable to stand it and determined to get it to stop. I couldn't. That's why I screamed at her to stop. Thank God at least I did not shake her. Then, shaking all over myself, I laid her on the sofa and sat across the room watching but saying and doing no more as baby cried and gasped and caught her breath and cried until Mama finally came home. I was yellow and the baby was yellow and we glowed in the dimness of the house from our strain. I have failed to do a good many things in my life. All of those things bother me still, but none so much as that evening alone with a baby for whom a father did and was nothing.

"La Salle de la Melpomène"

No quibbling over truth, not here. Memory is not merely selective. It is also tutelary, oracular. It is, in the end, as reliable as we are. The names and facts of my life as names and facts are insignificant. What we call history is something I slipped through. My life as I remember it to be is all I have to live on. I remember it as a plunge underwater, as a kite baffled and frantic in the wind, as a country-night sky pouring into my head every star, as smells of basements and bathrooms and black earth and lilacs and coffee and sex, as a hatred of mirrors, as a discarding of weighty thought, as stillness and persistence. All I know is of these things or states and how they made me feel. That would be truth in this book.

LIA PURPURA

SEPTEMBER

aid out perfectly where they fell in the tall grass, half sunk in the soft ground—the bones of a small cat. And how long did it take for the bones to clean, for the flesh to slip off and the eyes burn away? The shape the body made was placid-seeming, unlike the animals of prehistory, who, trapped in tar in the posture of shock, in half-light on a cave wall, are forever outrunning fire, weather, attack. In caves their broad, simple bodies are sketched in ochre flight: fear is the black cipher of an open mouth, the red oxide smudge on a flank. But I found these bones in the shape of sleep, of full and open expectancy, mid-stride in an airy leap. *Waiting for.* I learned it takes only days for a small animal's body to decompose at this time of year, to return itself to bone, to its simplest components—carbon, hydrogen, oxygen, nitrogen, sulfur. To press its outline back into the soft earth, which is a welcoming, rich place still, late summer. A home receiving the body in, expecting it.

ANNE McDUFFIE

WINTER WHEAT

I have seen wheat only once in my life. Only once fingered the stiff fan of its beard, plucked a kernel and held it in my mouth. I remember my grandfather's eagerness as he led us into the field beside his house to show us the wheat. I don't recall his explanation of how it grew, or how they would harvest it—just the cadence of his voice, easy and sure. He's telling us what he knows. The glare of the sun obscures his face as he twists the head off a wheat stem and bends down to offer it to me. I don't remember the house but how it stands at the edge of the wheat field, the cloudless sky, no shade anywhere but the kitchen where Grandma Charlotte stands at the counter with my mother, spooning out honeydew with a melon baller. She's filling the bowl between them with tiny, perfect orbs. It's not their field and not their house, but one of a series of rentals in the circuit of rural towns that they moved around every couple of years. Ritzville. Kennewick. Moses Lake.

Grandpa rarely talked to us like that. Mostly he told stories in which he starred as a big-screen version of himself. He saw Sitting Bull, he fired his pistol in a duel. He fought off wild dogs while delivering newspapers, and jumped a runaway train. During the war, he shot down Zeroes over Spokane and Seattle. He single-handedly saved the Fremont Bridge from being bombed—Zeroes again—on his watch with the Civil Defense patrol. When we repeated his stories to our parents, they went over them carefully, teasing out the few underlying facts. He did work for the Navy in Seattle during the war years, as a civil servant in Naval Supply. And maybe he did join the Civil Defense; many did. But the rest . . . they'd shake their heads, baffled.

Unlike most old people we knew, Grandpa rarely repeated himself. He always had new stories to tell, and the older we got the more he expected us to believe. The last time I saw him, he asked my husband about his work and then began to recount in earnest how he had carried out secret spy missions for the Navy, a briefcase handcuffed to his wrist. He wasn't senile, and he wasn't out of touch with reality; he simply preferred his version. We never questioned the truth of his claims because we knew it would only lead to an argument, and Grandpa could outlast anyone in an argument. Logic was no object, nor was history. He once insisted that the state of Idaho had rerouted a river, because its location on the map challenged his own recollection.

Every so often Grandpa told a story that seemed almost true, maybe was true. He told me once that he'd held over fifty jobs during the Depression, piecing together a kind of living from one part-time situation after another. I had some idea what he could do. I'd watched him repair restaurant chairs for Klinkerdaggers, hand-turning new legs on a lathe until each groove and swell matched exactly. He'd lost the tip of one finger, but his square, blunt hands moved with precision, cutting gingerbread on a jigsaw or sanding the curves of a freshly carved piece. You could see by the way he hefted the wood and sized it up, roughly caressing the grain with his thumb, that he was a natural craftsman.

We heard a lot about the house he'd built at Diamond Lake, and those stories were all true. My father told me about the summer he and his college friends came out to work on the house, how they swam in the lake and played bridge with my grandparents in the evenings. Their hair is still dark in the photographs, and they're clustered around picnic tables and card tables holding bottles of beer, or lying chastely side by side in sleeping bags. (My mother appeared in those photos—they must have been engaged by then.) Whole pages of my grandparents' album were devoted to the house alone: the foundation laid out on a shady, wooded lot and snapped from every angle, then progressive shots as they framed and built the walls, timber by timber, log by log. I think I remember that one or two photographs contained a small figure in a familiar plaid shirt, who faced the camera with his feet braced wide—or kept on working, face in shadow. But I'm not sure. My grandparents' photographs tended toward empty landscapes captured from a great distance. When they remembered to include themselves, it was usually to record a day's drive and to document their passengers on the excursion. Then they all dutifully lined up by a roadside sign, or alongside the car parked high on the shoulder, keeping the elusive view always at their backs.

Grandpa had a contentious relationship with my father; their stories rarely overlapped. Dad filled in the pieces Grandpa never mentioned: the bankruptcies and failed businesses, the times he moved their family from one depressed town to another in a fruitless search for a fresh start. He was still moving, still searching, all the time I knew him. Every visit, we roamed another town looking for another new address, another house, another field of wheat or alfalfa. Maybe this time there'd be horses grazing just out the back, or different birds mobbing another landlord's feeder. He presented these changes to us as though he'd arranged them especially for our entertainment—offered them to us like gifts. He wooed us with anything he could point to or describe, hoping maybe this was a place we'd want to come back to—never noticing that we kept coming back to him, wherever he was.

At his funeral, I was astonished by the grief of my older relatives and what they said when they stood to witness during the service. I didn't recognize my grandpa in their stories, though I could see glimpses of the man I remembered: a generous neighbor, good with his hands, always ready to work, to pitch in, to help out. They talked of a man who was known for his practical jokes, who loved a good gag: *Oh, we laughed. Clair could always make us laugh.* It's taken me a few years to dredge up a memory of my own: his deep chuckle, roughened by pipe smoke, the crinkles around his startling blue eyes. *Grandpa's just pulling your leg.* Did he ever say that? No one mentioned his stories, though they had all heard them. Or how, in later years, he was taken in by every sweepstakes offer, convinced he'd won our inheritance each time a fat packet arrived in the mail. He dreamed of leaving every grandchild with a new car and one last epic.

I brought my newborn daughter to meet him the year before he died. We had barely gotten out of the car when he started asking if we'd come again, and when. "Soon," I said. "As soon as we can." I realized as I said it that I would never see him again, and that I'd known that all along. I felt strangely relieved, as though I'd finally answered a question that had been nagging at me for a long time. We stood in the asphalt parking lot of his nursing home, already broiling in the mid-morning sun, while my grandfather tamped tobacco into his pipe and lit it. His oxygen tank wheeled and bobbled beside him each time he took a step, and he kept the clear tubing positioned under his nose while he smoked. The heat pressed in around me, the sun so bright I found it hard to see beyond the glare, and I felt like the child I was on all those long trips west, getting coaxed out of the car to admire the view. I longed to be back in the air-conditioned cool, my book in my lap, moving seventy miles an hour down an unfamiliar road. In my mind I was already on my way, passing all the fields of crops I couldn't name and all the towns where I would never live, moving toward the place where the rest of my life was waiting for me, somewhere just up ahead.

AMY TAN

CONFESSIONS

My mother's thoughts reach back like the winter tide, exposing the wreckage of a former shore. Often she's mired in 1967, 1968, the years my older brother and my father died.

1968 was also the year she took me and my little brother—Didi—across the Atlantic to Switzerland, a place so preposterously different that she knew she had to give up grieving simply to survive. That year, she remembers, she was very, very sad. I too remember. I was sixteen then, and I recall a late-night hour when my mother and I were arguing in the chalet, that tinderbox of emotion where we lived.

She had pushed me into the small bedroom we shared, and as she slapped me about the head, I backed into a corner, by a window that looked out on the lake, the Alps, the beautiful outside world. My mother was furious because I had a boyfriend. She was shouting that he was a drug addict, a bad man who would use me for sex and throw me away like left-over garbage.

"Stop seeing him!" she ordered.

I shook my head. The more she beat me, the more implacable I became, and this in turn fueled her outrage.

"You didn't love you daddy or Peter! When they die you not even sad."

I kept my face to the window, unmoved. What does she know about sad?

She sobbed and beat her chest. "I rather kill myself before see you destroy you life!"

Suicide. How many times had she threatened that before?

"I wish you the one die! Not Peter, not Daddy."

She had just confirmed what I had always suspected. Now she flew at me with her fists.

"I rather kill you! I rather see you die!"

And then, perhaps horrified by what she had just said, she fled the room. Thank God that was over. I wished I had a cigarette to smoke. Suddenly she was back. She slammed the door shut, latched it, then locked it with a key. I saw the flash of a meat cleaver just before she pushed me to the wall and brought the blade's edge to within an inch of my throat. Her eyes were like a wild animal's, shiny, fixated on the kill. In an excited voice she said, "First, I kill you. Then Didi and me, our whole family destroy!" She smiled, her chest heaving. "Why you don't cry?" She pressed the blade closer and I could feel her breath gusting.

Was she bluffing? If she did kill me, so what? Who would

care? While she rambled, a voice within me was whimpering, "This is sad, this is so sad."

For ten minutes, fifteen, longer, I straddled these two thoughts—that it didn't matter if I died, that it would be eternally sad if I did—until all at once I felt a snap, then a rush of hope into a vacuum, and I was crying, I was babbling my confession: "I want to live. I want to live."

For twenty-five years I forgot that day, and when the memory of what happened surfaced unexpectedly at a writers' workshop in which we recalled our worst moments, I was shaking, wondering to myself, Did she really mean to kill me? If I had not pleaded with her, would she have pushed down on the cleaver and ended my life?

I wanted to go to my mother and ask. Yet I couldn't, not until much later, when she became forgetful and I learned she had Alzheimer's disease. I knew that if I didn't ask her certain questions now, I would never know the real answers.

So I asked.

"Angry? Slap you?" she said, and laughed. "No, no, *no*. You always good girl, never even need to spank, not even one time."

How wonderful to hear her say what was never true, yet now would be forever so.

KELLY CHERRY

PLANET UNFLINCHING

t used to be an axiom that an object cannot occupy two positions at the same time, but now, of course, one may argue that in cyberspace it is possible to do just that. Perhaps someday it will also be possible to occupy the same position at two different times. At the dinner table, there between your two brothers, with your father and mother at either end and your mother's quietly hysterical twice-divorced sister seated next to you and plucking the corner off her paper napkin by increments, you will be both ten and seventeen. At ten you will eat your slice of ham with the slice of pineapple on top and your canned green beans and instant mashed potatoes and try to understand how there can be a God if he packs people off to hell like a Nazi routing trains to the Holocaust, and at seventeen you will have on pink pedal pushers and a pink shirt with three-quarter sleeves that dips in at the waist, and you will feel so sexy, so ready for something to happen—without understanding that this is what you feel, that this is why you can hardly be bothered to eat and can't wait to escape into your room and make a wish on the first star you see tonight from the dormer window that has a built-in bench in front of it. When you leave the table and enter your room, night will be nudging the window but not yet inside. Things happen when it is time for them to happen, you know. Or maybe not; maybe that is a sentimental notion, an instance of wishful thinking. But is there any other kind of thinking? How much really hard thinking, how much really cold logic, is there in this world? Maybe somewhere else there is a world where reason is never as soft as a bed, flat as a stale beer. Woozy as a woman who, to ease her back pain, has been washing down codeine all day with sips of the bad-tasting beer. The woman thinks she would get up if she could think of a good reason to, but damned if she can find a good reason. It would mean giving up being where she is, and who knows if where she would be would be better or worse. She could find herself in another world, and it might, I suppose, be a world unlike this one, where no taint of desire afflicts argumentation, where predication is not stained by untested assumption or hidden agenda. We will call this world Unflinching. On Unflinching winds reach hurricane speeds, and extremes of temperature occur with night and day. A green leaf is a rare example of moderation, a compromise between breath and poison, a pragmatic adaptation to circumstance. Unflinching is quite a world. People say it's a place they would like to visit, but most of them concede that they wouldn't want to live there.

DOROTHY ALLISON

FROM *TWO OR THREE THINGS I KNOW FOR SURE*

Let me tell you about what I have never been allowed to be. Beautiful and female. Sexed and sexual. I was born trash in a land where the people all believe themselves natural aristocrats. Ask any white Southerner. They'll take you back two generations, say. "Yeah, we had a plantation." The hell we did.

I have no memories that can be bent so easily. I know where I come from, and it is not that part of the world. My family has a history of death and murder, grief and denial, rage and ugliness—the women of my family most of all.

The women of my family were measured, manlike, sexless, bearers of babies, burdens, and contempt. My family? The women of my family? We are the ones in all those photos taken at mining disasters, floods, fires. We are the ones in the background with our mouths open, in print dresses or drawstring pants and collarless smocks, ugly and old and exhausted. Solid, stolid, wide-hipped baby machines. We were all wide-hipped and predestined. Wide-faced meant stupid. Wide hands marked workhorses with dull hair and tired eyes, thumbing through magazines full of women so different from us they could have been another species.

I remember standing on the porch with my aunt Maudy brushing out my hair; I was feeling loved and safe and happy. My aunt turned me around and smoothed my hair down, looked me in the eye, smiled, and shook her head. "Lucky you're smart," she said.

Brown-toothed, then toothless, my aunt Dot showed me what I could expect.

"You're like me," she announced when she saw my third-grade school picture. "Got that nothing-gonna-stop-you look about you, girl."

I studied the picture. All I saw was another grinning girl in dark-framed glasses, missing a tooth.

"No, look." She produced a picture I would find later among Mama's treasures. In this one Aunt Dot was a smooth-skinned teenager with a wide jaw and a straightforward glare, sturdy and fearless at fifteen as she would be three decades later.

"I see," I assured her, keeping my head down and away from her demanding eyes.

What I saw was a woman who had never been beautiful and never allowed herself to care. When she found me once, red-faced and tearful, brooding over rude boys who shouted insults and ran away, she told me to wipe my face and pay no attention.

"It never changes," she said in her gravelly voice. "Men and boys, they all the same. Talk about us like we dogs, bitches sprung full-grown on the world, like we were never girls, never little babies in our daddy's arms. Turn us into jokes 'cause we get worn down and ugly. Never look at themselves. Never think about what they're doing to girls they've loved, girls they wore out. Their girls."

"You ugly old woman," my grandfather called my grandmother.

"You ugly old woman," all my uncles called all my aunts.

"You ugly bitch," my cousins called their sisters, and my sisters called me.

"You ugly thing!" I screamed back.

The pretty girls in my high school had good hair, curled or straightened to fit the fashion, had slender hips in tailored skirts, wore virgin pins on the right side or knew enough not to wear such tacky things at all. My cousins and I were never virgins, even when we were. Like the stories told about Janis Joplin in Port Arthur, Texas, there were stories about us in Greenville, South Carolina. The football players behind the bleachers, boys who went on to marry and do well.

"Hell, it wasn't rape. She never said no. Maybe she said stop, but in that little bitty voice, so you know she wants you to love her, hell, love her for ten minutes or half an hour. Shit, who could love a girl like her?"

Who?

Beauty is a hard thing. Beauty is a mean story. Beauty is slender girls who die young, fine-featured, delicate creatures about whom men write poems. Beauty, my first girlfriend said to me, is that inner quality often associated with great amounts of leisure time. And I loved her for that.

We were not beautiful. We were hard and ugly and trying to be proud of it. The poor are plain, virtuous if humble and hardworking, but mostly ugly. Almost always ugly.

"You know Dot's husband left her," Cousin Billie told me once. "Came back after a while, then left again. Way she talked you'd think she never noticed. Some days I don't know whether to be proud of her or ashamed."

I thought about stories I'd been told, about women whose men left them or stayed to laugh out the sides of their mouths when other men mentioned other women's names. Behind my aunt Dot was a legion of female cousins and great-aunts, unknown and nameless—snuff-sucking, empty-faced creatures changing spindles at the textile plant, chewing gum while frying potatoes at the truck stop, exhausted, angry, and never loved enough.

The women I loved most in the world horrified me. I did not want to grow up to be them. I made myself proud of their pride, their determination, their stubbornness, but every night I prayed a man's prayer: Lord, save me from them. Do not let me become them.

KIM BARNES

WORK

1. Pie

My mother bakes pies for the Clearwater Café. Three
dollars a pie, five pies a day, two days a week. She
does this because it is winter, and because my
father, a lumberjack, will be laid off until spring. The tall
young cedar he harvests for poles become too brittle in sub-
zero weather to withstand the felling. They "snap like tooth-
picks," he says, and I remember the neighbor girl's arm,
snapped just so.

I miss his comings home, the inrush of dusky air, the diesel
scent and sharp smell of yew. The way he kisses my mother on
the lips, once, twice, three times. He sleeps until noon, but she
rises before dawn, sets the oven, dusts the counter with a fine
sift of flour. Today is lemon meringue, chocolate, banana,
coconut cream—pudding pies, winter pies, not dependent on
summer's fresh fruit. The huckleberries we picked in August

remain untouched in the freezer. Small and precious, impossible to cultivate, they are saved for family, for February when we might die for a taste of summer, for July when we know, finally, that the picking month is upon us, and we can let go our last reserve. Through the dead winter, they remain swaddled—double-bagged, triple-wrapped—their pungent perfume enough to taint the backstraps of venison, the trout in their currents of blue ice.

Crisco scalloped from its can, dough slapped and rounded, rolled to a disk, folded half and quarter, trimmed and finger-thumb-fluted, pricked against shrinkage, baked golden. With her husband out of work, she sees it as necessity, this labor of scalding, thickening, whipping the whites to stiff peaks. My mother believes in the silence and submission of her sex, her place at home. In our shotgun shack miles from town, surrounded by tamarack and lodgepole, she keeps my father's shirts chastely ironed, his canvas pants modestly patched and creased. She does not shear her hair or wear makeup to beg the attention of other men. She does not sin, except, perhaps, in the making of these pies, which she slides into the crate's dark interior before waking my brother and me for school.

Snow bows the tips of hemlock, slides from the downturned branches of fir, from the tin roof warming. Drifts pile higher against clapboard. The pies ride warm between us in the Chevy's backseat as our mother makes a first attempt at up the long driveway, the steep chute of ice to the road. "Hold them," she instructs. "Don't let them ruin." My brother and I steady the crate as the car slides back to its point of repose, and we begin another run.

All the long way into town, our bellies full of egg yolk sopped with toast, we breathe in the sugary steam. At the café, we wait as our mother hauls the pies to the door, hesitates a moment at her reflection in the glass, touches the apple of each cheek, disappears inside, where the men sitting at the counter wear Filson wool, green flannel, calked boots. Like our father, they are sawyers, loaders, limbers, swampers. They are Swanson and Tundevold and Larrabee. They are missing an eye, an ear, an arm, a half dozen fingers between them. When our mother returns, the crate is empty, her face flushed. She tucks a few bills into her wallet, says, "That'll get us a little farther."

When, at school, I open my lunch pail, I find a peanut butter sandwich, a thermos of hot chocolate, a tinfoil packet I unfold with great care. Inside, the scraps of her making, dusted with cinnamon and sugar, miraculously whole. These, I do not share. I lick the foil clean.

2. Tupperware

I am fourteen, the youngest of women gathered in Spokane, Washington, for the regional Tupperware convention. We sit in folding chairs at the center of the banquet room, surrounded by new products in Harvest Gold and Avocado Green skillfully stacked and balanced: celery crispers, ice cream savers, lettuce keepers, bread safes, Jell-O molds. All with a lifetime guarantee.

It is 1972, and my family has left the logging camps, moved to the small city of Lewiston. After a year of savage rebellion—fragrant baggies of marijuana, black lights, Hot Pink

posters, boys with Electric Blue eye—I have been sent north
to live with the preacher's clan in hopes I will *straighten out,
come back to the fold.*

As we sing the Tupperware song ("You can't beat it, don't
you try! It's the best that you can buy!"), we clap and har-
monize as we do at revival meetings, except no one is slain
by the Spirit, none cry out in the tongues of angels. Instead,
we are brought to a pitch of high keening by the nation's
top saleswoman, who paces the platform, provokes us into
liturgical response: "WHO's going to book one hundred
parties?" "WE are!" "WHO's going to earn a trip to Disney
World?" "WE are!"

Back at the parsonage, I fill out invitations and mail them
to the few young women who attend our small church. I help
unload the blue plastic suitcase, nest an attractive display,
serve coffee and squares of spice cake iced with creamy frost-
ing. I give my first demonstration, two thumbs running the
rim of a mixing bowl, pulling back the tab, burping out the
air, snapping the seal shut, sealing freshness in.

When, twenty-five years later, a friend asks, "What *is* it
about fundamentalist women and Tupperware?" I laugh. Imagine some reason to dress up, go out, get away—and not on Sun-
day. The cake spiked with cardamom. The prizes at the door.

That secret whisper of air.

3. Dirt

A year of waiting tables at Lewiston's first and only disco.
Black polyester skirt, dancer's leotard, three-inch-heels, four

p.m. to two a.m., then an hour to close down, clean up, drink the bartender's mistakes, smoke without interruption. Up at seven to make my college classes. My mother and father disapprove from a distance—a few miles, a chasm between us.

Exhausted, my grades wrecked, my financial aid in jeopardy, I say goodbye to twenty-dollar-a-night tips, put an ad in the paper: "College student desires housecleaning jobs. Reasonable."

The surgeon's wife, the dentist's, the wife of the supervisor at the mill: they need their houses clean. They have five bedrooms, four baths, a hot tub. Single-malt scotch and vodka in the freezer. They have five thousand Legos scattered across the carpet, miniature pinschers that shit behind the couch, a closet full of debate trophies, letter jackets, pom-poms. Cleaning out drawers, I find a suicide note framed in gold, the newspaper clues laminated in plastic—the oldest son, in the bathroom, with the knife.

When the husbands drop by during lunch hour, I hide myself in a bathroom, run water, lock the door. The wives surprise me, coming home to check on my progress, to find their men. I shine the broad leaves of philodendrons. From between cushions, I pinch dimes, the torn-open wrappers of rubbers. In the bottoms of their nightstands, I find *Hustler* and *Playboy*, books on how to keep your man wanting more. Sugary piles of sloughed-off skin, miniature moons of toenails thick and thin, cum-wadded Kleenex beneath the sheets, a dildo nestled between mattress and spring. I wipe around, dust over, arrange just so, leave be.

At the end of the day, I am gone. I'm home in my apartment, where dishes pile the sink, cat hair furs the corners. My hands smell of Pine-Sol and still I scrub them. At night I dream the songs of their lives—Bobby Bare eight-tracks, Conway Twitty LPs, the Grateful Dead on cassette—I've listened to them all, anything to fill the pure whiteness, the silence of my work.

4. Wood

We've borrowed, pawned, sold every ounce of gold jewelry not on our fingers, and still my new husband and I can't afford a movie ticket or pay cash for a beer.

I remember my mother's pies. I have the gift of her recipe, her way with crust. My ad in the paper brings one call for blueberry. A bag of frozen fruit takes the month's last few dollars. The first batch of dough is too tough, the second too sticky. I roll and patch, open the window to cool the oven-warmed kitchen. Mixed with sugar, a little flour, sprinkled with lemon, the watery blue turns to syrup. I brush the top crust with canned cream, slit a canvas of leaves and berries. When I subtract the cost of ingredients, I have made one dollar for each hour of work.

My next ad reads, "Firewood split, $10.00 a cord." I've become adept at swinging a maul, our own small house heated with red fir and larch. The elderly woman who calls has lost her husband, and her carport is filled with the last load pitched from his Ford pickup. "I want to use the wood," she says. "The warmth will remind me of him."

But it is my *man* and not me she has expected. As I pull on my gloves, she worries, especially about my *female organs*, which she believes may be damaged by such labor. During the four hours it takes me to split and stack the large rounds of tamarack, she brings me hot chocolate dolloped with whipped cream, macaroons fresh from the oven. I am sweating in the twenty-degree weather; my breath puffs out in sweet clouds.

The smell of sap, the sheen of honeyed wood, the smoke from the fire already burning, my father's words and instruction, how to penetrate the gnarled, unsplittable chunk: on its side, the bit aimed straight at the heart of the knot. The grain separates; the rounds fall into halves, then quarters. I feel the muscles across my shoulders, down the backs of my arms, whispering their sore promise.

When I knock on her door to tell her I've finished, she writes a check, her script tremulous, thorned. A five-dollar bonus, she says, because I've worked so hard.

It is enough, and I carry the check with me, folded and tucked. I stop by the store, buy dark bread, a gallon of milk, a cheap bottle of wine to share with my lover who awaits my return, a rough season's soup bubbling atop the stove. He raises the spoon to his mouth and listens for my step at the door.

KATHLEEN DEAN MOORE

MUSKGRASS CHARA

I used to love all smells. The smell of morning woke me smiling—air fresh as raw corn silk, cold in my nose. I loved the smell of clothes under a steam iron. Garlic baking. And the sea! I used to drive all the way to the beach just to breathe. My children would tease me. "Ah, smell the fish-packing plants," they'd rhapsodize, but it was true: I loved the sopping, salty air along the bay front where conveyor belts pulled heaps of shrimp from the holds of trawlers, and the air was all creosote and iodine. And the smells of my children, different every year: milk at first, and laundry detergent, then fresh grass from the neighbor's yard, pine sap and sewing machine oil, new textbooks, pears, and leftovers in lunchboxes, then perfume and a vague drift of cigarettes. Each friend's house had a different smell, and I knew without asking where my children had been.

What I remember of childhood, of being frightened at night and coming into my parents' bedroom, is the molasses smell of people breathing all night in a closed room. When my father was sick, I remember his terror of odors, his fury at careless nurses, the sorrow as he became more and more body, less and less mind, until the body was all there was left, and it too started to effervesce, releasing its cells to the room. Then, I didn't want him to have any smell at all, except rain maybe, or outboard motors.

Now I can be obsessive about smells. Some days, I move through the house on a rampage. I throw out the sour beer bottles and wash the recycling bins with soap. I scrub the place where the wastebasket sits and set a fan to blow air out the basement window. When my children come home at Thanksgiving, I boil oranges with cinnamon and light a fire to pull stale air from the corners of the house. They will not come in the door and think, "This smells like an old house. I had forgotten how old."

And every October, I return to a lake that lies at the base of a great escarpment forested with ponderosa pines that smell like butterscotch pudding. In the evening, I take my kayak onto this lake. I sit alone in my boat, smacked by waves from an evening wind. As the sun begins to set, I can pick up a certain smell of water that reminds me of so many years and so many streams. It's a green alga, I think. Maybe *Chara*. If my father were alive, he could tell me the name. It's a green smell, a dense smell of water after the sun has gone behind the mountains.

I paddle to the line where the mountain's shadow is moving across the lake, then slowly paddle with the shadow as it advances toward the eastern shore. This is where the scent lifts off the water, just where the night is covering the day. Nighthawks dive low over the water. Redwings call. I paddle just fast enough to keep up with the advancing edge of shadow, just fast enough to keep pace with the turning of the earth.

KATRINA ROBERTS

UNDERCURRENT

'm twenty-seven feet tall, stretched across the yellow stubble of cropped stalks. The baby in his carrier peers out, kicks and coos. Two and a half months, young as a lima bean, strapped to my belly to walk Cottonwood Hill up past twenty acres of wheat, yellow eye that centers our loop. By next fall, fifty houses—slated to stand where now mown rows like gold corduroy stretch up to the foot of the Blues—will block this view.

Scan the tar and weeds this morning: *short focus*, product of anger borne from Jeremy's tight-lipped goodbye, my *"Hush, the baby!"* before light. Perhaps a full moon over the pasture, pale pinkish cloud beneath orange will have buoyed his spirits. He loaded his flatbed with boards and pipes, but then as he drove out, I heard them spill with a clatter onto the gravel, truck grind to a stop, then more tossing of metal; then it geared up, climbed its stair of air and *blub-blubbed* off— expression of silent rage over thankless factory work. I count his fingers when he returns each night.

The baby, mesmerized by my gait, memorizes the black- and-white checks inside his Swedish swaddle; I climb with the sun. Tomorrow a crew will come to dig in pipes for the subdivision, rerouting our walk. On Kendall Ridge, we fol- low long black wires down while a magpie and small hawk spar for rank on looming poles; they dip and swoop crying *peeeeuw, peeeeuw.*

My shadow, first erect on the dune, then, when the crest smoothes, a streak of *purplegreyblack*, a smudge of self that Giacometti might make, or Modigliani paint, and . . . The van is almost upon us when I see: it swerves *not away*, but *toward*.

"*Fuck you!*" I shout, shielding our eyes from grit.

"*And you, too,*" I curse the yellow dog (*teeth bared, low gut- tural growl*) in the road where the hill flattens out. "*Get lost!*"

A plane circles, crop duster, but I trust it won't fall from the clouds or drop anything on us; the hawk rides thermals above telephone lines, will probably dive, but for mice.

Then, there in the lee in a fold of grass like a boat's wake: the housecat, cream and rust, seems to have run himself to sleep. But no, when I bend to look, no rise and fall. I turn my baby away, continue to walk. Here's the barn where they hang the sheep to skin at season's end. Here's the creek where the bull ambled through one morning. And here's the left we take to lead us back up to the farm.

Something's running through me and I'm not sure what.

JAMES GALVIN

✳

A SECOND TIME

It was the year I cut logs for the new house and roads, roads like veins that let the timber bleed. You wore a different shawl each day. It was the year I shot the white mare, and her filly, equally white, refused to follow the herd to winter pasture. It was the year you left me for the first time, before the aspen turned. Then it was the winter the sky couldn't get off the ground. East wind went down the chimney and filled the house with smoke.

The new house consisted of sticks and strings and numbers on scraps of paper. Facts are mercenary bastards. Spring was the fallacy that brought you back, but nothing in the world could hold you. The last storm we hauled feed to the snowbound horses. The white filly stood her ground apart. You fed that

rowdy gang instead, those bluejays, vainglorious thieves that
loitered in the pines behind the house. I wouldn't say you
tamed them, but they flew down to you for crumbs.

It took all June to haul foundation stone from the mountain,
to screen enough sand from the river for mortar. It was the
year we cut hay between squalls, and the aspen turned early,
their self-elegy, and the evergreens I'd cut turned into walls.
You scolded the aspen outside your window for staying green
when all the rest were gold. Now that you're gone a second
time I already know what it's like. It snows inside. Jays swirl
around the house like a blue shawl. Loud and bright they follow me whenever I go out—to the barn, the spring, even into
the patient woods.

It's been storming for a week. The quakies are bare except for
the one by the window, which is gold, in snow, and won't let
go its leaves. The evergreens are singed with frost so that each
is delineated, individual, each in its own doorway of ice. The
new roof is half finished. It snows inside. The early settlers
here made houses out of trees and tried to live. When they
starved out and moved on, they burned their houses down to
get the nails back.

VERLYN KLINKENBORG

JANUARY

Every evening just at dusk I carry two hay bales into the middle pasture. One goes into the high feed bunk, the other into the feeder just below it. Each bale is bound by two strings of sisal baling twine. I cut the strings near their knots, which were tied by a mechanical baler sometime late last summer in a Massachusetts hay field. The bale springs apart, and the hay falls into flakes. I coil the strings into a neat loop and put them in my pocket. There's at least one coil of twine in every jacket I own and another in the hip pocket of every pair of jeans. On this place, baling twine is the thread of life.

Not that it gets used for much. It ties down tarps and ties up tomato vines and rose canes. It piles up day by day in an empty grain sack or a cardboard box in the barn. The horses are easier to catch with a double length of twine-string as my farming cousins called it, then with a proper halter, and the horses are also gentle enough to be led that way. I know ranch hands in Wyoming who never ride out without a loop of the stuff—usually the orange plastic kind—knotted to a saddle-string or a D-ring. It's hard to describe the emergency that a length of baling twine would fix, but you'd know it if you ever rode into one.

And yet this is the common stuff that gives rural life its sub-stance, a token of what divides this way of living from any other, a reminder of what comes next, what comes every day. Coiling those sisal strands is one of the rewards of doing chores, as is standing among the horses while they crowd together and begin pulling hay from the feeders. The brown horses are mole-dark in their winter coats now, and the dapple-gray mare called Adeline looks ghostly white. Their long hair makes their ears seem especially small, and that makes them all look attentive, though they spend most of the day dozing broadside to the sun's low rays.

If you live with horses, you soon get used to the feel of a line lying across your palm and fingers—a rein, a lead rope, a lariat. It becomes second nature, what hands are for. You begin to feel for the life, the responsiveness in any piece of rope you handle, even a coil of baling twine, because when you work with horses, that line, no matter how stout or supple, is what connects you to them. It transmits the dexterity of your fin-gers, the guilelessness of your intentions. It becomes a subtle tool. It allows horse and human to moor each other.

Recently the neighbors' horses got out through a broken gate in the middle of the night. They trotted up the yellow line on the highway for a couple of miles, backtracked down a gravel road, and disappeared into the woods. We searched until three a.m., driving the back roads, walking the dirt margins, looking for hoofprints or fresh manure. The night was foggy and there had been no snow. In the end, the horses found us. They walked out of the trees and onto the road we had traced them to. They were wraiths until we haltered them. Then they turned into their old solid selves, a pony, a small mule, and three aging, swaybacked horses, all footsore. And who's to say what we turned into, standing there in the mist, clinging with relief to the lead ropes in our hands? The moon barely glimmered upon us, a knot of creatures on the edge of the winter woods, exhaling together, happy to be connected again.

LARRY WOIWODE

WINTER

I n our seventeenth year on a farmstead in North Dakota, a dozen miles from the nearest town, I decide to install an outdoor woodburning furnace, unaware that we're heading into the worst winter recorded in the state's history. The day my son Joseph and I finish the installation, I stand at the furnace as falling snow thickens with a clinging wetness and add scrap wood and branches to the cardboard going in the firebox with an orange gush like gasoline, then swing the door in when the heat gets so intense I have to jerk my head back from its grab at my face. My eyelashes cling at spots and I feel a bunched grip across my eyebrows.

"Crack the door for about ten seconds before you open it and then stay low when you add wood," an obliging advisor for the furnace company said, during one of my many phone calls for advice. The roar of the cardboard subsides; I add limbs, then logs, on this premiere firing of the furnace.

Joseph joins me and we study a gauge to the right of the furnace door. It measures the temperature of the water in a 400-gallon jacket surrounding the firebox. The operating range is between 160 and 170 degrees, I've read, and a vent on the furnace's side, near the front, covered by a grille, allows oxygen to enter to keep the burning lively. Behind the grille is a damper door that a solenoid slams shut. Or should, when a probe in the water jacket senses the temperature is 170. The minute it drops below 160, the same mechanism pops the damper open so the fire, smoldering between times, brings the water up to temperature again—or this is how the furnace reputedly works.

We watch for an hour, adding logs, the gauge barely nearing 100—a momentous amount of wood to heat four hundred gallons. The November day is darkening at five, although we're a month from our shortest day, and in the gloom and dark of snow Joseph and I return to the heat of my office. He is tall and solid, like my father, and goes to a chair and drops into it as I settle at the computer screen. He has inherited my uncles' languid Slavic ease, as I translate it, though he's met only one of them, so that he, like they, can appear at rest even when working—their minds entirely on the task, the parts of their body not involved off on vacation, and now he stretches his legs and crosses them at the ankles as he gives along his length like an uncle he never met. These bonds of blood.

Then his face comes alert with the light of a young person

with a congealing idea. "I know one thing that everybody who owns one of these boilers has in common."

"What? They all live in the country—away from cities and the like?"

"No."

"They want to be self-sufficient, or imagine they are?"

"No," he says.

"What, then?"

"They all have singed eyebrows, like you."

Before, to heat the house and office where I write, we used a combination of a propane furnace, two woodburning stoves, a length of electric baseboard, a kerosene heater and, when the weather turned worse, a milk house heater with a rattly fan. An outdoor furnace seemed the solution and, over and above that, wood is a renewable fuel. Propane or kerosene or heating oil, all petroleum products, can't be replaced, along with coal or peat or plutonium rods.

We've planted thousands of trees on our farmstead and plan to plant more, and not out of guilt. This rolling plain scraped by glaciation, all but treeless, needs any planting it can get to hold its soil. Across the landscape trees lie where they fall and half-mile tree rows, put in as shelter belts, go dead. The trees around our farm were planted sixty years ago, during the Dust Bowl days, and most of them, Chinese elm and ash, are dying. And what do you do with a dead tree? Dump it in a poisonous landfill? We cremate them for the heat.

On a night when Joseph is marooned in town, due to a blizzard, the temperature, with wind chill, reaches a new low, minus 85, and as I wake with a jolt and check the digital clock—3:00 a.m.—I know something is wrong. The wind has throttled up so much our bedroom feels insubstantial from drafts—never this way before. I get my clothes, pull on my boots and coveralls, my face mask and wool cap with earflaps, and go out.

I know it's way below zero when the hair in my nostrils is Brillo with my first breath. In cold like this you don't breathe through your mouth or your lungs feel scorched, as if you inhaled a wigwam of smoke. The scorch arrives though I haven't breathed that way, my hand still on the door.

A chill grips my back as I realize I'm at the epicenter of something awful. I can't see the closest building, not even the furnace, and remember the tales of farmers who had their wives pay out a rope tied to their waists as they left for chores, so they were certain to find their way back, and some didn't. So their wives went to look and were lost, too.

Let light be my guide, I think, dimly seeing a shifty glow from the bulb on the furnace. To establish this end of the rope I turn on the light above our front steps. The corner of the house is a lee, I find, as I step into the tearing snow. Instantly my forehead hurts. I put a glove over it and lower my head and seem to mark time in the wind coming straight from the north, the approximate direction I want to go.

I get to the furnace, out of breath, out of air, about to lean against it when I see that the snow, winding in such a whirlpool it draws sheets straight up past the furnace light, has been plastering the airtight door and melting, forming a nubbly coating of ice. Stalactites the size of an arm, stained yellow in an overflow from combustion, I tell myself, run from the bottom of the door to the ground. I grab the handle and jerk and the door pops open with a clatter like plate glass smashed.

The fire is almost out, the gauge down to 90. *How?*

On the side panel I flip the switch that turns the solenoid on and off. Nothing happens. I should hear the damper clang shut when I do that, because it should be open for burning, with the temperature of the furnace so low. Has the circuit breaker blown? No, the light, which is on the same circuit, is burning. I seem to remember reading about a smaller fuse inside the control box.

If it's dead I can remove the side grille and prop open the damper door. Which means monitoring the furnace every hour, to make sure a boil doesn't begin, and I'm so worn out from working all day in the cold I'm not sure I can do that. The wind is up to such a pitch it's all I hear. I start for the house, whisked from behind in a way I don't want to be in snow so deep, and bend over with a glove above my eyes like a scout, as if I'll be able to see what I'm about to hit.

Inside it feels like suburban Detroit in December. The batteries in most of our flashlights are dead, I remember, used up over a time of no electricity, and I forgot to get replacements. Two pocket flashlights work, I discover, the better of them the one my wife keeps in her purse, pathetic. But two lights as my

rope ends so far have worked. I tread through the kitchen, trying to keep from shedding snow ("It's clean snow!" people
say, when they hate its messy melt), and jog down to the basement. Somewhere is the right socket for the bolts that hold on
the louvered cover.

No, the socket set is in the garage, I realize, and get one of
the mini-flashlights, take a breath of temperate air, and step
outdoors. On my way to the garage I have to climb over a
drift, and once in the garage I roll the door back down. Even
here it feels warm. The car looks stalled in a ditch, from snow
that's seeped in and drifted around it. Socket in hand, I climb
a drift that steps down from one touching the eave of the
garage, and the best I can do is crawl, then roll to the furnace.

To remove the louvered cover I have to take off a glove, and
just as my hand goes numb I see a difficulty in the glow of the
furnace bulb and my mini-beam. Through a silver-gray sheen
that flickers and dims as it thickens—a layer of active snow—
I make out ice at the base of the damper door.

I go to the house for the other pathetic flashlight, the last
one, grab a huge screwdriver, and return to the curved
cocoon carved by wind in the snowbank around the furnace. The ice is so hard it takes fifteen minutes to chip it
away with the screwdriver, but at least my hand has recov-
ered on the trip to the house, and feeling kicks in as I work.
I flip the switch and the door doesn't clang. I check the
gauge on the furnace, down to 80. With this wind the pipes
in the house will be affected soon, because in a kind of
counter-wrap of memory to the cold I'm caught in, I remember how cool the basement felt.

A mechanical part of the damper seems frozen, perhaps the rod that acts as a lifter to push it open, because I can see it bow with strain when I toggle the switch. I turn and head for the dim glow on the house and inside head down to the basement. Yes, cold. I find what I'm looking for—my soldering torch. I fire it up in the entry and the second I step out the door it's snuffed. I let it leak gas all the way to the furnace, jerk open the door, and hold the torch near the last of the coals. It springs to life. I run the tip of its flame over the linkage, afraid of getting too near the top, which might fry the solenoid, then remove the screwdriver, which I've been prying beneath the vent door with, and try the switch again. Nothing.

I bang on the vent with the screwdriver handle, lave it with heat from the torch, and watch drips of water freeze before they're full enough to fall, that cold. I lie on the ground, out of the worst in my cocoon, and find I can hold the torch close enough to the damper from there. Then I watch as the blowing snow starts to form a fuzzy layer over my coveralls, forming a drift of me.

I'm not sure how long I wait for the torch to do its work but soon I know I have to sleep. Life, brief as a breath, over? Carole, Joseph, Newlyn and Ruth and Laurel, dear daughters, it may be by a row of words you remember me, or maybe not. Or images, once my body is gone. You'll have to resolve the distinctions between the two for yourselves, if I can't keep the torch on target, get us heat, undo the miscues that brought us to this, so you'll know it wasn't my interior and its revolving search for words that held me here, but you.

Then the damper springs wide with a clang.

TED KOOSER

IN NEBRASKA

FROM *LOCAL WONDERS*

This prairie is polished by clouds, damp wads of fabric torn from the hem of the mountains, but every scratch shows, from the ruts the wagons made in the 1850s, to the line on an auctioneer's forehead when he takes off his hat. No grass, not even six-foot bluestem, can cover the weather's hard wear on these stretches of light or these people. But though this is a country shaped by storms—a cedar board planed smooth with the red shavings curled in the west when the sun sets—everywhere you see the work of hands, that patina which comes from having been weighed in the fingers and smoothed with a thumb—houses, sheds, machinery, fences—then left behind, pushed off a wagon to lighten the load, a landscape of litter: the boarded-up grocery store with leaves blown in behind the door screen, its blue tin handle reading RAINBO BREAD, the sidewalk heaved and broken; the horseshoe pits like graves grown over with crabgrass and marked by lengths of rusty pipe; the square brick BANK with its windows gone, even the frames of the windows, its back wall broken down and the rubble shoveled out of the way to make room for a pickup with no engine.

You read how the upright piano was left upright by the trail, the soundboard ticking in the heat, how the young mother was buried and left in a grave marked only by the seat of a broken chair, with her name, Sophora, and the date scratched into the varnish, and only a lock of her hair to go west. There are hundreds of graves like that left in the deep grass, on low rises overlooking the ruts that lead on. I tell you that everything here—the auto lot spread in the sun, the twelve-story bank with its pigeons, the new elementary school, flat as a box lid blown off the back of something going farther on, the insurance agent with his briefcase, the beautiful Pakistani surgeon, all these and more, for some reason, have been too burdensome, too big or too small or too awkward, to make it the rest of the way.

KENT MEYERS

THE NIGHT TRUCKS

The cattle trucks came at night so that they would arrive at the stockyards in the morning. Their lights down our long driveway in late winter cut shadows across the upstairs bedroom where my brothers and I slept, the web of the naked elm in the front yard moving slowly over the walls like an ineffective net. Shadows of crooked branches slid over the wall above my bed, over the ceiling, over my sleeping brothers, over the model cars and airplanes we had built and placed on shelves, over the chifforobe where we each had a drawer to store personal things. The gray Formica kitchen table with its wavy patterns of white seemed almost to disappear in the moving shadows. It had come to our room after Dad brought home from an auction sale the great black wooden table that had made Mom cry when she saw it, but which she couldn't refuse because the family had grown too large for the smaller table.

The shadows made the bedroom seem underwater, light coming down through a broken surface, from a distant world. I watched them for a while, then climbed down from the bunk bed and walked through them as they rose over my bare feet from the floor. For a while, before going downstairs, I stood at the window over the porch roof to see the great trucks, framed by their orange running lights, descend the long driveway and pull idling into the yard.

Dressed in coveralls and overshoes, I went out to diesel smoke in the cold air, and throbbing engines, and the drivers' faces in their mirrors as they labored at the wheels, backing around the granary, twisting the trailer so that it eased, with a sigh of air brakes, up to the wooden chute placed at the barn door, through which came the muffled sound of moving animals.

Steam filled the barn. Men and beasts moved obscurely in a white fog lit by dim bulbs, the cold air gusting through the door, heightening the smell of manure. Hooves clattered on the wooden chute. Steers tried to go up two at a time, grunting, snorting, until someone at the chute forced one of them back. The whole barn heaved and roiled. The animals approached the chute head down, legs ready to spring away, until one made the move, and then others followed.

We'd sorted them during the day, gathered them close to the barn and then walked among them, forming judgments. When young, we were just cutters, bringing the ones Dad wanted to see to his inspection, and then, if he decided, chasing them into the barn. The cattle tried to dodge back into the herd and we followed them, singling them out. Even at a young age we could tell one steer or heifer from another, and eventually we'd cut the one Dad sought. He'd look at it, make a decision.

As we got older we learned without formal training, simply by the repetition of finding in the herd the ones he wanted to see, to recognize for ourselves which ones were ready. Then we brought them forward without his orders, and as we got older still we joined the discussion with him, pointing out aspects to a particular steer that made it finished.

We didn't particularly like selling cattle. It was exciting, of course, the dark night, the immense trucks, the contained sense of secrecy and large event in it. But we had walked among these cattle for almost a year, pulled their ears as we paced the bunks, named many of them, learned their idiosyncrasies. There was always a feeling of loss in selling. At the same time we knew it was necessary, like so many other necessary things. The day after the cattle were sold we'd all listen to the morning market reports on WCCO radio to see how well we'd done, to wonder if we could have done better.

And then, always, within a few months, the new calves would arrive, frightened, snorting, scouring, running from the daytime trucks that released them to huddle against the windbreak. And we would feed them. And they would grow used to us. They would grow tame. They would grow fat. Until we would walk among them, judging, dispassionate and critical, and nod our heads, and chase certain of them into the barn.

The year after night came, my brothers and I walked alone among them, having completed the final cycle. We sold them in batches, as Dad had always done, the finished ones first, then feeding the remaining ones for a few more weeks, sorting again, feeding, the trucks coming down the long driveway, going away, coming. Like so many other things, we discovered that we knew how to do this. We no longer needed Dad to make the final decision. We could look at a steer and tell a finished one from an unfinished. It surprised us. Perhaps it shouldn't have, given how long we'd been doing it; the surprise was in discovering what we hadn't known we knew. It was a small pleasure, and perhaps a foolish one, to discover such competency in a year of such loss.

Then the final truck came. By then the haymow was empty of all but a few bales of hay. The silo was empty. The corncribs had only a few piles left. We had planned it that way. We knew what was needed to finish the final herd.

Hooves boomed in the metal trailer. The trailer rocked and swayed. One by one the last cattle leaked away through their own fog, flesh turned insubstantial as shadow. They disappeared through the cloud of their own warm breath, through the chaos of their own confusion, until the barn stood empty, rags of mist in the rafters, and the sound of a diesel engine shifting through its gears and axles echoes from the county road—a rectangle of orange and red running lights, headlights pointed away. We watched. Listened. Then turned toward the house. Snow creaked under our overshoes. The stars were cold.

SVEN BIRKERTS

OPPOSITE OF SOUTH

I am, in all of my deepest identifications, a Northerner. Genetic background goes a long way toward laying the base. I am a first-generation Latvian American, and both sides of the family, as far back as we can trace, hail from places no more than a hundred kilometers on either side of the fifty-seventh parallel. All of the stories I grew up with, from the lives of my parents and their ancestors and from the books that my mother read to me, were somehow rooted in the geography and climate of that part of the world. Simple primary saturations: forests, winters, and the surges of the Baltic Sea, which has always figured in my imagination, rightly or wrongly, as cold and gray. And while my first vocabulary was Latvian, those sounds forever holding the deepest emotional associations, I have nevertheless always thrilled to the words *north* and *northern* whenever I have encountered them.

The word for *north* in Latvian is *ziemeli*, which derives directly from *ziema*, for "winter." Northerners—*ziemelnieki*—were winter people, people from the place of a winter. But the Latvian word, compelling as it is, is narrower and less suggestive to me than its counterpart. *Ziemeli* invokes too directly the frigid core of the concept of north and insists on physical endurance almost exclusively, curtailing so many of the rich peripheral associations.

North. I am at a loss to account for the full biography of that one-syllable construct in my verbal consciousness. I can only marvel at the complexity of resonance I have funneled into the word. I mean not only the background sensations of family history and lore—subtract the elusive essence of north from these stories, and they change their nature entirely—but also an elaborate, subtle ethics of stoicism, which, if I pursued it diligently enough, would probably turn out to be a metaphysics complete with founding principles.

North. Simply and obviously it is the opposite of south, a definition I sometimes call upon as a personal shorthand device to help me get closer to the feeling, the psychology, of what I want to explain. In therapy—itself at some level a betrayal of the Northern ethos, as I understand it—I often rely upon a caricature of my opposite number, the man I so often long to be: the vivid, flash-tempered Sicilian who moves through life by way of emotional explosions, discharging strong feelings before they settle, turn into sediment, or crystallize and grow hard and hurtful edges. What I am really talking about, of course, is my own character, my genetically transmitted, culturally reinforced way of taking in and giving out emotion, my essential rigidity, my held-in nature—my Northernness.

If I am right in making this large-scale geographical, or latitudinal, observation—if I am not simply projecting upon and extrapolating from the merely personal—then I might argue that the essential Northern character, with its deep Lutheran reticences, its iron-flanged stoicism, holds itself counter to the whole paradigm of our progressive, melioristic, therapeutically-oriented millennial culture. Insofar as my images of North encode a message, an assumption about life, it is that circumstance is fundamentally adversarial; human relations are difficult; resolution (never mind transcendence) is unlikely; and the best one can do is to keep one's own counsel, hold fast while enduring disappointments and defeats, and accept that the highest human goal is to greet fate with dignified composure.

Where did I pick this up? Since earliest times, from observing and listening to my people, hearing their stories, taking in the inflections of admiration that quickly became part of my instruction book for living. "And he never said another word to her, never told her how he felt. Can you imagine what strength that took?" Always a moral, always an implied code of behavior. Whatever the account, whatever twist it took, I never failed to get the sense of a self enduring, holding firm, and—most compelling of all—masking its pain.

Do I still subscribe to this worldview? No, not consciously, anyway. Indeed, in many ways I live my life against it—I hope for clarified relationships, trust in the possibilities of growth and improvement (in the self, in the world), long for transcendence in any number of ways. But I also know that my bedrock intuitions, the ones I sometimes try to counter so strenuously, are a product of my Northernness. I feel them whenever I cannot get past myself in a difficult emotional situation, when the inner obstacles don't yield. But I also know that they have come to my rescue, have helped me bear down on a hard task, hold off gratification, and mobilize resistance when I've needed it most.

For a hundred good reasons, to which I mainly subscribe, our culture has demonized repression. Repression is unhealthy; it is the sclerosis of the emotional life, one of the main sources of human unhappiness. Why is it, then, that I respond so much more intensely to art that is premised upon restraint? Clear lines. Characters who understate their pain and hold their secrets, who tighten themselves against the harshness of the world. On the personal plane, why am I, psychologically educated as I claim to be, still stirred by the taciturn, the inhibited, those who seem to accept that it is their lot to be solitary in the world?

I think of the face of the actor Max von Sydow, so familiar in its cast. I see traces of my father's face there. The ascetic nose, the bitter grimace. Hints, too, of Joseph Brodsky's face, which I never tired of watching years ago when he was my teacher, the line of his mouth at once a wince and its containment, the forward set of the lower jaw, so I imagined, a determined damming of some strong feeling. Stoicism, austerity, and—yes—privacy. All of these faces, I realize as I picture them, propose their own self-containment. They are not turned toward the world with some expectation or desire of completion. They do not await the answering other, and for this reason they remain mysterious. Private faces in public places, wrote W. H. Auden, another Northerner, are better than public faces in private places.

What I am moving toward saying—I see it now—is this: that these various attributes are all, for me, tokens of inwardness. In my mythology, harshness and remoteness sit guard over a susceptibility heightened by solitude. This is the compass needle's true north, I'm convinced: the self in isolation—silent, all emotion, thought, and perception contained, held, amplified within their enclosure, even as the strain of the containment signals to others what they cannot possess.

SHERMAN ALEXIE

WHAT SACAGAWEA MEANS TO ME

n the future, every U.S. citizen will get to be Sacagawea for fifteen minutes. For the low price of admission, every American, regardless of race, religion, gender, and age, will climb through the portal into Sacagawea's Shoshone Indian brain. In the multicultural theme park called Sacagawea Land, you will be kidnapped as a child by the Hidatsa tribe and sold to Toussaint Charbonneau, the French-Canadian trader who will take you as one of his wives and father two of your children. Your first child, Jean-Baptiste, will be only a few months old as you carry him during your long journey with Lewis and Clark. The two captains will lead the adventure, fighting rivers, animals, weather, and diseases for thousands of miles, and you will march right beside them. But you, the aboriginal multitasker, will also breast-feed. And at the end of your Sacagawea journey, you will be shown the exit and given a souvenir T-shirt that reads IF THE U.S. IS EDEN, THEN SACAGAWEA IS EVE.

Sacagawea is our mother. She is the first gene pair of the American DNA. In the beginning, she was the word, and the word was possibility. I revel in the wondrous possibilities of Sacagawea. It is good to be joyous in the presence of her spirit, because I hope she had moments of joy in what must have been a grueling life. This much is true: Sacagawea died of some mysterious illness when she was only in her twenties. Most illnesses were mysterious in the nineteenth century, but I suspect that Sacagawea's indigenous immune system was defenseless against an immigrant virus. Perhaps Lewis and Clark infected Sacagawea. If that is true, then certain postcolonial historians would argue that she was murdered not by germs but by colonists who carried those germs. I don't know much about the science of disease and immunities, but I know enough poetry to recognize that individual human beings are invaded and colonized by foreign bodies, just as individual civilizations are invaded and colonized by foreign bodies. In that sense, colonization might be a natural process, tragic and violent to be sure, but predictable and ordinary as well, and possibly necessary for the advance, however constructive and destructive, of all civilizations.

After all, Lewis and Clark's story has never been just the triumphant tale of two white men, no matter what the white historians might need to believe. Sacagawea was not the primary hero of this story either, no matter what the Native American historians and I might want to believe. The story of Lewis and Clark is also the story of the approximately forty-five nameless and faceless first- and second-generation European Americans who joined the journey, then left or completed it, often without monetary or historical compensation. Considering the time and place, I imagine those forty-five were illiterate, low-skilled laborers subject to managerial whims and nineteenth-century downsizing. And it is most certainly the story of the black slave York, who also cast votes during this allegedly democratic adventure. It's even the story of Seaman, the domesticated Newfoundland dog who must have been a welcome and friendly presence and who survived the risk of becoming supper during one lean time or another. The Lewis and Clark Expedition was exactly the kind of multicultural, trigenerational, bigendered, animal-friendly, government-supported, partly French-Canadian project that should rightly be celebrated by liberals and castigated by conservatives.

In the end, I wonder if colonization might somehow be magical. After all, Miles Davis is the direct descendant of slaves and slave owners. Hank Williams is the direct descendant of poor whites and poorer Indians. In 1876 Emily Dickinson was writing her poems in an Amherst attic while Crazy Horse was killing Custer on the banks of the Little Big Horn. I remain stunned by these contradictions, by the successive generations of social, political, and artistic mutations that can be so beautiful and painful. How did we get from there to here? This country somehow gave life to Maria Tallchief and Ted Bundy, to Geronimo and Joe McCarthy, to Nathan Bedford Forrest and Toni Morrison, to the Declaration of Independence and Executive Order No. 1066, to Cesar Chavez and Richard Nixon, to theme parks and national parks, to smallpox and the vaccine for smallpox.

As a Native American, I want to hate this country and its contradictions. I want to believe that Sacagawea hated this country and its contradictions. But this country exists, in whole and in part, because Sacagawea helped Lewis and Clark. In the land that came to be called Idaho, she acted as diplomat between her long-lost brother and the Lewis and Clark party. Why wouldn't she ask her brother and her tribe to take revenge against the men who had enslaved her? Sacagawea is a contradiction. Here in Seattle, I exist, in whole and in part, because a half-white man named James Dox fell in love with a Spokane Indian woman named Etta Adams and gave birth to my mother. I am a contradiction; I am Sacagawea.

STEPHEN DUNN

TWO

Scruples

Since the early eighties more students in my Literature &
Ethics class, a freshman seminar, say they would press a
button that would kill a nondescript peasant in another
land, for which they would receive one million dollars and the
guarantee of never being caught. They respond anonymously
and must give a reason. Four out of twenty-five would in
1982. Eleven out of twenty-five in 1995. Reasons: Because it
would set me up for life. Or, It's just a one-time thing. And
once, Because it's a doggie-dog world. Afterward, I point out
that the question is designed only to see if they are murderers.
By semester's end, I'm pretty sure I know who they are, these
murderers, and it all switches to me—that age-old imperative,
to discover what's right and to do it. I've given a murderer an
A because of incontrovertible intelligence. Yet I've graded
down at least a few because their logic, however sound, was

without heart and I didn't like their faces. And I can't say how many times I've given up on some of the decent ones—their correct, inherited, annoying positions unchanged by drama or dialectic. In the early seventies, no one I knew would press the button. I love that it wasn't high-mindedness back then, merely the obvious, and that so many wished to do good. Experience took years to show us what we could not sustain.

Saints

Those who earn their names know what suffering is . . . and elect it anyway. They love without ambivalence one shining thing, yet some—the even more saintly—are tortured by the manifold richness of the discernible world. I've known one secular saint. I watched him fast so an idea would swell. I didn't want to be him, though once or twice, by design, I've felt that strange sumptuousness born from doing without. For him it must have been an imagined feast, like a wafer on the tongue. For me: just another something for the body to have known before it dies and becomes dust. Saints, like revolutionaries, walk headlong into the cool, dry wind, are always serving a hidden flame, are terrifying because of what they do not need. The saint asks, What will you die for? The revolutionary adds, For what would you kill? Either way, sacrifice is an ugly business, as ugly as history itself. Choose between these terrible things, history often says. We are only commentators until, for us, it comes to that choice.

PAUL ZIMMER

THE TRAINS

enry David Thoreau's tranquility was interrupted
daily by the sound of the train passing near Walden,
reminding him of things he did not wish to think
about. "The whistle of the locomotive penetrates my woods
summer and winter, sounding like the scream of a hawk sailing over some farmer's yard." The old clinkers must have been
especially invasive, clanging and spouting soot and cinders
into the trees and onto the board-and-batten houses near the
tracks.

There have been no trains in our valley in southwestern
Wisconsin for more than sixty years; the final run on the fifty-
two-mile Kickapoo Valley & Northern branch line tracks
from La Farge to Soldiers Grove passed through in 1939. I
was five years old and growing up far away in Ohio when the
last train ran the bankrupt line. I guess it was a sad occasion

and the local bands played funeral dirges as the engine paused at each station.

All of the KV&N track was pulled up for scrap metal during World War II and only a few old stations and traces of the throughway are left. Ben Logan, the novelist who grew up in this area, tells me that on damp days the sound of those old trains winding through the valleys came right up to your ears and made you feel the sadness of the fog. It brought you up from whatever you were doing. Just to imagine that mournful hooting in the woods makes me understand Thoreau's complaint—but now, strangely, I envy his annoyance. I would give a great deal to be able to grumble about such interruptions. They would provide more frame to the landscape than the remote wisps and distant droning of high-flying jetliners over our ridge.

But I start this piece on 12 September 2001, and today I would give anything to hear the distant drone of the high liners and see their contrails crisscrossing overhead. The skies are empty and we are in national shock, mourning death and devastation as we begin to gain determination. We are at war, and we are told that it is likely to be long and cruel. In a few days or weeks, when we have gathered our wits and resources, we will be mounting our response, sending young men and women off to distant battlefields. Their loved ones will bid them goodbye. It will be the fifth war of my generation's time, and perhaps the worst.

Why do I sit at my writing table at a time like this? Because it is what I know how to do. Perhaps I should admit that I long for another time, sights and sounds I never knew or deserved to know, steam trains gray and slinking in the rain or blue and buoyant in the sunlight, the whistle of solemn engines winding through misty woods and fields in the valley below.

My orders in 1953 were to report to the army's base near the atomic test grounds. I was not going to war, but I was headed toward the unknown and particular danger of my era. I had been ordered to participate with a small group of men as military witnesses to the testing of these ultimate weapons. I did not know what this meant, but I was aware of what the bombs had done to Hiroshima and Nagasaki. The army wanted to test the reactions of soldiers to atomic explosions, and we were to witness detonations at very close range.

What I saw and experienced in Nevada does not matter at this moment. What I want to remember here is what I felt—or what little I felt—as I rode the train west from Ohio. I was twenty years old and this was my first train journey alone. I had taken a few days' leave from the army to visit home on my way to Nevada. I said hello and goodbye to my friends. My mother tearfully held me for a long time at our house, but she did not go to the station. My father, who never cried, took me to the train and solemnly shook my hand as I stepped up into the coach. He tried to say something, but the engineer was clearing blast pipes on the big engine, so we smiled and waved at each other through the din. Then he turned and walked away quickly with his head down.

I was a shy, taciturn young person and had learned in basic

training to attract as little attention as possible to myself. Frightened and trying to be brave, I was also numb with uncertainty. The trip took several days and I must have changed trains in Salt Lake City. We passed through grand vistas, deserts, and mountains I had never experienced, but I paid little attention. I nibbled candy bars and ate the sandwiches my mother had packed in a shoebox. Without speaking, I pointed to my selections of soft drinks from the vendor's cart. Mostly I kept my head down and talked to no one.

What was I thinking? I cannot recall. I was doing my duty, traveling toward danger, preparing myself to be staunch. I had a book, an anthology of great short stories, and I had some vague notion that I wanted to be a writer. This was my first experience of Chekhov, Saki, Huxley, Conrad, Maupassant, Colette, Mann, Turgenev, Salinger, Porter, Hemingway, Faulkner. Frequently I was puzzled by what I read, but when I finished the book, I started it again.

There was a young woman with a baby in the seat across the aisle. The baby was fussy, and she struggled to comfort it. At one point, in frustration, she appealed generally to the passengers, asked if someone could help her open a can of baby food. She had forgotten a can opener. I carried an army C-ration opener on my key chain. When no one else came forth, I motioned to her that I could give assistance. She smiled with relief and thanked me when I handed the opened can back to her. She told me that her husband was also in the army; she wanted to have a friendly chat, but I did not know how to respond. I blushed and put my nose back into my book of stories. I must have opened half a dozen cans for her during the trip, working the sharp little blade around their rims, then handing them back without a word.

When I made my way to the restroom at the end of the car, I kept my eyes straight ahead and looked at no one. How can I explain my extreme reticence? I was so lonely and unpracticed, so far from home. I did not know how to speak, nor did I have anything to say. Occasionally I gazed out the window, but mostly I read.

I remember pondering and rereading Joseph Conrad's story "Youth," the old man's narrative of his perilous experience as a young seaman on a storm-wracked, burning coal liner. I wondered what he meant when he said toward the end: "I remember my youth and the feeling that I will never come back anymore—the feeling that I could last forever, outlast the sea, the earth, and all men; the deceitful feeling that lures us on to joys, to perils, to love, to vain effort—to death."

I think about myself as that disoriented young man on the train, as I think of the young people who are loading their gear, saying goodbyes, and heading toward the highly ambiguous future with so little knowledge of the past. I think of what they must do in the days and months ahead, their silence, their fear and determination. I stand in a meadow and look up, wishing for vapor trails in the crisp autumn sky. I listen longingly for the clatter of old trains in the valley below.

DAVID HUDDLE

MEN AT NIGHT

We loaded up to make a night jump. It was after sunset when we boarded the planes. One tall, gangly trainee accidentally pulled the handle of his emergency chute and sent the thing billowing out down the aisle of the plane. He came walking back down the ramp of the C-130, carrying a bundle of white parachute cloth in his arms. From over in the shadows, Sergeant Dixon began yelling at him.

We sat on the planes a long time before we took off. We couldn't see outside, but we knew it was dark, and even the Jumpmasters at the rear of the plane were nervous. We flew for what seemed like hours, and when the doors finally opened, there was a blast of wind and noise, but there wasn't any light coming in, and the darkness out there roared at us. We stood up, checked the equipment, released static lines from each other's backpacks, and handed them forward. We hooked static lines and checked them. Then we stood by, watching the red light. The Jumpmaster signaled the first man to stand in the door, and that man took the crouching position, with his hands and one toe outside the plane, facing out into the darkness. We waited for the light to change to green. But it didn't.

After a long while the Jumpmaster pulled the first man back out of his crouch. The doors were pulled closed on both sides of the aircraft. The command was passed back along the lines of us, each of us shouting it to the man behind him, "Unhook static lines. Sit down."

The C-130 landed back at the air base. It was the first time any of us trainees had landed in one of those C-130s. The landing was rough and frightening, the plane bouncing and fishtailing on the runway. The rear ramps were let down for us. They did not tell us why the night jump did not take place.

Outside in the dark around the C-130s, the men began grumbling while we took off chutes, packed them up, and threw them to men waiting to receive them on deuce-and-a-half trucks. Then we formed up to run back to the training field.

It was a clear night. There was a thin moon. The long paved road out around the air base gleamed like a trail of pewter in front of us, the dark grass flattening out on either side of us. First there was silence while we ran. Then two men began talking and cursing very loudly, while others in the ranks shouted at them. At the rear of the formation a fight broke out, we could hear scuffling, and Sergeant Dixon and Sergeant Mitchell dropped back to see about it. We kept running in the dark, but the steady cadence was broken. Men continued shouting and talking in the ranks, a few laughing loudly. A shrill voice back in the ranks began to make sounds I couldn't really fathom. I was afraid while I ran. Sergeant Mitchell came bulling up through the ranks, shoving men out of his way and shouting to us, "Shut up, you assholes, you shitheads!" His face was swollen when he reached me, and he seemed to have grown larger in size, so that when he grabbed me with both hands and flung me out of the formation onto the dark grass, I knew that he had enough strength in him to kill me easily. I spun and crouched and waited for him to come after me, but he went on up through the ranks, shouting, "Shut the fuck up!"

I trotted back into the running formation. Men moved over to make a place for me, and soon Sergeant Houghton came up beside the ranks. He began calling a simple cadence, just loud enough for us to hear him. "Yo lef! Yo lef! Yo left, ri, lef!" he called, and his voice worked to calm us. The chaotic shuffling in the dark became a steady, unified pacing, every boot hitting the pavement as one boot. It was so dark I could barely see the man in front of me, but I knew I was all right now. I was in step with a hundred men, each of us nearly invisible to the others.

SCOTT ELY

RANDOM

arrived at a base camp near Saigon in 1969, just after a nasty Tet. I walked up to an ice cream stand with another soldier, who was dressed in faded jungle fatigues and carried a rucksack and a rifle. He was tall and thin and did not look like he had an ounce of fat on his body. Except for my shiny new fatigues, he could have been my double. After we bought vanilla ice cream cones, I asked him what he was doing in base camp. He licked his dripping cone and pointed at his teeth.

"Sniper shot the guy in front of me in the head," he said. "I caught his skull fragments in the mouth. Man, I got a week in base camp. And new teeth."

For the first time I realized what it was going to be like, the randomness of it all. We had practiced ambushes in basic training. Sometimes I was told that I had lived because of a good reaction and sometimes I was told that I was dead because I had reacted too slowly or had made a mistake. One of the training cadre had been the sole survivor of a unit bombed by mistake by American planes. He had pointed out with a smile that at the time of the bombing he was on R & R. I had not paid much attention to him. Instead I had listened to my instructors, counting on surviving because I would be quick and smart.

I told him that I was going up to Pleiku, located in the mountainous region of the country. I asked him what to expect.

"It's not so bad," he said. "Up and down, up and down."

He walked away with a bounce in his step.

I wondered what he was carrying in his rucksack. Whatever it was, it could not be heavy, perhaps a change of clothes, a book. I had no books. On the plane ride over I had read Dostoevsky's *The Devils*. I donated the book to the Red Cross girls when I stepped off the plane. Something for soldiers to read in hospitals, they said.

While we were waiting to be loaded onto a plane to Pleiku, another set of Red Cross girls handed out brand-new books. I chose a copy of *Howards End*. I began reading it, sitting cross-legged on the steel floor of a C-130, packed in with other soldiers. When I reached the middle of the book, the novel started over again. The publisher had dumped these defective copies on the troops. I wondered how many soldiers never even got to the middle.

I lay in a clump of bamboo outside of Pleiku and watched the shell fragments, glowing red in the night, come sailing toward us. They cut down the bamboo above our heads, and the stalks fell across our bodies. It was harassment and interdiction fire, our guns, fired at random points in the bush. It was a game we played with the enemy, designed to make his free movement uncertain and difficult. Theoretically we were safe, our position marked on a map down in some bunker. But sometimes the gunners made mistakes, and tonight we were within the kill radius of the rounds.

As I raised my head, I knew I was making myself vulnerable. None of us wore helmets or flak jackets. We were a recon team. We needed to be able to move fast and make no noise. We were soft targets, softer than the underside of a woman's breast. The fragments jumped out at me, and I was mesmerized the way I was as a child when I watched a 3-D movie in Atlanta, peering at the screen through a pair of special glasses as spears leaped out of that one-dimensional surface.

Someone pushed my head down into the bamboo leaves, which had a dry smell, like old newspapers.

"You gonna get your damn head blown off," a voice whispered in my ear.

Recently I talked with a young archaeologist. He was home on a visit from digging for bones in Laos and Vietnam. He had become an expert on downed aircraft. We talked of F-4s, A-1Hs, and AC-47s. I was comfortable speaking with someone who knew the names of these things. He was intimately familiar with the ordnance the planes carried and the mines they dropped. American pilots dropped enormous quantities of these mines, so many that they indifferently referred to them as "garbage." The mines could be dropped from the air without detonating and packed enough explosive power to blow off a foot. And there was the BLU-42, known as a "spider mine," which threw out eight tripwires upon impact. To this day the spiders lie in wait for the unwary.

He worked on the Ho Chi Minh Trail at major arteries where the action was hot during the war. There were plenty of North Vietnamese bones, but few American remains. Whatever the team found was shipped to Hawaii for identification.

He told me how they made field identification of skulls and teeth. Oriental incisors are wedge-shaped. But then so are the incisors of Native Americans, so he could never be completely certain. And you can stick a pencil up the nasal cavity of an American skull, but it will not fit into a Vietnamese skull.

He surveyed the sites and supervised the dig. Instead of using a computer, he made his maps of the site by hand. He told me that if he took the time, he could make a beautiful map. I imagined him sitting in his tent at night, working on the maps in the light from a gasoline lantern, charting the location of those bones.

He told me about unexploded cluster bomblets and how Vietnamese have built houses out of the containers. He talked about the heat and malaria. His voice rose with excitement as he told me how he had seen Vietnamese workers blown apart by unexploded mines. They were after the metal and the high explosive, which they used for cooking.

Then we talked about how he and I looked at the world differently. How we were beyond the reach of things that trouble ordinary people. And I wanted to tell him to be careful, that there was a line he should never cross, that once you go over you cannot go back.

JUDITH KITCHEN

✳

STANDARD TIME

We've stopped saving daylight. Now, in the dark diminished hour of five o'clock, light hovers somewhere over the lake, a second horizon floating above the first, bright for a lingering moment, then gone. It comes again in early morning—earlier morning—when we don't yet want to be awake. Oh we know that it helped our grandparents on the farm, helped them milk and feed in the milklight of a November sunrise, but we have left all that behind.

Daylight. Day delight. The calypso of four years old, early to rise into the dawn. The wide expanse of lawn where the Conscientious Objectors planted their long rows of lettuce. More than a victory garden: feeding the war, but not fighting it. Scud and scuffle of hoes, my father showing them how to lift, then pull against the grain. My brother in his three-wheeled baby buggy. No rubber for a fourth wheel. And down the road, Johnny Haar, gassed in World War I, his face twisted into a smile. Drool down his chin, and his indecipherable sounds. Not quite a wail, not quite a moan, though my mother says *see how happy he is.*

Not a farm, but next door to a farm. Cornfields and pasture. Cows restless in their stanchions. *Mooooo.* They really do sound like the storybooks. Shifting of rumps. The call rises at the far end of the barn. Clank of metal as the cow swings her head, back feet splayed. A ripple of flanks. *Moooo.* The answer, close now, louder, slobber of sound.

That was all before. When everything rose early. A rooster who haunted the rafters. When everything seemed large and familiar and unchanging. Then there was kindergarten and the world grew as small as a word. C-o-w. Which led to h-o-w and v-o-w. Which led in turn to the confusion of *low* and *mow* and *sow* and *tow*. And back to *now*. And later *bough* and *through* and *tough* and *thorough*. Small as a word, and unfamiliar.

Dawn over the Cascades. Three thousand miles away, I see it happen. Though I know you really can't see the mountains till noon. Gray in the morning, a filtered gray, all gauze and cautious cloudcover. Three thousand miles and three time zones, and still I can call up sunlight on snowcap.

Sundown, nightfall: the compound words of active disappearance. I picture the Olympics, their dark serrated edges outlined in pink and gold. And then the solid dark. Eleven o'clock, which only days ago was midnight: the motion-sensored light in the backyard snaps on. My brother opens the sliding glass door and looks out. Raccoons, he thinks. So he listens for something—a rattle of lids, a scratch of claws on the cement patio. I see myself in the premature light of morning, looking for evidence. What was out there in the night? My imagination includes the raccoon, the deer that stare back unafraid, apples falling behind the fence, the last long stretch to the solstice. This, I suspect, is nostalgia for the future.

Two hundred years ago, a day had its own slow cycle, full and round as the arc of the sun in the sky. No one conceived of today's digital dislocation. And then, with the Industrial Revolution, suddenly time belonged to someone else. The world shifted. Protestant time: doctrinal and unrepentant.

The long reach back to four years old—conjured memory—is not the same as nostalgia, which presumes a sense of time passing, the sense of self that says *mine, my time, my time*, over and over, a litany of hours. No, that was before time slipped through the fingers and made itself felt in its very dissipation. The sun rose, and fell. The men came with their tools, went back again to their quarters. My mother took down the clothes from the line with their hint of folded sunshine. My father came home from work and took up his hoe. Up one row, down another. What is a weed? What is a sun-ridden sky, and a world beyond it?

Time stops. Suspended there where to sit all afternoon on the front step is simply to sit all afternoon on the front step. Is to register the sound of duration in birdcall and breeze. Is to hear the blurred wings of a lawn mower, a dog punctuating the silence from two blocks away. One bark. A syncopated beat. Then two more. Then nothing. But a nothing full of the bark that did not follow, an ellipsis of sorts. And then, when you least expect it, when the throb of sunshine is all you can sense, another bark. Fainter, and less insistent.

Afternoons filled with time, as though it were solid and you could save it in your pocket. As though you could part it, like a curtain, and find yourself inside another room. Sometimes you did. You stepped right inside the pages and they held you up. Wherever you were, the book was all that contained you as you clambered over the locked garden wall. It knew you better than you knew yourself.

But some books were better than others. You knew enough to know that, even then. Some took the words that had floated free above you and anchored them to circumstance. The wall grew thick with vines. It became *your* secret.

Some were better than others, and you held the key—a huge black key that turned in the lock and allowed you entry. Indeterminate time, until your mother called you back for dinner, until bedtime came in its lockstep pace.

Those were the books that mattered. They were in you, the way waves, incessant, after a while cease to be sound. Even now, you can call up their timelessness. Not only *The Secret Garden* and *Little House on the Prairie*, but the chronicle of your maturation: *East of Eden*, *The Great Gatsby*, *Light in August*—west and east and south opening themselves to you long before you mounted the steps of the train, long before the summer you and your friend drove her sister's old Renault into Wyoming, where you had to wait two days for foreign tires to be shipped to Dubois from Cheyenne. West and east and south and suddenly there you were: in Dublin itself, its wet streets slick and shiny in the streetlights, seeming to leap from the pages of Joyce. Were you really there, or did the book take visible shape? You shivered a little in the rain and were glad of its physical reminder. You stepped back into time, into deadline and decision and detail.

Who were those men from the CO camp? They came from Brooklyn, from Buffalo and Pittsburgh, brought together in our town through their shared refusal. Some were communists—innocent idealists of the sort that only America can produce. They were city men who knew nothing of farming. If they'd been from the west, we know they would have been pressed into fighting fires, building dams, clearing trails in the national parks. But in the east they were herded into a barracks and farmed out to do their farming. My father was one of them.

Or not one of them, not quite. He was a physicist in a necessary job, so he was allowed to stay at home, allowed to go to work each day. He moved freely in and out of society. The best of both his worlds. By rights, they should have resented him.

I would have sensed it. I'd have felt their backs stiffen when they tossed me into the air. I'd have seen their eyes cloud over whenever he came home, riding his bicycle the long seven miles, saving gasoline. They would have looked away, busy with their weeding. Instead, they looked up, called out the latest news on the radio. And they welcomed his hoe, adding to the rhythm of the long summer evening. Light languished. None of them knew—not even my father, the physicist—that Los Alamos was looming.

Here's what they thought: all wars are the same, and all are inhuman.

Some books are better than others. I say it into the void. I say it into an atmosphere filled with the explosive shards of theory. I say it in the face of a vocabulary that daunts even the dauntless, a jargon I cannot wrest from its abstract origins. Some books are better than others. They know more of the human heart, and more of its heartlessness. They are haunted by water. Haunted by what they cannot escape. Heart-rending. They are not cultural constructions. They are Johnny Haar— the pure, individual cry of the singular first person. His war was not the same—and it was inhuman. Time twists and conjoins like a Möbius strip, catches up from behind and places its shoes in its own parenthetical footprints.

We could name them: those brave voices that stand out from the crowd. We could name them, but our lists would not tally. Still, we would know what we mean: someone was there before me. Some one.

The body wakes in its old time zone. Shaken awake. All afternoon you sat on the step while the sun swept the sky. All afternoon you relived time. Dean Stockwell played Colin, you remember that. And now you see him on the screen, an aging man, a few years older than you are. Your mirror, if you needed one. Though anything will do: "Blue Suede Shoes" or "The Wayward Wind"; paper dolls, the Brooklyn Dodgers, S&H Green Stamps. Green War Savings Stamps. My father's yard laid out in tidy rows: corn and carrots and onions and beets. The handwriting of a generation.

Yesterday the tall young woman who didn't know how to hold a pen. Caught it up in her fist, then twisted her wrist in order to print a couple of words. Where was the Palmer Method of her youth? That spiral of O's uncoiling like a Slinky. Something lost, something skittering away. So this is what it is to see time fly. To count the years, then the months, then the days. To feel the press of time even as the minutes quicken, even as everything moves in doublespeed, fastforward, a race to the finish.

Now there is only the page—and the way the day stops at the brink of it. You have no words for what the greatest writers do, and hardly any words for how they do it. But you know what it is to turn back the hands of the clock, stare out of your bedroom window into one long evening hour when the men are leaning on their hoes, talking softly about everything that will matter for the rest of your life. The heft of their words, the urgency of tone as they talk about missing their wives, about violence and war and the way they have had to look deep into their own capacities. And then your mother calls through the screen—coffee and cake—and they all come, laughing, into the house. Their sounds will weave through fifty years, faded and forgiving. You've forgotten their names: those men who would not fight. You wonder if they might have been mistaken. You know that you don't know what drove their moments of decision. All you can hear is the grate of metal on rock, the small *harrumph* as a clump of dirt is pulled from the aggregate. The war ended and they went away. The mouse ran down. You went off to school.

JANET WONDRA

THE WAR AT HOME

There they are, in the kitchen, she washing, he drying, talking the adult talk that is both without interest and oddly comforting. What matters is that it runs on, is not about us, that the tone is even, not a drone, but a hum, of life continuing. It is adults talking adult talk to each other so my sister and I can go about our lives under the canopy of these tall people. The room is a little dim although the kitchen light is on; from this I can tell it is winter, when night seeps through the cracks around the windows and mixes with the kitchen light, darkening it, the way a drop of blood in a glass of water will diffuse, making the whole glass not water anymore but something slightly sinister.

Who knows where I am. Maybe at the dining room table doing some homework or making a drawing. Or maybe I'm sitting in the alcove near the vegetable bin, or playing on the floor outside the kitchen, on the rug. But wherever I am, I know that my parents will always do the dishes after dinner, my mother always washing. This is the time when they unload their day, reveal the pattern to each other and the details that make the pattern, and even when my sister and I are older and doing the adult thing—being generous—and offer to do the dishes so they can rest or take their evening walk, they say, *No, this is our time together, when we talk.* This is the fixed quality of the family, the thing that holds us to the foundation, that makes us firm and whole. We are glad, really, to have more time to be our selfish selves, and we've made the gesture and have been given the great boon of their saying no.

But lately I stand outside that kitchen door again and think about the darkness, of my parents not as big people magically created so I could be born, with no more life or history than I had, but almost as strangers, who lived for thirty years before I arrived. Who had been to war.

My mother did not go to war—she was at home waiting to be my mother. But my father did, and we knew this growing up, but had no sense of it, the light in the kitchen was a little dim because it was dark outside, and even the curtains couldn't hold back that much darkness, pressing the way that water presses constantly against the concrete sides of a pool, not violent or sharp, just constantly asserting its desire to break through. And unaware of this danger, this past, my sister and I played.

We had our problems—a fight with a friend, fear of school, the vague but constant discontent of childhood, which is something like wanting to be free while knowing that the outside is too big and fierce for someone so small, but wanting out anyway, how a cat will cry to go outside, and then, on the other side of the door, will immediately cry to be let back in. We went about our business, my sister and I, growing up, denying our parents had any part in making us what we were, blaming them for any part of ourselves we disliked, and we set out into the world to be buffeted in our own right.

I stand outside the kitchen door still and watch my parents and try to imagine where they were before I was five, seven, singing little songs to myself, all dreamy dreams. But what I consider now is that when I was born, the war was only seven years back, and for my sister, only five years before. Five years is just a moment ago, especially for something so fierce, so all-encompassing as war, a world war. I remember asking why it was a world war instead of just a war, why there were only two, why there were two at all. I saw the world spinning against its black theatrical curtain, and the blue-green of it turned to red and flame, and my fear was that the planet would explode, because I had seen the science films of solar flares and molten lava pouring down the sides of volcanoes at night, and didn't every country have to be fighting every other country for it to be a world war? And how could everyone be so mad at everyone else, all at once? And whose fault was it? And was my father angry? And if not, why did he fight? And how was it that the earth didn't explode and was spared so I could live on it and watch the wind blow the tall pecan trees into a frenzy at night when I was supposed to be going to sleep but instead was blinking out the window into the dark?

My father had gone across the water to Europe, but still he had come back to be my father. His cousin—his close friend—

had been blown up in a troop ship, and I knew this and I watched Donald's mother, my Aunt Johnnie, for signs of persistent sorrow. What I saw was dailiness, carrying on, but it was hard to know adults, no matter how much you watched and listened. Mr. Kerwin had been in an Italian prisoner-of-war camp, but you would never know it because he was mostly just very handsome and a joker and the father of four handsome sons we played with. But then, at a barbecue, when the youngest son, joking around, let a marshmallow he was roasting fall into the fire, Mr. Kerwin grabbed him up, by the upper arm in a grip you could tell was inescapable, and said, *You must never, ever waste food that way again*, and we hushed and were afraid. Later our parents told us it had been very bad in the camp, so it made sense that Mr. Kerwin felt so strongly about food, but for us, not that many years before *Hogan's Heroes*, it was a mystery. War made you into someone who seemed normal and calm, but like the earth, you had layers all the way down, and sometimes—who knew when?—the lava would pop right through.

There were just too many questions, and if you asked them, the grown-ups got cross or impatient, and then you couldn't find out anything, so sometimes it was better to make up your own answers. Even though it would be years before I would learn about the scientific method, I came up with hypotheses and silently gathered data to match against them, the way you take a piece of a jigsaw puzzle and try it against the hole you hope to fill, turning it this way and that, imagining the shape of the piece you're looking for, the color, the pattern. And if there was a war movie, and my father was in the room, I would watch his face, out of the corner of my eye, to see if anything showed—skepticism, fear, sadness—or if a story was forthcoming or an exclamation like *That's not the way it was at all*. But very little came clear.

When we were growing up, my parents would pause, as if listening to something in the distance and say, *That was one*. And we'd ask, *One what?* And they would say, *An earthquake, didn't you feel it?* And it wasn't until I had been through a major earthquake myself that I began to sense those little tremors. An initiation. The war was like that, I think. Ever after, it was a lens you looked through.

It sounded as if my mother mostly had fun during the war, although war-related fun, so maybe it didn't count: dancing with boys at the USO—a kind of patriotic duty, after all; what girls did for the war, at least back then—and I seem to remember something about going to the Red Cross to make bandages and knit socks. And, of course, writing my father, who was overseas. So there was a cast over all this lightheartedness, but it was hard for us to see, because after all, wasn't she just waiting for my father, passing the time with those other boys? God or someone else had decided in advance that my father would not get blown up and therefore would be coming home, so how could there be any true worry or apprehension, any sleepless nights or anxious waiting, and how could we imagine the level of fear or the stress of constant not-knowing because, after all, the war was just a brief interlude before my father began the long, golden story of being our mustached parent. And of course, the mustache was part of the story, because he had grown it on the troop ship over, or maybe it was coming back, but in any case, he had never shaved it off, even though we would beg and wheedle, because we wanted to see what he looked like without it, because we wanted to make him do what we wanted for once, because we wanted to alter the plodding monotony of steady family life.

What we didn't consider, what I think about now, is how hard my parents worked to create that steadiness, the very thing I sometimes hated and did everything I could to turn topsy-turvy. The dailiness, the one foot in front of the other, the predictability of school every weekday, mowing the lawn once a week in summer, and once every two weeks all the rest of the year, the dutiful visits to grandparents and other relatives, the daily dishwashing. How I longed for something to happen! The big emotions, the big event, the upheaval—anything. But only a few years back, bright in their memory, was the war, years of it, when my father should have been dancing with my mother instead of getting trench foot, when my mother should have been rolling silk stockings up her legs instead of applying leg makeup and drawing a seam up her calf with an eyebrow pencil. Maybe their wish was that nothing big would ever happen again.

So we struggled on, the children rampant, the parents longing for restraint and a little peace and quiet. In the newspaper cartoon or on television, the quintessential 1950s father, his feet on the ottoman, says, *Could I just have a little peace?* It's not much to ask. My grandfather had fought the war to end all wars, then my father had fought his. A little peace, as if it has to be measured out in grains, precious, too costly for us to have our fill.

WANG PING

BOOK WAR

discovered "The Little Mermaid," my first fairy tale, in 1968. That morning, when I opened the door to light my stove, I found my new neighbor, a girl a few years older, sitting under the streetlight, a book in her lap. The red plastic wrap indicated it was Mao's collected work. She must have been there all night long, for her hair and shoulders were covered with frost, and her body shivered violently from cold. Another loyal Maoist, I thought to myself. Then I heard her sobbing. I got curious. What kind of person would weep from reading Mao's words? I walked over and peeked over her shoulders. What I saw made me freeze in fear and excitement. The book in her hands had nothing to do with Mao; it was Hans Christian Andersen's fairy tales, the story of "The Little Mermaid." Since I heard the story in my kindergarten, I was determined to read it myself someday. Just when I was ready, the Cultural Revolution began. Schools were closed, books, condemned as "poisonous weeds," were burnt on streets, and the rest were confiscated.

My clever neighbor had disguised the "poisonous weed" with the scarlet cover of Mao's work. Engrossed in the story, she didn't realize my presence behind her until I started weeping. She jumped up, fairy tales clutched to her budding chest. Her panic-stricken face said she was ready to fight me to death if I dared to report her. We stared at each other for an eternity. Suddenly she started laughing, pointing at my tear-stained face. She knew then that her secret was safe with me.

She gave me twenty-four hours to read the fairy tales, and I loaned her *The Arabian Nights,* which was missing the first fifteen pages and the last story, but no matter. The girl squealed and danced in the dawn light. When we finished each other's books, we decided to start an underground book exchange network. With strict rules and determination, we had books to read almost every day, all "poisonous" classics.

Soon I excavated a box of books my mother had buried beneath the chicken coop. I pried it open with a screwdriver, and pulled out one treasure after another: *The Dream of the Red Chamber, The Book of Songs, Grimms' Fairy Tales, Romeo and Juliet, Huckleberry Finn, American Dream,* each wrapped with waxed paper.

I devoured them all, in rice paddies and wheat fields, on my way home from school and errands. I tried to be careful. The consequences could have been catastrophic, not only for myself but also for my entire family, had these books fallen into wrong hands. But my "enemy" was my own mother.

Once she discovered I had unearthed her treasure box, she set out to destroy these "time bombs," combing every possible place in the house. It was a hopeless battle. My mother knew my habits, my little tricks. I couldn't outsmart her. Whenever she caught me red-handed, she'd order me to tear the pages and place them in the stove, and she'd sit nearby, tears in her eyes, muttering: "This is for your safety, everyone's safety." And my heart, our hearts, turned into ashes.

When the last book was gone, I went to sit in the chicken coop. Hens surrounded me, pecking at my closed fists for food. As tears flowed, the stories became alive from inside. They flapped their wings and flew out of my mouth like mourning doves. I started telling them to my siblings, friends, and neighbors; stories I'd read from those forbidden treasures, stories I made up for myself and my audience. We gathered on summer nights, during winter darkness. When I saw stars rising in their dimmed eyes, I knew I had won the war.

LAWRENCE MILLMAN

BOOKLESS IN BIAK

Once, in the Ecuadorian Amazon, I was obliged to lighten my baggage prior to boarding a seemingly lighter-than-air plane. I wouldn't have minded giving up my waterproof poncho, my hiking boots, and my chloroquine tablets, but when the pilot asked me to leave behind Waterton's *Travels in South America* and Alec Waugh's *Hot Countries*, I became rather upset. What if I were laid up in some remote jungle hut? I wasn't worried about dying, but I was worried about dying without a book to read.

Of all the maladies capable of striking down a traveler in a foreign land—malaria, blackwater fever, typhoid, sleeping sickness, and so on—the one I fear the most is being caught with nothing to read. Let the monsoons play havoc with my itinerary, the national airline go on strike, and the foreign land itself prove unabashedly dull: a good book or indeed a bad book will always save the day. Nor do I even need to open this book. Simply the knowledge that it's there, waiting to be opened, is enough.

Not too long ago, on Biak Island off Irian Jaya, I turned the last page of Charles Darwin's *Voyage of the Beagle*. I wasn't too concerned about this because I figured I still had an unread copy of Graham Greene's collected short stories lodged somewhere in my rucksack. I was mistaken. There was no Graham Greene in any pocket, nook, or corner of my rucksack. There was no book at all, in fact.

I was still more or less unperturbed. Biak is not the North Pole or the nether Sahara but the gateway to eastern Indonesia, and thus an important traveler's way station. My bookless condition would only be temporary. Or so I told myself to keep up my morale.

My first thought was to visit the airport. Like other airports in Irian Jaya, it doubled as a concession stand and sold such native curios as spears, carvings, and charms made from chicken feet. I figured it'd sell books, too. I even imagined finding a copy of Peter Matthiessen's account of his 1961 Irian Jaya trip, *Under the Mountain Wall*, a book I'd always wanted to read. Or failing that, I'd buy a thriller or two, preferably by Simenon, whose Inspector Maigret novels I'd been able to pick up in such far-flung locales as the Outer Hebrides and Coeur d'Alene, Idaho.

Sad to say, the concession area of the airport was closed. It opened only for international flights. The next such flight, I learned, was two days away and happened to be the flight I was booked for. Those two days suddenly loomed before me like ten years in a Siberian gulag.

I hopped a *bemo* for Biak town, otherwise known as Kota Karang, City of Coral. Here, among an assortment of shacks and jerry-built houses, among Chinese traders, Indian tailors, and Javanese durian merchants, among ubiquitous piles of penis sheaths ("You wish to try on?" one waggish salesperson asked me), I looked for something akin to a bookstore.

An hour's search turned up no local equivalent of B. Dalton. It didn't even turn up the local equivalent of a drugstore or a newsstand. In fact, it didn't turn up any printed matter at all. Well, that's not exactly true—a travel agency did offer me a colorful brochure on the beaches of Bali, along with an out-of-date ferry schedule for Yapen Island . . .

The telltale symptoms of my malady were beginning to assert themselves. Palpitations. Profuse sweating. A sort of *horror vacui* taking over my thought processes.

Then all at once I saw a ray of hope—a small house with several books in the window. Eagerly, a bit anxiously, I entered what turned out to be a shop run by local missionaries. Its selection of titles consisted entirely of religious texts for school-age children. In my desperation, I probably could have managed a religious text, even one for a school-age child, but not a religious text in Bahasa Indonesia, a language I neither spoke or read.

The clerk was a Yapen Islander named Isaiah, one of perhaps half a dozen Isaiahs I encountered during my stay in Irian Jaya. I told this particular Isaiah my predicament. I'd settle for any book in English, any book at all, I said.

Isaiah knitted his brow. In those knit lines I saw my last hope dashed to pieces. Then he brightened. He went to the rear of the shop and brought down a book from an upper shelf. "You are maybe interested in bondage, sir?" he inquired politely.

I had an image of leather-clad missionaries gleefully tying up new converts and then having their way with them. It wasn't the right image for the book Isaiah handed me, however. This book was a dusty old Penguin paperback of Somerset Maugham's *Of Human Bondage*.

I'd read Maugham's novel at age sixteen and even then found it a bit cloying, long on sentiment and short on genuine drama. There was no telling what my reaction to it would be now, twenty-five years later. But I didn't care. I plunked down my rupiah, thanked Isaiah profusely, and strode out of the shop, my prize clutched lovingly to my chest.

Never mind that I ended up being too busy in Biak looking for cockatoos in a forest reserve and watching a firewalking ceremony in Adoki village to read *Of Human Bondage* again. Or even to crack it open for a single momentary brush with Maugham's prose. What mattered was this: at last I had a book in reserve, a buttress against the whims and uncertainties of travel, indeed, of life itself.

RON CARLSON

DISCLAIMER

This is a work of fiction, and any resemblance to actual events, locales, or persons, living or dead, is merely coincidental, except for the restaurant I call the Wild Chicken, which was a real place actually called the Blue Bird, a drive-in fast-food joint I always drove past on my way to Debbie Delucca's house. I always liked the Blue Bird, all the lights on late at night, because I knew that I was going to get a cheeseburger and a vanilla shake, so many of which I enjoyed with Debbie Delucca herself, or alone if I was driving back late from her house wrecked from all the couch time with her. The couch time I put in this book was real, too, as was the couch itself, a kind of overstuffed deal with Debbie's mother's big red and blue afghan on the back, a blanket that wanted to get caught in the gears and dragged into the evening's activities quietly and inextricably, a beautiful bold coverlet with a repeated pattern of red geese against a blue sky. Of course, the Blue Bird, which I have called the Wild Chicken, and where I stood so many mid-nights under the fluorescent lights picking red and blue threads out of my hair waiting for a cheeseburger and a vanilla shake, is now a Custom Tile Outlet, a place you can go if you want your fireplace to look like the one in any Hilton.

I also should add here that Debbie's house is real, based on her real house, a green-sided thing on the corner of Concord and Eighth South that had a long shallow porch where I stood so many nights that year whispering with Debbie, giv-ing Mrs. Eisenhour across the street a little show, I guess, as we would stand some nights for an hour saying good-bye and *I love you* and *I can't believe I've met someone like you* and *That was dreamy in there on the couch, I love you so much* and other direct dialogue which I've used in the text absolutely verbatim, probably the easiest thing of all the things in this book to write because everything we said is alive within my head after all these years, things actually said on the chilly fall nights there on Concord as we twisted closer, so lost some nights that we'd wipe our moist noses on each other's necks under the huge munificent blessing of the ancient poplar tree in her front yard, a real tree that held up the sky for a half a mile in every direction, a giant that dumped its leaves in unending ten-ton squadrons that fell like some kind of perfect setting for us, a backdrop, a movie; if it could give up its ten million golden secrets, a blizzard of leaves, then we could be in love, a tree as gone as the house in which Debbie Delucca lived, under the blades for the inter-state years ago, a tree we'll never any of us see again.

No coincidence is going to bring that tree back, nor Debbie Delucca, who was my close associate all those years, the young person with whom I invented modern love, love as we know it. Love which so many people dabble in today, but do not study or understand or allow to course through their veins like some necessary thing. We were the last people to use love right. She's now Debbie Delucca Peterson somewhere in St. Clare, where she does who knows what. I can't imagine, though I've tried. And what am I going to do, go into the ShopMart down there and run into her at the little lunch counter they've got over by the children's department as she sits quietly sipping some chicken noodle soup and reading this very book and nodding at how accurate every word is— the things she said, the things I said in return? As I'd sit down beside her and order a vanilla shake, not even wanting their fake version of one of the world's great treats, not even real ice cream, nor real vanilla, but wanting to say the words the way I did so many nights under the bright lights of the Blue Bird Cafe, *vanilla shake*, to see if she might turn to see who's talking like this, looking up from a book that I'm sorry now I even wrote, really sorry, because I see it for the first time: you can't get anything back. No coincidence at some lunch counter and twenty minutes of conversation with a girl you once knew, some woman sitting there, and you know the exact location of every mole on her body, is going to make one thing in this real world different. If you want the coincidence where some character based on me gets the amazing girl back and has his heart start again after so many years, you're going to have to look in a book.

MICHAEL MARTONE

CONTRIBUTOR'S NOTE

Michael Martone was born in Fort Wayne, Indiana, where he was known, in the womb, as Missy. At birth, Michael Martone was named Michael Anthony Martone, the Anthony being his father's name and the name of his grandfather on his father's side. Names his parents called him, recorded in the extensive Baby Book (he was a firstborn), included Dolly, Peanut, and Bug. His grandfather on his mother's side called Martone Gigi-tone (the "g" is hard) all of his life. He was known as Tony's boy or as Patty's boy or as Junior's (Martone's father being known as Junior or simply June) or as Tony and Patty's boy. He was baptized at age six weeks as Michael or more exactly Michaelus, the Latin version of Michael. Though he was named Michael, Martone was soon being called Mickey by his parents and then by his grandparents and his aunts and uncles and cousins. As a child growing up in Fort Wayne, Indiana, which is also known as the Summit City, he assumed he was named Mickey by his father after Mickey Mantle, the New York Yankee baseball player, as a kind of homage to Mickey Mantle or a charm to aid Martone as he inaugurated his own peewee baseball career. It turned out that Martone's father—he told Martone when Martone asked—had named him Mickey after a good friend of his, Mickey Allen, who lived across the street from Martone's father's boyhood home on Brandriff Street and who died when he, Mickey Allen, was fifteen. Martone's father had been a pallbearer for Mickey Allen's funeral, the first time Martone's father ever served in that capacity. In the summer, then, when playing Little League and later Pony and Colt League baseball, Martone was known as Mickey by his friends and teammates and by their parents and by the coaches and people who lived near the parks and watched the games. His family called Martone Mickey all the time, not just in the summer, but in school Martone was known as Michael because that was Martone's official name, recorded on his records. It was shortened to Mike by his teachers and Martone wrote "Mike" in the top right-hand corner of his papers all through school. To this day, a few of Martone's classmates from fifth grade still call Martone not Mickey nor Mike but Monk when they see him. At all his high school reunions when he is called Monk by someone, Martone will be reminded of that afternoon years before when on the playground he imitated a monkey to endear himself to a group of kids and got called Monk for the first time. The name Monk began as a teasing joke but turned into a certified nickname after Martone drew a simple monkey character based on the Kilroy graffiti and then doodled a whole pantheon of Monk character variations from history, literature, and popular culture. General Monkarthur, Sir Monkalot, St. Francis of Monkssisi, the Monka Lisa, Monkinham Lincoln, Monkleberry Finn, Marilyn Monkroe, and even the Monkles before the Monkees debuted. At the reunions, the few men and women who remember Martone as Monk don't remember why they remember him as Monk, and every five years Martone reminds them of the story. Martone chose the name Joseph for a confirmation name after reading through lists of saints' names and their stories. At North Side High School almost everyone except for those few still calling him Monk from elementary school or Mickey from summer baseball leagues called him Mike. Martone discovered Janine Burke liked him when in Mr. Humphrey's English class he, Mr. Humphrey, caught her writing Mrs. Michael Martone and Mrs. Janine Martone and Janine Martone on the inside cover of a notebook and made her read what she had written to the whole class. Mr. Lewinski, Martone's brilliant and very formal senior year English teacher, called Martone Mr. Martone and did so even when, years later, Martone visited Mr. Lewinski, who was completely blind and slowly dying from diabetes, in the hospital. When Martone graduated from high school, his diploma read "Michael Anthony Joseph Martone." All of those names were read by the vice principal, who was annoyed by the number of names and told Martone so during the commencement rehearsal. But Martone didn't know of any other time when he would ever use all of his names and submitted them again on the forms for his under-graduate and graduate diplomas. In college, Martone belonged to *The Mikes of America Club*. For a nominal fee, the club, based in Minneapolis, Minnesota, sent Martone a certificate and a quarterly newsletter. For years, Martone, a member in good standing, carried a card he would produce at parties that said his name was Michael "Mike" Martone. In college and graduate school, Martone would always answer "Michael" when a professor asked what he went by. He had thought of himself as a Michael, really, ever since Mr. Lewin-ski's class in which he, Martone, first thought he might like to write and had thought about his *nom de plume*, his pen name, and practiced (as Janine Burke had done in another English class) a signature, his signature with the upward looping "h," "l," and "t." His family still calls him Mick but will force themselves to refer to him as Michael when speaking about him in third person to people who ask. For years now, since graduate school, where he met his wife, who always has called him simply Martone, Martone has thought of himself as Mar-tone. Friends call Martone Martone, a strangely intimate con-struction in the way children in Tuscaloosa, Alabama, where Martone lives now with his wife who still calls him Martone, call Martone Mr. Michael, that mix of formality and famil-iarity. Martone got married in a civil service at the Story County courthouse, in Nevada, Iowa. Along with his soon-to-be wife, Martone had to sign papers and register at the clerk's office before going into the courtroom. There was actually a big, ancient book both of them had to sign. Martone was not surprised to see that there were places that needed to be filled in labeled "Bride's Name Before the Marriage" and "Bride's Name After the Marriage." His wife, who has several pet names she calls Martone but refuses to let him share or use them in public, kept her name. Martone was surprised to discover that there were also spaces that asked for "Groom's Name Before Marriage" as well as "Groom's Name After Marriage." The possibility that there was this possibility of taking on a new name had never occurred to him. At that moment, he couldn't think of what to call himself and simply signed Michael Martone twice. Martone and his soon-to-be wife and their two witnesses waited their turn in the courtroom, sitting in the jury box while the judge, who was going to conduct the service, sentenced someone to the county lockup. After the prisoner was led away, the judge asked Martone if there were rings and said he hadn't thought so when Martone said there weren't. Then he said, "Do you . . . " prompting Martone, with an urgent head nod and a raising of his eyebrows, to answer, to fill in that blank he had left floating in the air with a name, any name.

DAVID SEDARIS

ME TALK PRETTY ONE DAY

At the age of forty-one, I am returning to school and have to think of myself as what my French textbook calls "a true debutant." After paying my tuition, I was issued a student ID, which allows me a discounted entry fee at movie theaters, puppet shows, and Festyland, a far-flung amusement park that advertises with billboards picturing a cartoon stegosaurus sitting in a canoe and eating what appears to be a ham sandwich.

I've moved to Paris with hopes of learning the language. My school is an easy ten-minute walk from my apartment, and on the first day of class I arrived early, watching as the returning students greeted one another in the school lobby. Vacations were recounted, and questions were raised concerning mutual friends with names like Kang and Vlatnya. Regardless of their nationalities, everyone spoke in what sounded to me like excellent French. Some accents were better than others, but the students exhibited an ease and confidence I found intimidating. As an added discomfort, they were all young, attractive, and well dressed, causing me to feel not unlike Pa Kettle trapped backstage after a fashion show.

The first day of class was nerve-racking because I knew I'd be expected to perform. That's the way they do it here—it's everybody into the language pool, sink or swim. The teacher marched in, deeply tanned from a recent vacation, and proceeded to rattle off a series of administrative announcements. I've spent quite a few summers in Normandy, and I took a monthlong French class before leaving New York. I'm not completely in the dark, yet I understood only half of what this woman was saying.

"If you have not *meimslsxp* or *lgpdmurct* by this time, then you should not be in this room. Has everyone *apzkiubjxow*? Everyone? Good, we shall begin." She spread out her lesson plan and sighed, saying, "All right, then, who knows the alphabet?"

It was startling because (a) I hadn't been asked that question in a while and (b) I realized, while laughing, that I myself did *not* know the alphabet. They're the same letters, but in France they're pronounced differently. I know the shape of the alphabet but had no idea what it actually sounded like.

"Ahh." The teacher went to the board and sketched the letter *a*. "Do we have anyone in the room whose first name commences with an *ahh*?"

Two Polish Annas raised their hands, and the teacher

instructed them to present themselves by stating their names, nationalities, occupations, and a brief list of things they liked and disliked in this world. The first Anna hailed from an industrial town outside of Warsaw and had front teeth the size of tombstones. She worked as a seamstress, enjoyed quiet times with friends, and hated the mosquito.

"Oh, really," the teacher said. "How very interesting. I thought that everyone loved the mosquito, but here, in front of all the world, you claim to detest him. How is it that we've been blessed with someone as unique and original as you? Tell us, please."

The seamstress did not understand what was being said but knew that this was an occasion for shame. Her rabbity mouth huffed for breath, and she stared down at her lap as though the appropriate comeback were stitched somewhere alongside the zipper of her slacks.

The second Anna learned from the first and claimed to love sunshine and detest lies. It sounded like a translation of one of those Playmate of the Month data sheets, the answers always written in the same loopy handwriting: "Turn-ons: Mom's famous five-alarm chili! Turnoffs: insecurity and guys who come on too strong!!!!"

The two Polish Annas surely had clear notions of what they loved and hated, but like the rest of us, they were limited in terms of vocabulary, and this made them appear less than sophisticated. The teacher forged on, and we learned that Carlos, the Argentine bandonion player, loved wine, music, and, in his words, "making sex with the womens of the world." Next came a beautiful young Yugoslav who identified herself as an optimist, saying that she loved everything that life had to offer.

The teacher licked her lips, revealing a hint of the saucebox we would later come to know. She crouched low for her attack, placed her hands on the young woman's desk, and leaned close, saying, "Oh yeah? And do you love your little war?"

While the optimist struggled to defend herself, I scrambled to think of an answer to what had obviously become a trick question. How often is one asked what he loves in this world? More to the point, how often is one asked and then publicly ridiculed for his answer? I recalled my mother, flushed with wine, pounding the tabletop late one night, saying, "Love? I love a good steak cooked rare. I love my cat, and I love . . ." My sisters and I leaned forward, waiting to hear our names. "Tums," our mother said. "I love Tums."

The teacher killed some time accusing the Yugoslavian girl of masterminding a program of genocide, and I jotted frantic notes in the margins of my pad. While I can honestly say that I love leafing through medical textbooks devoted to severe dermatological conditions, the hobby is beyond the reach of my French vocabulary, and acting it out would only have invited controversy.

When called upon, I delivered an effortless list of things that I detest: blood sausage, intestinal pâtés, brain pudding. I'd learned these words the hard way. Having given it some thought, I then declared my love for IBM typewriters, the French word for *bruise*, and my electric floor waxer. It was a short list, but still I managed to mispronounce *IBM* and assign the wrong gender to both the floor waxer and the typewriter. The teacher's reaction led me to believe that these mistakes were capital crimes in the country of France.

"Were you always this *palicmkrexis?*" she asked. "Even a *fiuscrzsa ticiwelmun* knows that a typewriter is feminine."

I absorbed as much of her abuse as I could understand, thinking—but not saying—that I find it ridiculous to assign a gender to an inanimate object incapable of disrobing and making an occasional fool of itself. Why refer to crack pipe or Good Sir Dishrag when these things could never live up to all that their sex implied?

The teacher proceeded to belittle everyone from German Eva, who hated laziness, to Japanese Yukari, who loved paintbrushes and soap, Italian, Thai, Dutch, Korean, and Chinese—we all left class foolishly believing that the worst was over. She'd shaken us up a little, but surely that was just an act designed to weed out the deadweight. We didn't know it then, but the coming months would teach us what it was like to spend time in the presence of a wild animal, something completely unpredictable. Her temperament was not based on a series of good and bad days but, rather, good and bad moments. We soon learned to dodge chalk and protect our heads and stomachs whenever she approached us with a question. She hadn't yet punched anyone, but it seemed wise to protect ourselves against the inevitable.

Though we were forbidden to speak anything but French, the teacher would occasionally use us to practice any of her five fluent languages.

"I hate you," she said to me one afternoon. Her English

was flawless. "I really, really hate you." Call me sensitive, but I couldn't help but take it personally.

After being singled out as a lazy *kfdtinvfm*, I took to spending four hours a night on my homework, putting in even more time whenever we were assigned an essay. I suppose I could have gotten by with less, but I was determined to create some sort of identity for myself: David the hard worker, David the cut-up. We'd have one of those "complete this sentence" exercises, and I'd fool with the thing for hours, invariably settling on something like "A quick run around the lake? I'd love to! Just give me a moment while I strap on my wooden leg." The teacher, through word and action, conveyed the message that if this was my idea of an identity, she wanted nothing to do with it.

My fear and discomfort crept beyond the borders of the classroom and accompanied me out onto the wide boulevards. Stopping for a coffee, asking directions, depositing money in my bank account: these things were out of the question, as they involved having to speak. Before beginning school, there'd been no shutting me up, but now I was convinced that everything I said was wrong. When the phone rang, I ignored it. If someone asked me a question, I pretended to be deaf. I knew my fear was getting the best of me when I started wondering why they don't sell cuts of meat in vending machines.

My only comfort was the knowledge that I was not alone. Huddled in the hallways and making the most of our pathetic French, my fellow students and I engaged in the sort of conversations commonly overheard in refugee camps.

"Sometime me cry alone at night."

"That be common for I, also, but be more strong, you. Much work and someday you talk pretty. People start love you soon. Maybe tomorrow, okay."

Unlike the French class I had taken in New York, here there was no sense of competition. When the teacher poked a shy Korean in the eyelid with a freshly sharpened pencil, we took no comfort in the fact that, unlike Hyeyoon Cho, we all knew the irregular past tense of the verb *to defeat*. In all fairness, the teacher hadn't meant to stab the girl, but neither did she spend much time apologizing, saying only, "Well, you should have been *vkkdyo* more *kdeynfulh*."

Over time it became impossible to believe that any of us would ever improve. Fall arrived and it rained every day, meaning we would now be scolded for the water dripping from our coats and umbrellas. It was mid-October when the teacher singled me out, saying, "Every day spent with you is like having a cesarean section." And it struck me that, for the first time since arriving in France, I could understand every word that someone was saying.

Understanding doesn't mean that you can suddenly speak the language. Far from it. It's a small step, nothing more, yet its rewards are intoxicating and deceptive. The teacher continued her diatribe and I settled back, bathing in the subtle beauty of each new curse and insult.

"You exhaust me with your foolishness and reward my efforts with nothing but pain, do you understand me?"

The world opened up, and it was with great joy that I responded, "I know the thing that you speak exact now. Talk me more, you, plus, please, plus."

BARBARA MALLONEE

SEMI-COLON

Shadows stir; the season shifts. As I sit in the first winter sunshine, reading the morning papers, the print rises up, coldly poised, perfected in a way that the writing I am next to read is not. In stacks of student essays, language flies across the open page as wildly as the last brown leaves across the campus quad. Pens in hand, the faculty gear up to rake the prose about, trimming a sentence here, planting commas there, carting off redundancy.

As winter chill sets in, I look at warm young faces and wish it were the semi-colon they yearned to learn. A point I think a fine point they think much too fine a point. They are still tilting at words, and even I have to admit that as an object of study the semi-colon seems obscure, its place in the path of paleography lost in the dust of time.

The mark was used by Greek grammarians in the schools

of Alexandria. By the end of the fifteenth century, British pundits and three generations of Venetian printers named Manutius were using it and other punctuation marks to regularize pauses in print. For three more centuries, it flourished, even on rough American shores. In the twenty-first, if it has not perished in practice, in praise it is long overdue.

What kind of name is "semi-colon," really? The mark hasn't the braking power of a colon and might be thought half of its worth were sectioning speech the sole function of punctuation—but it is not. Like the question mark (?), the exclamation point (!), and the colon (:), the semi-colon (;) amplifies the power of the period (.). It has its peculiar purpose. Most punctuation marks arose as aids to elocution; the semi-colon serves not the outspoken orator, but the silent writer solitary at his desk. While speech streams forth like birdsong, rows of prose take slow root in the fields and beds and pots of print. Brought from the old world to brave the new, the imperturbable semi-colon upholds the virtues of cultivated thought.

It engenders a well-bred economy. Even in an age awash in information, a sentence is a dear commodity. Overseen by the semi-colon, the well-tended sentence can hold any number of things: "apples, prunes, persimmons; linen and lace; pheasant, roast beef, goose; eggnog, brandy." Under the framework of a single sentence can also be gathered two or more sentences' worth of useful thought. Wrote, for example, Ben Franklin, "When men are employed, they are best contented; for on the days they worked, they were good-natured and cheerful, and with the consciousness of having done a good day's work, they spent the evening jollily; but on our idle days, they were mutinous and quarrelsome." Less capacious, more terse was Francis Bacon: "Prosperity is the blessing of the Old Testament; adversity is the blessing of the New."

A mixed blessing, to be sure. Adversity occasions the troubles that become our daily news. At home and abroad wars rage over civil rights, civic wrongs, guns and arms, forests, disease, the homeless, the infirm, the illiterate, the neglected, the abused, the unemployed, the poor. Writers have long arisen to address their contentious times. A tart Samuel Johnson could pen, "I have found you an argument; I am not obliged to find you an understanding," but all writers work that harmony might grow.

With the swift stroke of pen or pencil, the semi-colon subdues strife. It does so not by stilling or ignoring opposition; within a grammatic arena, it coolly balances hotly contested views. Franklin D. Roosevelt owed to this small mark a great deal, for he distilled into one measured sentence the New Deal: "The test of our progress is not whether we add more to the abundance of those who have too much; it is whether we can provide enough for those who have too little."

"Simplify, simplify," wrote Henry David Thoreau, who labored in the cold drafts in winter to refine a harvest of fruitful thought. "The intellect," he argued, "is a cleaver; it discerns and rifts its way into the secret of things. I do not wish to be any more busy with my hands than is necessary . . . My instinct tells me that my head is an organ for burrowing as some other creatures use their snout and forepaws."

As the first snow falls, the fall semester almost over, I look at young heads bent over rows of prose. Education is an investment their parents feel it prudent to make. Wrote E. B. White in *One Man's Meat*, "School buildings are heated by wood stoves except the high school, which has a furnace. At the end of the year, the account stood: for fuel, $459.44; for teachers, $2600.40. Thus, it costs one-sixth as much to heat pupil's bodies as their minds, minds being slower to kindle."

At a time when too few have food and fuel for mind and body, young people have still the luxury of learning to cultivate thought. In a world where one man's meat is always another man's poison, the semi-colon survives each vanished era. It has great staying power for it knows the habit of accommodation. Under its classic tutelage, wit is expended, wisdom grows.

STEPHEN COREY

EXPERIENCING

The plastic cap from a soft-drink bottle slides off a kitchen table, knocked by an arm reaching for something else.

Two ants scurry their weave along the asphalt sidewalk that runs below the summer arts colony's grand old hotel looming on the hillside, some forty yards away, and above the mile-wide lake slapping its weed-choked shore sixty yards in the other direction.

My foot jiggles, suspended twelve inches above the floor by virtue of my one leg being crossed on the other knee while I sit in the rocking chair in our vacation apartment's living room.

The four young dancers, clothed in brilliant pink-unto-fuchsia ballet garb, sweep and glitter and leap across the broad, deep, raised stage of the roofed outdoor amphitheater.

All of these things—bottle cap, ants, foot, dancers—were observed by my seventeen-month-old granddaughter, Mary McClain, within the space of a single July day. I, in turn, observed her observing, and my first retrospective thought was about the great-seeming democracy in a young child's sensory intake of the world: all is intriguing, or all is frightening, or all is . . . ?

A grandfather and a bottle top are one; ditto the pas de deux of ants and of human beings.

But this was only my initial take on McClain's seemingly boundless attentiveness and delight that day. (Among other things, she also licked ice cream from a plastic spoon and rainwater from a park bench.) As I focused more carefully, more exactly, on my recollection of her various enthusiasms, I recognized—or believed I did—certain gradations of appreciation.

The cap caught McClain's eye with its falling and rolling, which led her to it as something of a size she knew she could grasp and hold. Motion was likewise what brought the ants to her attention, but because *their* motion did not stop—when was the last time you saw an ant pause to rest?—McClain's interest did not flag for a greater period of time. She did not try to touch the ants as she followed their slow but furious track along the sidewalk, as if she knew there was something in them that could not be held, knew the distinction between living and nonliving.

My foot was touchable in its bouncy-mechanical dance, probably because my granddaughter understood it was a part of, or at least "caused by," me. Her response in being drawn to my foot was more playful than possessive (the cap) or amused (the ants). She grabbed, tugged, pushed, tugged.

The dancers, in motion as were all the other things I've described here, did what none of those others achieved: they struck McClain into immobility. When I carried her to a line of sight with the stage, standing off to one side at the top of the amphitheater built to hold five thousand, behind all the rows of wooden, pew-like seats, and then managed to direct her attention toward the people moving on that stage, she froze in classic dropped-jaw fashion. She held that oddly adult pose for at least a minute, perhaps as long as two, before she began to dance in my arms and to smile and jabber—words were still pretty much beyond her—in response to the music and gliding bodies. Within another five to ten minutes she was ready to get on with her life, squirming and shouting to let me see that fact quite clearly; but for much longer than was the case with the cap and the ants and my shoe, she was fully drawn toward a certain little world-within-the-world.

I want to say that my granddaughter, scarcely able to speak and still liable to tip suddenly backwards onto her bottom when she walked, experienced art and beauty as she sat in my arms and was immobilized by orchestral sounds and by lithe, colorful young women dancing. Not that McClain understood these things or qualities, but that she experienced them. I want to say this, but I know I should not. And yet I have.

The same day she saw the dancers and all the rest, McClain walked straight into our kitchen table, nicely positioned at forehead height for a seventeen-month-old, and she experienced pain—no question there. Perhaps beauty is, or can be, the same: a visceral connection between the body and something it encounters. And perhaps art, which creates beauty willy-nilly—no matter what else it might also create—can likewise come to us from the very beginning at this physical level. If so, then whenever we may come to art (and thereby to beauty) in later times at different levels—emotional, rational, rhetorical, and so on—we will be coming not just to something outside us, but also to something already embedded within our bodies' most basic, natural, and necessary responses to living.

BARBARA HURD

MOON SNAIL

No very small animal can be beautiful, for looking at it
takes so small a portion of time that the impression of it
will be confused. —*Aristotle*

Surely Aristotle's wrong. If a moon snail isn't beautiful,
it's not because it's small. This shell I've just lifted out
of sand, in fact, is a graceful whorl of bluish grays that
pale toward white. When I turn it to the sun, the luster of
plum glazing the aperture shines almost luminescent. It's been
at sea for a while, no trace of the creature inside. I run my
pinky finger up into the emptied chamber. If I were a still life
painter, I'd paint it with other objects whose interiors beckon:
geodes, kiwis, bells. Forgoing the richness of Dutch masters—
a polished table, a pitcher, a lemon, and always the yellow
light pouring through a window—I'd set my easel up on the
beach, frame my objects with pieces of driftwood, position
them in a tangle of seaweed. Drawn as I am to the evidence of
departure, my painting would include prints in the sand—
crab claws, human feet, dog paws, the wide and meandering

band the moon snail leaves behind. Beauty, it seems to me, must have something to do with movement both inward and away.

Moon snails are carnivores. They kill with their feet and their tongues. Sensing a nearby clam just under the surface of sand, a moon snail pumps water in rippling waves to its retracted foot, which soon emerges as a swelling gelatinous nub that grows into one of the largest of all snail feet, four times the size of its own shell. A shapeless, boneless appendage smeared with mucous that keeps pulsing, spreading forward and sideways until the shell itself sits slightly lifted, almost encircled, and the pulpy thing with its whorled carriage oozes forward. The propodium—the front edge of the foot—plows the sand aside, much like a cowcatcher on the front end of a train.

I try to imagine a clam, wonder whether it can feel the unstable sand above, the sense of something large approaching, about to make a tomb. And then the foot shoveling down, settling on, wrapping around, like a live and fleshy blanket.

A clam is a bivalve; it can shut its shell, stay closeted until danger has passed. There's plenty of room inside, and no way for a moon snail to pry anything open. The foot tightens around the clam. Perhaps for a moment there's great stillness.

And then the moon snail's tongue—coiled, studded with small rounded teeth, rasp-like—begins to lick a small hole in the clam's shell. It licks and licks and once in a while it tongues a little juice. The juice corrodes. The giant foot clenches the clam. The tongue grazes and scrapes and finally breaks through, making a neatly beveled hole.

Just below, trapped inside its hinged shell, the clam must feel a sudden trickle of sand, a poof of air. And then the prod of a long proboscis.

What does it look like, that initial suck? Does tissue bubble, a dimple rising into the proboscis? A dimple that spreads and deepens until the body is nothing else, just this rising and rising like a small spout of gray tissue drawn up into the straw, the mouth, into the body of the moon snail, which looms above it?

Perhaps my painting must be a diptych. In the second panel, the aftermath: emptied clamshells with neatly bored holes near their hinges.

And maybe the moon snail itself, when hunger's been replaced by threat and it needs to gather up that large and fleshy foot and disappear inside itself. An approaching starfish can trigger its retreat, as can the nearing plow of another snail or a gull's growing shadow. The foot starts to contract its muscle, expel water from its flesh. It grows dry and begins to recede into the shell, which looks now much too small to hold it. When the last protruding nub has been pulled inside, the operculum, a horn-like oval door, closes, seals the snail inside and out of reach.

It can't breathe for long with such a thing inside. Its gills are pressed against its heart and stomach, smushed against the inside wall. It must feel claustrophobic, crowded by the very thing it needs to stay alive.

Once the moon snail has shown its foot, it's not possible to call it beautiful. Aristotle notwithstanding, this has nothing to do with size but with unseemly proportions and the reminder that need so often vulgarizes form. My painting, I see now, should be a triptych. I'd want the last panel to suggest that a certain beauty recedes when hunger and threat intensify. There'd be sand dunes in the distance and a horde of snails in the foreground, their insides grotesque and efficient, on the verge of suffocating themselves.

REG SANER

BREAKFAST WITH *CANIS LATRANS*

Ancient apprehensions stir in our bloodstream. From time to time—helpless to say why—we feel an ominous, all-but-subliminal sense of some lurking *thing*. Lying low, yet edging closer in this world where life is cheap and ruinously dear.

Just now, mid-January, my dawn mood is quite other. Against the mesa's snowy slope, which in the open shadow of 6:50 a.m. is still sky blue, sparse clumps of leafless twigs poke forth, forlorn and bleak against (as our ski resorts love to report) "ten inches of new." So the slightest motion thus backgrounded by snow is a cinch to pick up; even that of a distant hunter whose guile has evolved a pelage the color of straw fields and dusk.

Through binoculars I follow its moves, watch lives taken and swallowed whole, though can't tell whether of voles or deer mice, just see that their bodies were big enough to need some real chomping before getting helped by convulsive gulps further down the gullet. Quite a process for the coyote doing the gulping. And for its prey. Thorax impaled by giant teeth, skull crushed till brain oozes from nostrils and eye holes. Eaten alive. Not a fate I care to share, except with an empathetic shudder. Yet points of view do transform us, the way a hand is changed in coming to rest on another.

This coyote's success rate soon has me wondering. "How many tries per kill?" During the thirty-five or forty minutes I follow its critter quest, every other pounce pays off. Slightly better actually. Out of ten tries, six kills. Clearly, this particular *Canis latrans* is on a roll.

This morning, down past a swath of ponderosa well below the mesa rim, my lone-hunting coyote descends, making alert sweeps; right, then left, trotting comfortably through snow that brushes its long belly hairs and clings. The hunter then slows, raises a thoughtful forepaw poised like a setter on point. Head cocked, ears forward, using everything it's got: sight, scent, and hearing keen enough to detect under that snow a living morsel. Sometimes *Canis latrans* will place both forepaws on a boulder for a more elevated view, or may stand atop one on all fours, so as to read what's written over wind-crusted snow. Often the page is empty. Other times, its scholarly gaze deciphers a text that speaks comfortably to belly juices.

Depending on the season, coyote scat may contain chokecherry pits, wild plums ill-digested, grass stems con-

torted but unchanged—I've even seen, inexplicably, a
Kleenex—but year-round its bulk comes from the hair of
small rodents. Rain then sluices fresh scat down to tufts and
twists of wooly stuff which, if on a trail, sooner or later gets
flattened by hikers. Yet few hikers notice it and still fewer
could name its source. As for me, I smile at coyote presump-
tion in using scat to claim a trail made by humans, but also
read there a fuzzy sort of world story. Between the need of
coyotes to eat, the need of deer mice and voles not to be eaten,
I find in those rather pathetic hair wads a scenario we suppose
we're not part of. Yet three days ago on one of winter's most
blue-and-silver mornings I was out hunting tiny lives myself.

An all-night wind, a west wind that really knew how, had
packed earlier snows into what skiers call "breakable crust,"
the kind that holds your weight, then suddenly doesn't. Everywhere around me wind's fluent past was evident as blown
snow, still miming one-way, downslope currents of a night
that roared. On the lee side of rocks, streamlined drifts made
boulders into stones meteoric, furiously speeding in place.
Behind every squawbush, dead-fallen pine trunk, or clumped
yucca the whole mesa slope was plumed with flying white
streamers now lying motionless.

On the expectation that broad patches of wind-packed
crust would be perfect for tracking deer mice, I had worn
boots and gaiters, and—under sun half an hour high—soon
found readable treks aplenty. Each delicate impression evoked
a deer mouse's four minuscule footpads and teeny claws, all
rimmed—in that early light—with the subtlest tinge of blue
shadow. So far so good; but so good as to puzzle. Though I

often find a few mouse tracks here and there over snow, this
unusual variety of trails was a surprise. Why all the nocturnal
traipsing?

Curiosity set me to reading the almost-visibly-timorous
meanderings in hopes of an answer, perusing their wavery
hither-and-yon with growing respect, even fascination. Each
trail seemed daring, and in direct proportion to the distance
covered. One powdery stretch made that span dramatic. After
stitching their seam across drifts, the roving paw prints ended
abruptly where disheveled snow read "owl," whose "stealth
feathers," as I call them, had allowed it to glide with the
soundlessness of shadow. Plainly legible on the snow, a
pounce-mark evoked the owl's sudden clutch of talons, dither
of wings. Day's blinding refraction of multifaceted sunfire
made a stark contrast to the darkness in which the owl's low
and wide-eyed night patrol had found its target.

Every now and then I come upon narrative variants: blood-
speckled snow, tufts of rabbit fur tossed about. Other times,
a telltale scatter of feathers, ones designed for speed, thus
quite unlike plumage whose downy edges evolved for silence.
Even eagles, hawks, and falcons need to be wary of them,
because a raptor alighting to feed on a kill can easily fall prey
to an owl. Fair enough. A sort of retributive justice. But owl
against mouse? Foolishly I felt it one-sided. Raptors aren't
into *noblesse oblige*, and Dame Nature's no lady.

Yet the world we reason about isn't the one we live in. As
my boots plunged through white crust I quit seeing those traces
of deer mice as "cute," and began reading even their fifteen-
foot journeys as very nervy affairs. Longer travels—ten, twelve

yards—became positively daring. Each trail emerged from the base of a yucca and, after wandering right, left, and even roundabout, disappeared into the base of another—for reasons known to anyone whose shins have been pricked to bleeding by a narrow-leaf yucca's stilettos. Neither foxes nor coyotes care to poke a snout into such dense bouquets of pain, which is why, crisp as cuneiform, those mouse trails emerged from and disappeared into a burst of evergreen spikes.

But why all those sallies out from cover into the dangerous open? Though the smallest animals keep busiest, what could those mice find to feed on? The tracks often veered as if aimless. Then I realized. Seeds, of course, a main food for deer mice. From upstanding stems of winter-killed grasses, last night's wind had stripped seeds by the millions—which the fastidious forepaws would batten on like manna. There might also be the occasional bonus of an insect overtaken by late-afternoon chill-down and slowed to a standstill. Countless times I've watched birds feed at leisure on flying insects that have unwarily set down atop snowfields whose ice granules quickly induced the torpor that rendered them easy pickings.

So seeds explained the journeying, while making mere hunger seem perilous. Amid crust so sun-drenched that my darkest glacier glasses felt like none at all, I began plunging around in search of last night's longest, death-defying mouse trek. Twelve yards had been impressive till I found and followed a twenty-yarder. Eventually I spotted—and with rising astonishment followed—a far more epic outing. It wound about, past naked squawbush and hawthorn, past sullen boulders now dripping snowmelt, past the potential sanctuary of yucca after yucca to a length of fully sixty yards! Silly as the idea of deer-mouse heroism might seem, it didn't to me. Seeing how the pulsations of a heart small as a juniper berry had sustained those tiny paws on their long night of travel, my own heart filled with commensurate admiration. Countless animals play out their roles in life incomparably better than do some of us humans, so attributing "greatness" to a mouse didn't seem absurd. In any case, while tracking the longest set of paw prints I felt myself following a better mouse than I am a man.

Now, bushy tail held parallel to the snow's surface—surely for maximum stealth—my coyote eases forward through tall grasses—big bluestem, winter-changed to brownish orange—and stops, freezes. Takes a single, carefully slow step further. Again holds *perfectly* still. Considering the stakes on both sides, that stance is quite dramatic. Then the leap—stiff-legged and high into air to pounce with forepaws and snout right on target. Although such a comic bound skyward amuses me every time, I'm not the munchable target at ground zero. As inscribed eons ago into the brains of small rodents, it must be the ultimate bad dream, which to realize is to share.

For some seconds the coyote's muzzle stays buried, frantically scattering snow, snuffling around after prey that somehow escaped. The head then does a fast scan every which way. Also a bit comic. Whereupon it launches upward, landing on a spot seven feet from the first pounce. No good. Once more the mouse or vole gets away. Again the scanning business.

Having spied no clues, *Canis latrans* surprises me by casually trotting twenty yards west to assess a fresh surface.

There the very first leap pays off. And the next. And the leap after that. Each time, however, the coyote is careful to interrupt his or her moments of snuffling, worrying at, then jawing on and tenderizing its victim.

Abruptly the head snaps toward me. Steady gaze. I don't stir. Then does a typical coyote scan all round, so as not to become prey itself. Mountain lions? Oh, yes. Bears? Those, too. *Canis latrans* is nothing if not circumspicuous.

Clearly, no predator can snap the spine of a live creature while still carrying one now defunct. So after kill number five my well-practiced coyote buries it and trots to a nearby stand of straw grasses as if scenting further prospects. But failing to score, returns, digs up the victim it had put in cold storage, and has me talking to myself: "Just how many can its belly hold? It'll have to mouth-carry this latest catch, won't it?" Oh no. Down a pulsing gullet goes the latest kill. Whereupon my coyote trots toward a ravine way below me, and soon disappears into gray thickets of naked willow and hackberry.

How old is fear? Surely far older than humans. Innate as predation? Perhaps. And that would put it far back as the Cambrian; thus, "awful old" seems a safe bet. In fact, as one plausible hypothesis has it, predation explains the so-called "Cambrian explosion," when forms of animal life multiplied exponentially. If indeed such devouring and being devoured suddenly threw animal evolution into fast-forward by selecting for mobility—vital to both hunter and hunted—every open mouth makes the predator/prey cycle a thought to get lost in.

As was this breakfast walk with *Canis latrans*. All the while, amid sky-blue shadows still sensuously long over snow which—elsewhere—the just-risen sun has turned quite pink, I couldn't help sharing both a coyote's survival moves and a small rodent's quivering, cowering role in this precarious world. A world you can get snatched out of at any moment—into explosions of pain. Our primeval past is nearer than we think.

Gradually, confusedly, waking from a daydreamy meditation on the archaic source of our forebodings, I glance toward my house. My den. Centrally heated. Fireplaces to boot. Shelves with plenty of food. Well-roofed, insulated, insured. All of it sits on land stolen by killing off Indians. Five minutes below me, there at the foot of the mesa.

CHARLES BERGMAN

AN ANIMAL LOOKS AT ME

We live in a time when animals are defined largely by their absence. Most people encounter animals only at dinner, or as pets—and neither of those seem quite "animals." In the West, animals have always been a problem, but things got especially bad after Descartes, whose philosophy reduced the family dog to a clock with a tail.

Our old certainties are not so certain anymore. What are we to do with the creatures for whom our philosophies and attitudes have been so inadequate, so confused, and often so cruel? Should we protect them? Some species have rebounded from the brink of extinction. Even endangered animals have become troublesome, but in a surprising way. What if they recover? How many do we really want around, anyway? When they become inconvenient or bothersome, should we ship them off—or maybe even kill them off—like mountain lions when they wander into the backyard pool, or like Canada geese which annoy people so much in our parks?

One famous anthropologist, Claude Lévi-Strauss, has said, "Animals are good to think." Yet we seem not to know what to think about animals—which is one reason, perhaps, that most people prefer not to think about them at all. I would like to propose that the beginning of thinking about them lies in their eyes.

None of this was on my mind when I stepped into the marsh. It is deep background for anyone who cares now about animals. It came into focus in the eyes of a little-known waterbird hiding in a Mexican marsh.

I was in the state of Sonora, close to the United States border, south of Yuma, Arizona. Called the Ciénega de Santa Clara, the marsh is huge. Ciénega means "hundred waters" in Spanish. This marsh is the largest wetland in the state of Sonora, and arguably the best wetland on the entire 14,000-mile Colorado River. It's a huge island of water in a Sonoran sea of sand—50,000 acres, or three and a half times the size of Manhattan Island.

The ciénega is in the delta of the Colorado River, one of the most neglected and abused landscapes on the North American continent. After the United States built about one hundred dams and diversions on the river, Americans turned their back on the delta in Mexico. Some twenty million people in the American Southwest depend for their lives on the Colorado River, but few of them could even tell you where the river delta is. Even the maps of the Bureau of Reclamation, which built all the dams on the river, end at the border with Mexico. It's as if, for Americans, the river ceases to exist once it crosses the border.

It's not easy being a wetland or water bird in the American desert, where our big-gulp culture sucks up every drop of water for farming, faucets, and city fountains. That's why this area has one of the greatest rates of extinction in the world. Endangered species in the desert are the modern equivalent of the outlaws of the Old West. They live on the edges and margins of our culture. And these endangered creatures have done exactly what the old outlaws did—they've fled to Mexico. The American Southwest has about fifty endangered species, and large populations of around twenty-five of them can be found hiding in Ciénega de Santa Clara. Quietly, surprisingly, this Mexican marsh has become an almost miraculous refuge.

This evening, I'm on the eastern shore of the marsh, where I've been helping biologists and locals count birds, especially endangered birds. I've spent many hours on this marsh, and it's one of my favorite wildlife places on the continent.

Eared grebes are not endangered. But when I see one swimming alone in a small pond in the marsh, I step right in with my tripod and camera. I want to see if it will let me photograph it. The eared grebe is a small, duck-sized waterbird. It has a black crest, which it raises frequently, and rich chestnut flanks. It has a pointed beak, and it dives and chases fish.

The grebe is in full breeding plumage, and is especially beautiful in the late desert light. It is named for the spectacular flare of yellow feathers on its face. They seem to radiate out from its bright red eyes.

When I set up my tripod in the middle of the pond, the grebe does not try to flee or fly. Instead, it swims a bit nervously along the reeds, then comes out toward me. I simply stay in place, with the sun at my back. I watch the grebe through my lens. As is the case with animals, you have to let them teach you how they will be photographed.

I turn to one of my friends and ask him what he calls this bird in Spanish.

"*Pato marijuana*," he says with a little laugh. It's the marijuana bird, named for the vivid red eyes, which look bloodshot from smoking dope.

The grebe is tentative, but assertive. It approaches me. It comes right up to me. Soon it is within just a few feet. And it is looking right at me. It looks at me carefully. Fixes me in the eye. Its eyes are crimson red, liquid as pools of blood.

Forgetting about the camera and lens, I return the grebe's stare.

In the grebe's eyes, I see myself being seen. For the time that we look at each other, I exist in the grebe's world. I find myself in other geographies and alive in other lives. I have been caught looking. As Freudians and voyeurs know, there is power in looking. That is why, I think, it is so unsettling to discover yourself in the eyes of another animal. It upsets our normal stance with animals. We look at them. We take their measure. An animal looks at me. It disturbs my sense of human superiority, my human arrogance. We don't truly know ourselves until we see ourselves in the eyes of another creature.

Recently, philosophy has begun to try to return the gaze of the animal. The animal gaze, for example, forms a pivotal moment in the emergence of environmental ethics. Aldo Leopold summarizes the lesson of his famous "land ethic," his new view of the place of humans in nature, in the "fierce green fire" of a wolf's eyes. The look of a wolf reveals to him what it means to "think like a mountain."

French post-structuralist philosopher Jacques Derrida has been obsessed with what he calls "the question of the animal." The animal has been banished and forgotten by Western philosophy, he says. But Derrida watches it re-enter philosophy in his bathroom. The philosopher realizes one morning he is standing naked in front of his cat, which looks at him studiously. Derrida describes feeling a shiver of shame—an antidote to humanism's unbounded pride and denial of the animal. "As with every bottomless gaze," writes Derrida, "the gaze called animal offers to my sight the abyssal limit of the human."

It's a gaze that looks two ways. The creature looks at me. It is a being as I am. Its look distills the incontrovertible fact of animal being. I look back. I am something, but I am not everything. The world looks different, and full of being.

This evening, the red-eyed grebe finally darts past me. I am absorbed in its face, even as it swims away. In its flashing yellow feathers and its glowing red eyes, I might as well have been looking into the bright rays of fierce desert sun.

SUSANNE ANTONETTA

THE HUMAN ROAD

A pod of five gray whales swims into our harbor in Bellingham Bay, a detour in their annual Alaska migration. Our bay is polluted with mercury and chlorine from the Georgia-Pacific plant, which produces toilet paper, treating the paper with chlorine to make it whiter. The plant sends a nonstop cumulus of chemical-smelling steam into the air, as if it's manufacturing another brand of sky. I accept the plant as part of the landscape, like the Northwest's chronic real clouds, and in my acceptance I find a kind of betrayal.

Some twenty thousand gray whales remain on the earth, a number no longer small enough to be called endangered. Who knows what will become of the grays? They, and the orcas here, seem to be losing the ability to reproduce. They suffer from *encroachment*, from *viability issues*.

I take my son Jin to a park that crescents along the water, to watch the whales. He's close to three and I keep thinking about his developing memory. My earliest memories are from his age. The whales are strips of black rubber separating the water now and then: moving spumes. When they surface and blow, the crowd claps. A young girl in jeans has climbed onto a boulder and dances there, a slow undulating arm-waving feet-on-the-ground dance, a Northwest expression of ecstasy. A businessman in a navy suit holds binoculars to his eyes and a cell phone to his ear. I see women in suits and heels, tie-dyed kids from local communes. Everybody's here.

"Watch this," I say to Jin, "remember this," over and over, because the whales are too theoretical for him, refusing to carry their bodies where we can see them clear. Jin chases the dirty-looking gray gulls that march full-on in front of us. I want him to record the whales for the future. His lens takes in other images: a small circle of women in Indian print dresses beating drums; a young man with blond dreadlocks writhing in front of them; another dancer. When people approach the women to ask what they're doing they say the whales are spirit guides, like angels, who come to humans to teach them to live at a higher level of spiritual evolution.

The human outlines on my Honda's dashboard—reclining, with sketchy lines to show air blowing either to the head, the torso, or the feet—Jin has come to call *angels*. I don't have a clue where he learned the word. "Turn on angels," he says, when he wants to press the buttons.

Whales have followed a different evolutionary path from ours, beginning on land and then becoming, in the water, one of the great predators of the Eocene—archeocetes, huge crocodile-y monsters with gaping teeth—before mellowing into these toothless mammals that live in social groups and nurture their young. Gray whales are a baleen whale, a simple class of whales also called *mysticetes*. They feed through a baleen, a spongy scrim in the mouth that sucks in seawater and filters out the tiny organisms they eat—porcelain crab larvae, ghost shrimp. Like all whales, grays are mammals and intelligent, large-brained, with a much larger brain than ours (a fact I suspect the whale drummers would tell me lots about if I asked them), but compared to other whales they're relatively slow in evolving, having lived in their present form for some twelve million years, leaving their Eocene form twenty million years before that. Using baleen is a peaceful way to feed, compared with other members of the whale family, who might stun prey such as schools of mackerel with sound waves, then dive and eat.

When the whales surface you can see, with binoculars, the crust of thousands of barnacles on their backs, the quick dives of birds that live off the smaller lives whales carry, kelpweed and bladderwort tangled on their flukes. They're like islands, or planets, so whole and different they absorb our projections the way stars do: some people I know say whales are aliens from other worlds, come to teach us how to evolve so we can join with them. The spaceships they see hovering over us travel to contact the whales, besides doing other things, like abducting people. A hairdresser I know tells all her clients about her own abduction. A grueling experience, she says. "But they won't come for you," she adds, parting hair, "unless you're spiritually ready."

Whales vocalize about many things—food, danger, mating— through a system of sounds with names like *hauntings* and *trumpets*. And they click and whistle and sing, in two-tone themes that build toward nothing and sound (to us) both complex and primeval, yanked from the ocean floor. The orca pods housed in our Northwest waters have individual dialects, and one pod member takes on the job of teaching the young of the group how to vocalize. Whale species that like to sing have whales in each group that sing more than others, more accomplished singers; the rest listen more, falling out into performer and audience. Humpback whales have a common breeding song made up of four to ten musical themes— sequences of notes—that each singer changes so that each year the song evolves, as the males follow each other's improvisa- tions and add their own. Speeded up a lot, the humpbacks sound like birds. Speeded up somewhat, they sound just like human music. Scientists like Donald Griffin of Harvard call this *musical intelligence*.

I have been reading about metabolism lately, the timing of our bodies—heartrate, bloodflow—by which we learn to time the earth around us. Our body's speed is the clock that invents us. What's faster than our body rhythms, like a shooting star, is fast; what's slower is slow. I learn that to the whales, with their slow metabolisms, humans appear speeded-up, so the dancers greeting the whales with their swaying scooped-arm movements would look to the whales at sea jerky, spastic, desperately flapping.

What do the whales see when they see us on shore? Something too quick, too nervous to be alive. Perhaps they would want to comfort us humans, though not for the reasons we imagine. Whether they think about us, in any way we would find intelligible, is the real question that keeps us glued to the cool grass at Boulevard Park.

Watching these whales feels like a lesser form of what I feel looking at my young son: the drive to know his consciousness, his growing humanness; the thoughts that are always sifting in his head, turning dashboard figures into winged swoops of grace—or maybe to him angels are just slouched sketches of the human, supine. To know his mind. To know.

Jin has begun asking questions, in the endless perseverant way of small children. Why is it dark sometimes? and I tackle the earth's rotation, the question of days and nights. Why is it *today*? and I begin again. What is tomorrow? and again I'm talking, sorting through the facts, offering what seems plausible to him. (The earth is like a big ball and it turns around and there's the sun again . . .)

Why is tomorrow *tomorrow*? he says, with mounting frustration, and the questions keep coming in an infinite regress of questions, to the point where language dissolves utterly— it's clear that he's not asking about planets and turning at all—and another explanation of time will only result in a plaintive, Why is tomorrow *tomorrow*? Why?

I always cheat at the end and say, Why are you *you*? knowing I'm tired and punking out, resorting to an unfair existential feint.

I imagine it is thirty years from now, and Jin and I stand on the shoreline again. I can show him where he once saw gray whales: where they spouted and rolled and heard the too-fast bird chirps of humans crying to them on shore. Anglo-Saxon poets once called their whale-filled Atlantic *whale-road*—the mammals were that plentiful—though the whales they saw, like the sperm, are now almost extinct, and the rolling backs of tankers have taken their place.

If we hum, we might speak with whales' voices, inventing the same tunes. They are so much us they could write our symphonies; isn't it funny to know that, now that they're largely gone? Of course, when we talk about the grays in that future, it will depend on how we talk: *Let's put it this way, they weren't able to adapt; it's nature's way*, we could say, which is to say: *We are nature now*. Or maybe there'll still be this village-worth of them, clinging to their strip of coastline, their movement foreordained as my son's.

Human-road, we could say to all we see, where to?

ANN PANCAKE

CAPITAL REALISM

Every home in my neighborhood in northeast Thailand had a television or at least a stereo, but not one had drinking water, sewer system, garbage collection, mail delivery, or telephone. My neighbors watched sitcoms while they boiled rice over charcoal braziers. They lived in cinderblock boxes jammed with extended families, traditional wooden homes swaying on stilts, and corrugated metal shanties, and a triangular loft over a cement truck garage sheltered a slew of young women, a bigger slew of little kids and puppies, and a quadriplegic beggar with the best sound system in the vicinity. I had the nicest place on our road, but even it was built of boards that didn't meet. Trashfire smoke and dust storms gusted through my floor-to-ceiling cracks. Yet in the field behind our mud road jutted several acres of new bungalows, bright blue with red tile roofs. Not a soul lived there, and they were protected from the people already in the neighborhood by walls speared with shards of glass. Weeds mounted those walls. Vines lipped around the shattered bottles. The bungalows waited for the rising middle class to do their rising.

I'd noticed all over the country billboards promising buildings like this. Handpainted skyscrapers and condo developments, always white, to contrast the contemporary reality of Asian Third World gray. One such billboard stood at the end of our road, over a swamp dump where little boys paddled around on discarded chunks of Styrofoam. Under the skyscraper pictured on the billboard, black stick people scurried about toting tiny black briefcases. I called this genre "capital realism."

I came to Thailand in 1992, in the heat of the country's rush to First World status, a breakneck hurtle towards what optimists would call industrialization or modernization, but what I came to view as a kamikaze plummet into the kind of hypercapitalism that one only sees in more muted and benign forms in the West. Thailand was global capitalism under an X-ray and construction the national pastime, careening along nonstop everywhere, with few environmental restrictions and no apparent safety regulations. The college where I taught, for example, had no building, no place. It was a ghost operation superimposed on a vocational high school. But behold, my supervisor reassured me the day I arrived: the college was under construction across the highway. It would be seven stories high, he gloated, the tallest building in the province. It would be even higher than the Royal Hotel downtown. I gazed across the highway at the partially completed "sky-scraper" I would later find on the billboard at the end of my road. It rose from the swamp like a giant refrigerator. The family name of the real estate magnate who owned the college was emblazoned in four-foot-tall letters across one end. An enormous red bow adorned the other. I noticed immediately in the New Seven-Story Building a disconcerting bulge.

I had never seen before and would never see again more workers labor any harder in worse conditions for as many hours as I saw in Thailand in 1992. In my neighborhood, village loudspeakers rousted everyone at first light, frantic rapid-fire rat-a-tat Thai. I would hear three different broadcasts simultaneously, each in the hysterical pitch of a two-hour-long used car commercial or coverage of the Kentucky Derby. All the neighbors, even the children, walked outside, leaned away from their houses with their hands on their hips, hacked, and spat the night's accumulation of pollution out of their throats. The loudspeakers pattered and wailed until the national anthem at eight—that's the only thing I recognized—but for the two and a half hours before eight, I imagined them exhorting, "Develop! Modernize!" And by eight o'clock, if not earlier, everyone seemed to be doing precisely that.

Even though I couldn't peer into the factories, the plants, I still saw everywhere the ground-level grunt makers of rapid industrialization, the people who bore it on their backs. They squatted in truck beds on sacks of sand and lime, their heads protected against the sun and dirt and exhaust by rags, towels, plaid sarongs. They came in both genders, their skin darker than the skins at the college, faces knobbier, their arms and legs ropy with fatless muscle. They came in all ages, the elderly, their bare feet splayed like dinner plates, broken toenails and teeth, and the children, collecting bus fares, pumping gas at Shell stations, and, of course, working construction, their faces hardened years before their bodies would catch up, so that they looked like midgets or dwarves. As I walked to and from my office in the vo-tech school, I watched the construction of the New Seven-Story Building, wondering if it would ever measure up to its capital realist ideal on the billboard along my mud road. Most of the work was done by boys monkeying through a vast bamboo scaffolding and by women who carried shallow baskets of rock and cement on their heads. All lived in temporary aluminum shacks thrown up near the construction site, and they never had a day off. I studied the bulge in the New Seven-Story Building from a distance.

Capital realism flourished. Huge signs featuring tiers of spec homes, inevitably white with the inevitable red tile roof, two stories, landscaping, a garage. Gazing upon the housing development would be a modern Thai nuclear family, stick-figure father, mother, ten-year-old son, eight-year-old daughter, all clad in Western clothes. My neighborhood, too, was under perpetual construction, and because it was not only unzoned but also not segregated by class, as it would have been in the States, I could observe the whole gamut of house-building. In addition to the brand-new bungalows, new upper-class homes began to jostle against old wooden ones. At the other end of the social scale, shack dwellers shifted to rows of what looked like self-storage lockers. And one night, just after dark, I walked home and passed a partially completed block home, superior to the cells and shacks, but far short of the capital realist models. A whole family pitched in to build it. Father, mother and two sons, only six or eight years old, mixing concrete under a glaring portable fluorescent lamp.

The view on my routine bus rides to Bangkok for visa "problems" was a sort of four-hour-long construction movie: project after project after project, state-of-the-art heavy equipment, manual laborers in a state of collapse. Much of the ground along the road had been beaten into a blizzard, no place to settle, the earth in air and air in earth, confused. And on the long approach to the Bangkok city limits, dust so choked the air that the people squatting along the road waiting for their own buses looked like apparitions—materializing out of the haze for seconds, their eyes screwed against the dirt, the backwash of traffic wafting the plastic bags they clutched in their hands, before they vanished again behind the displaced soil. The constant tearing up of the ground and pouring of concrete. The paving of a nation.

In the *Bangkok Post*, I read stories of collapsed multistory buildings, of hastily clapped-together shopping centers and office complexes and hotels. I followed the erection of the New Seven-Story Building with increasing paranoia. Other articles cited percentages of buildings in Bangkok not up to regs, inspectors paid off, eyes averted, in the frenzy to make that Third to First World vault. I regarded the bulge in the New Seven-Story Building where I'd soon be spending eight hours a day. I began photographing capital realism when I saw it, dazzling five-star hotels in Bangkok slums, shopping malls tottering over rice fields, and once, up near Chiang Mai, a painting of a golf course and an obese Caucasian business-man with a blond Dutch-boy haircut, wielding a scroll of blueprints in his hand. Under this billboard, back in real life, huddled a long stretch of desolate hovels.

Late one afternoon, the pickup truck bus dropped me at the end of my road, where a newly middle-class family had completed its capital realist dream home just a few days before. It stood directly across from the cement truck garage with the loft and the quadriplegic beggar. Since the morning, the family had elevated a patch of ground beside their new house, about the size of two double beds. They had rolled sod onto it to make a "yard." As far as I knew, the next nearest "grass," in the suburban U.S. meaning of that word, grew on the army base golf course across the city. No one was home in the new house, but six neighborhood residents were admiring the capital realist microlawn. Two stray dogs slept on it, a third sniffed it, a fourth pissed, and a pair of chickens scratched up the turf.

A year or so after I left Thailand, the Royal Hotel collapsed. In the U.S. media, Thai news rarely warrants notice, but the Royal Hotel generated enough horror and blood to earn a few lines. I squinted at the photos in an absurd effort to identify people I might know. The Royal Hotel. The second highest building in Nakhom Ratchasima province after the New Seven-Story Building. I thought about twelve-year-old masons and that faint, but unmistakable, bulge.

Five years after I left, the Thai economy collapsed too, along with Japan and Korea, and Malaysia, and Indonesia . . . Capitalist domino effect. As usual, after the initial catastrophe, I found news of the fallout scarce, but a few weeks later I had lunch with friends who had just traveled in Thailand. In a tea shop, they said, they had met a Thai man who told them the country had sold every last natural resource: every tree, every mineral, every gem. Empty. And for that reason, he said, Thailand would never recover. I knew this didn't literally happen, but I also knew the spirit of it was close enough.

I think of them, back in 1992, hurtling along towards some capitalist glory, the promise of wealth and comfort and even democracy that countries like the United States assured them would accompany "modernization." A nation trying to make in fifteen years an economic leap the United States made in one hundred and fifty. Dragons and Tigers. Keeping up with the Kims. I think of the sacrifices so many were making, not just the laborers but the beggars, and the farmers, and the democracy protesters, and the culture, and the land itself. And I was never convinced the sacrifice would be worth it, even if Thailand did "catch up" to the West. But they didn't. They sacrificed and then went downhill. And who benefited? Thai elites? I don't know. But certainly global corporations, heavily invested in by Americans, and American consumers like myself.

Capital realism. I became a connoisseur of such billboards. I went out of my way to visit them, catalogued them in my journals, mounted my photos in albums. Offices, banks, hotels, apartment high-rises, shopping malls, and always, on the bottom border of the paintings, humanesque figures scuttled about. Often, on closer inspection, I would see that the artist not only didn't include eyes, noses, mouths; he didn't even bother with an oval for a face. For heads, he daubed a few black smears.

PICO IYER

JET LAG

FROM "NIGHTWALKING"

Not long ago in Damascus, I lived for a few days on muezzin time: long silent mornings in the Old City before dawn, walking through labyrinths of dead-end alleyways, in and out around the great mosque, and then long hot days in my room sleeping as if I were in my bed in California. Then up again in the dark, the only decoration in my room a little red arrow on the wall to show which direction Mecca was.

I went on like this for a while—watching the light come up in the mosque, seeing the city resolve itself into its shapes in the first hours of light, and then disappearing myself, down into a well—and then, after a few days, something snapped: at night, by day, I could not sleep. I stayed up all the way through a night, and the next day couldn't sleep. I drew the curtains, got into pajamas, buried myself inside the sheets. But my mind was alive now, or at least moving as with a phantom limb. Soon it was dark again, my time to wake up, and at last, at 2:00 a.m. or so, reconciled to my sleeplessness, I picked up an old copy of *Fear and Loathing in Las Vegas* and began to read.

From outside, in the fourth-floor corridor, the sound of a door being opened, then closing. Furtive rustles, a circle of whispers. The thump of a party, forbidden booze, female laughter. The ping of the elevator as it came and opened its doors; the sound of the doors closing again, the machine going up again and down. Sometimes I went to the window and, drawing the curtains, saw minarets, lit in green, the only tall monuments visible across the sleeping city. Once, putting away the story of Dr. Thompson and his Samoan, I opened the door to check the corridor, but there was no one there. No footsteps, no figures, no anything.

Hours later, I was in an Internet cafe in Covent Garden, not sure of who or where I was, having not slept for what seemed like weeks, and hours after that, in Manhattan, where I'd lived in a former life. My bags had not arrived, and so I was wearing clothes not my own, bought with an airline voucher. Outside, a drill screamed in the harsh summer light—"recon-struction," the Front Desk said—and I tried to push myself down into sleep, somewhere else.

A little after midnight—I was just coming to life and light now—I went out and walked to Times Square, where there was still excitement. A man was cradling his girl's head in his arm, and kissing her, kissing her softly. She stooped down to get into a cab, and he leaned in after her, kissing her again, as if to pull her back.

The cabdriver, with a conspicuous slam, put on his meter, and the car pulled away. A woman nearby was shaking her breasts at a male companion, who looked as if he belonged to another world from hers. He watched her in delight, the screens and lights all around exploding.

The man who had been kissing, kissing his girl, eyes closed, straightened himself up as the car disappeared around a corner, looked around—taxis, crowds, from every direction—and then walked across to a telephone as if to start the night anew. Crowds streamed out of theaters so one could imagine for a moment this was New Year's Eve, the center of the world. The hushed, deserted mosque of the Old City of Damascus—I'd been there yesterday morning—was a universe away.

I walked and walked through the city in the dark, seeing a place I could easily imagine I'd never seen before, let alone lived in for four years. At Sixty-second and Broadway, a man, tall and dark, suddenly raced out into the street, and I stiffened, my New York instinct telling me this was an "incident." But it was just a group of cheerful men from the islands, playing cricket under the scaffolding of a prospective skyscraper at 2:00 a.m.; the man fielded the ball in the middle of the empty road and threw it back as if from a boundary in Port of Spain. Around the all-night grocery stores, the newsstands, people were speaking Hindi, Urdu, who knows what language, and epicene boys were wriggling their hips to catch the attention of taxis.

Elsewhere—last night in Damascus again—people were huddled on stoops, against buildings, bodies laid out as if no longer living, scattered across the steps of shuttered churches. A woman crouched on the steps of an all-night market, three suitcases in front of her. A man reciting to himself, outside a darkened theater. Another wheeling a suitcase across a deserted intersection—2:57, says the digital clock outside the bank.

I'd never seen these signs of poverty, this dispossession, in all the years I'd lived here, but in the dead of night a kind of democracy comes forth. The doorman says hello to me as I pass, and the night manager of a McDonald's laughs at a drunken joke as if he's never heard it before at 3:15 a.m. On the floor of the same McDonald's, a group of kids sits in a tribal circle.

On Sixth Avenue, as I walk, a clutch of Japanese tourists, twenty or thirty of them, following a woman under a flag, stand silently, waiting for the light to change. As soon as it does, they walk across, en masse, as unfathomable as everything else here, off on some kind of night tour.

An all-night guard is saying something about a colleague who got lost. A tall, tall girl with a model's ponytail is hailing a cab on Eighth Avenue. A woman with a shock of blond hair, a leopardskin coat, is traipsing after a man in a suit, while another woman sits up and goes through her worldly possessions: a bundle of blankets beside her on the street.

I could be in Manila again, I suppose, on the night side of the world. Certainly I feel as if I've never seen this place around me, even when I lived here and worked many a night till 4:00 a.m., taking a car back through the deserted streets before awakening and coming back to the office after dawn. When the light comes finally up, and I go to breakfast at a fashionable hotel across from where I'm staying, the friend who greets me tells me that there was an incident last night, a mass murder in an all-night fast-food store. Five bodies discovered in a pool of blood; it was on all the morning news shows.

"That's strange," I say (in Damascus now, Covent Garden?), "I never would have guessed it. I was out in the street last night, walking and walking; the city never looked to me so benign."

M. J. IUPPA

DAYLIGHT SAVINGS TIME

That autumn day was much like today's weather. Air pungent and sharp with its smells of wet leaves and earth and distant chimney smoke is loaded with melancholy, just lingering to be breathed in and set loose in a sudden gush, a thought of someone not quite forgotten, someone whose embrace felt dangerous and ticklish like electricity, like power surge before blackout. Someone so reckless, so wild, so willing with promises and kisses that you were swept away in a late October hour that happened completely. One hour that repeated itself, minute by minute, and forgot that you were in the wrong place at the right time. One hour that turned back on itself, so you could save face, pretending you weren't there.

*

You were alive and every minute counted. Sitting in the front seat of a 1968 Volkswagen bus, waiting for a man you hardly knew to come back three times in his forgetting something—a phone number, a pen, a message left on his desk—you nodded your head at him like a dopey car doll that signals directions from the dashboard. You said *Hurry up* in a patient way, but you knew better. This was going to be a long two-hour trip.

No one tells the truth about love. Talking matter-of-factly seems banal, like proving a right angle or finding the equal distance between two lines. You were listening to *his* love story, feeling the sun warm on your face and neck, thinking about your own. The two-lane highway was slowly rising into the foothills of the Alleghenies. Staring straight ahead, you saw the windswept trees and fields hanging on to skeletons of milkweed, and bristles of burdock made everything he said sadder. Things were sticking to you. You could barely talk. Not that it mattered. He could and did until he realized his voice. He became silent.

The thrum of the bus tires on pavement was soothing. The road was pulling away from everything you knew and opening up to the unexpected. He kept checking his rearview mirror, watching the highway lines breaking up like Morse code. You were looking ahead into that ever-changing sky. In the distance, you spotted a large maple tree standing all alone in

the middle of a field covered with black leaves. Look at that!
What kind of a maple is it? He had an answer for everything,
but not this time. You asked him to pull over. He stopped the
bus on the soft shoulder, in front of the tree, but still at a field's
distance. You slid out of your side, leaving the door ajar. His
door clicked shut, not a loud sound, more like someone flip-
ping a Zippo lighter shut. Strangely in the instant of that
sound, the tree exploded into flight. You watched hundreds of
starlings disperse into wind. The maple stood empty, except
for one.

There is always one. One left to know this. One left to keep
quiet.

BRENDA MILLER

GETTING YOURSELF HOME

Y ou're in the bed of a stranger. Well, not a stranger, really—he's your boyfriend, after all, you agreed to this designation just the other day, both of you content from an afternoon of careful courtship, the binoculars passed from hand to hand as you watched the trumpeter swans and the snow geese sharing a field in the Skagit River plains. But now his face, when you glimpse it sidelong, looks so rigid, the mouth shut tight, the head tilted up and away. Even those creases around his ear, those lines you once found endearing, now seem a deformation. Even if you could see each other clearly, your glances would knock sidelong off each other, deflecting, and you can hardly imagine now the first time you made love: not the sex itself, but the kiss that preceded it—so long, so breathtaking, your head arched back, the body's tendons giving way without a thought.

But now you feel dangerously exposed, your body huddled under the covers: how has it come to this so quickly, so soon? You wrap your arms around your naked chest and long for your flannel pajamas, but they're at your own house, hanging on the hook behind the bathroom door, you can see them so clearly, along with a vision of your new kitten wandering the house by herself, still so bewildered by these rooms, mewling into the dark—did you leave on a light? did you fill her water bowl?—she's frightened, you imagine, and baffled by your absence.

It's three o'clock on a winter morning, foggy, the roads slick with ice. You turn in the bed, away from the man and his thick arms, his muscled chest, the wrists powerful from days spent with hammers and saws. You open your eyes and begin to calculate each of the moves it would take to get you out of here: the flip of the blankets, the swing of your legs onto the floor, the search for your clothes crumpled on the chair by the desk, gathering those clothes in your arms and tiptoeing over the creaking planks to pull them on in the other room—the boyfriend muttering from his side of the bed, or not making a sound, his eyes tightly closed, his head twisted away. And then the search for your purse, your shoes, your keys, your coat, standing with all these things by the doorway, trying to decide whether or not to say good night, and finally just fleeing down the stairs and out the door to your car, the windows covered in a thin sheet of ice. You'd have to scrabble for the lock, nicking the paint, then inside put the defroster on high, jumping out again with scraper in hand, hacking away at the windows, your hands aching with cold. Finally, the creep up the dirt driveway, dipping your head to peer under the scrim of frost, accelerating too hard so the back end swerves as you pull out onto the road. Then the road itself: pitch dark, slick, the air veiled with fog so the high beams do not illuminate so much as blind as you make your clumsy way home.

Just the thought of it exhausts you, and when you contemplate even the first of these moves—the turning back of the covers—you realize the impossibility of even such a simple gesture, one that will lead you out of here and back where you belong. You dare not move a muscle, so you blink back the darkness and try to navigate how you got here in the first place, scrolling in your mind, but all you get is a procession of men from your past—they parade before you, one after the other, all of them turning to smile briefly, forlornly, their foreheads puckered in disappointment.

You shut your eyes. Take a deep breath. You try to remember what your meditation teacher told you about the breath: how you enter your true home with each inhalation, each exhalation, a cadence old and plain as those worn-out concepts of love, of compassion. So you try it: you breathe in, you breathe out, but there's a glitch in your throat, a mass in your chest, and your body feels nothing like home, more like a room in a foreign hotel, the windows greasy, the outlets reversed, the noise of the street rising like soot. The body's no longer an easy abode, not in this bed, not with two strangers lying in the dark and waiting—breath held—for morning to finally arrive.

PAUL LISICKY

AFTERNOON WITH CANALS

t's the hour when the heels are inevitably blistered, when we've strolled past as many canals, funky houseboats, and tall, glamorous windows as we can for one day. Even the obsessive pleasure we've taken in trying to perfect our pronunciations of *Prinsengracht* or *Leidesgracht*—the burr of those "g's" scratching the backs of our throats—is no longer of interest. All those rainy pavements, those brooding clouds blown in from the North Sea: we're sodden, saturated, and we can't help but wish to be warmed, to feel the heat of a candle's flame drying us out from inside.

"So now what should we do?" I say.

My boyfriend leans against a stone wall in his leather jacket. He shifts his weight from leg to leg. He holds me entirely in his gaze, brows raised, a hint of mischief in his grin. We know it's too early to head back to the guest house. We shrug at exactly the same moment, tensing our shoulders, then laugh, nervous but relieved we've been thinking alike.

Of course, it shouldn't come as any shock that we're strolling past these burnished cherry red boxes (I think of elegant Japanese furniture) inside of which handsome men, in varying degrees of light, lie back with their hands latched behind their heads or on their stomachs. Now that we've calmed down—the fingers fill with blood; the pulse slows— we're tempted to walk downstairs till I'm reminded of my tattooist's instructions: no steam room, no hot tub. I press my hand to the freshly pierced flesh, bewildered that the crown-capped heart will be on my arm for the rest of my life.

Then my boyfriend's arm is around my waist.

Just across the hall, inside one of the boxes, sits a man with an amazingly hard chest. A honeyed light shadows the planes of his rough, bearded face. What does he want? Is it just me, or am I simply in the way? Are we, together, two large Americans with our shaven heads, just the ticket for a dreary, low-lit afternoon? We try our best to read him, the flares of interest, the averted eyes, as he shifts inside the frame of the box, soulful and startling: a Vermeer in the flesh.

Only hours ago we stood before a still life in the Rijksmuseum. Tulip, dragonfly, conch shell, lemon peel: all of it entered me, soaking through my skin and bones, like dye. If only for a moment, I stood before the easel, missing paints. Poppy seed oil, lead, red upon blue—twilight falls, while just outside the window, on the other side of the wall, horse-shoes clomp on cobblestone, bakers pound their dough.

Time hurries away from me as I try my best to still it, to anchor it within its frame.

We walk around the system of boxes. It takes us but two minutes to find out that our dear Vermeer is gone, his space empty. We look at each other and shrug, smile. No matter. Maybe this is what we'd wanted anyway. Without saying a word, I draw my arm over his shoulder and lead him inside the box. It doesn't take long. The warmth beneath my fingers, the density and heft of his muscles—he feels like gold in my hands as I touch my lips to his neck. His palms press against my skull. Then what: a kick against the wall? We laugh. So many footsteps down these halls, so much longing and release, little cries, and breaths pulled in, while far from the range of our hearing, the car horns beep, the motorboats chug in the canals, cell phones ring, forks chime against the dinner plates of Amsterdam. "*Prinsengracht*," he rasps. "*Leidesgracht*."

We walk down the street again, arm in arm this time. In two days we'll be back on the plane, rushing off to meetings, appointments. My feet hurt inside my shoes. But we've framed time at least: we'll travel back inside it, again and again, and beyond.

MARY PAUMIER JONES

SIENA, BURNT AND RAW

Obscured by thick cloud cover, the Tuscan sun is nowhere in evidence. Rain falls; stops. It sprinkles again. The air holds maximum moisture, softening edges, making distance and form palpable if sometimes deceptive. In this light the buildings ringing the famous piazza are not the bright color we have been conditioned to expect by travel guides and postcards. Still the bricks are a shade so distinctive as to have taken its name from this place: Siena, sienna. The stones of Florence are gray and masculine in comparison; the marble of Carrera, unearthly white.

The name for the color sienna did not come into use until later, but the iron oxide limonite clay from which it comes was abundant from antiquity in Italy and other places. Cave painters at Lascaux extracted and used it, creating forms that take our breath away today, 15,000 years later. Yellow-brown in its raw state, sienna clay reddens when its water is removed by heating. Burnt sienna: color of Tuscan sun even in cloudy shade. Remember it from crayon boxes?

Natural pigments naturally vary tremendously from one place to another. The sienna from terra di Sienna was particularly valued through the ages for its rich hue and jewel-like transparency, caused by the silicates in the clay. Leonardo used transparent sienna in the delicate gradations of his *sfumato* technique, Caravaggio to achieve the depth of his chiaroscuro. But clay mines, sadly, are finite resources. Those in the Siena hills that yielded the pigments of Michelangelo, Botticelli, Rembrandt, Vermeer, and on and on are used up now. Since the 1940s, natural sienna has come mainly from Sardinia and Sicily, and from the Appalachian Mountains. Still called sienna, no longer Sienese.

At Lascaux the fungal "green and white sickness" caused by so many visitors endangered the paintings and necessitated closing the cave. History turns. An exact replica, painstakingly built, still inspires our awe while saving the original.

High-quality earth pigments become rarer every year. Purists and standard makers insist on the superiority of the natural. Many experts, however, say that lower-quality natural pigments are really inferior to the high-quality new synthetics. To get the look of the sienna of the old masters, they say, you'd be better off using a rich-hued transparent synthetic iron oxide paint, first developed by—what else?—the auto industry.

Nor is the crayon box sacred. Last year burnt sienna was one of five hues Crayola nominated for retirement to make way for new colors. The others—blizzard blue, teal blue, mulberry, and magic mint were voted off the island, and have been replaced by jazzberry jam, wild blue yonder, inch worm, and mango tango—names not without a certain poetry perhaps, but a little lacking in historical resonance. Loyal fans of burnt sienna, however, raised the hue and cry. Prevailing in their Internet vote, they kept burnt sienna in the box.

SAMUEL HYNES

FROM *THE GROWING SEASONS*

Summer only has one date when you're a kid—the Fourth of July. That was true in the country on the Heggs' farm and it was true in town. But the way you celebrated was different. The town Fourth began a long time before the date, when fireworks stands appeared along highways beyond the last houses, the junkyards and the used-car lots. That was because it was against the law to sell fireworks inside the city limits. We rode our bikes out Cedar Avenue to where the hasty sheds and tents stood with their red-white-and-blue "Fireworks" signs, and there bought skyrockets, Roman candles, pinwheels, cherry bombs, torpedoes, ladyfingers, half-inchers, inchers, and even two-inchers, and rode back into town with our stuff in paper bags in our bike baskets, and sticks of the rockets standing up like flagstaffs.

Morning comes early on the Fourth of July in town. I wake

in the half dark before dawn to the sound of the day's first explosions, a distant rattling stutter; somewhere in far-off backyards other kids can't wait. I dress and take my sack of firecrackers downstairs and out to the back steps. Chuck is already there, sitting silently, with his own sack. We can't begin yet; there has to be a period of waiting, like Christmas morning, until the folks are awake. The best times are always delayed by adults, every kid knows that. Then the lights go on in the kitchen and the pots rattle and the radio begins to play, and we can begin.

I start with my littlest crackers, the strings of ladyfingers; they go off together in a rattling rush, *pop-pop-pop-pop*. In other backyards I can hear other kids doing the same thing, making the neighborhood crackle. When the little ones are gone I build a miniature village out of strawberry boxes in the dirt. Then I put one-inchers under the houses and blow them all into the air. I rebuild the village and do it again. The destruction is very satisfactory, like being God when he's angry. I like the drift of the smoke and the smell of burned powder. But Nellie makes me stop, not because of the noise or the splintered village but because I'm making a puddle where she hangs the laundry to dry.

After lunch I meet my friends in Apple Alley. We find empty tin cans in garbage cans, set them up in the alley with a two-incher or a cherry bomb underneath, and blow them high into the air. Cherry bombs under cans make parents nervous: "What if the can explodes? Don't stand too close! If it doesn't go off, don't pick it up!" We know fireworks are dangerous, we've read about accidents, and will find them again in tomorrow's papers: ANOKA BOY LOSES FINGER IN FIREWORKS ACCIDENT, GIRL'S DRESS CATCHES FIRE FROM SPARKLER, ROCKET BURNS GARAGE DOWN. It's the danger that makes it fun, that and the noise.

At Powderhorn Park the Fourth of July is an all-day carnival, with running races and music and speeches by politicians. We don't go to the daytime part—that's the time for kids in the alley with their own fireworks, and anyway my father doesn't like speeches, he says they're all lies—but after supper we walk together to the park for the fireworks, a family among other walking families, slowly because there's lots of time, it's still daylight, joining folks who converge out of side streets, the crowd thickening until it flows into the park and onto the hills that circle the little lake, making a great bowl of waiting people.

The sunset slowly loses its color behind western trees, and the high sky turns a darker blue. Birds settle in the trees, bats swoop low in the half darkness and girls squeal and cover their hair because a bat might make a nest there, and the families wait quietly, except for the children, who stir restlessly and ask, Is it dark enough yet? *Is it?* and light sparklers that burn like lightning bugs on the far hills. Down below on the island in the lake shadowy figures move, and flashlights blink. And the crowd, denser now, waits.

The last light is gone from the sky, and stars are out—it must be dark enough now! A sudden sizzing streak of fire and smoke climbs the night air and the first rocket bursts overhead, and the crowd on the hillside sighs one "Ah-h-h-h," because it has begun. And then another and another, each one bursting as

the one before fades in a scatter of sparks, all the possible vari-
eties of rocket, surprising us, delighting us—"Ah-h-h-h,"
"Ah-h-h-h," "Ah-h-h-h"—the ones that burst and spread fingers of smoke that burst again at the fingertips, the ones that
spread bright worms of fire, the ones that explode with a bass
thunder that rumbles and echoes in the hollow of the hills, the
ones that open and linger like chrysanthemums, the necklaces
of lights that float slowly down, fading from brightness as they
fall, the blinding white ones like a million flashbulbs or the
end of the world that catch our rapt white upturned faces on
the hillsides and hold them for a moment fixed in pure light,
and then return us all to the darkness.

The last rocket is always the best of all—burst after burst,
the echoes rebounding, and then another burst just when you
think it is all over. And then it is. The families rise slowly in the
sudden silence and fold their blankets, and walk home through
the dark, still streets, not talking much, purged by the high
splendors they have seen, satisfied that another Fourth is over,
another summer has been celebrated with a proper hullabaloo.

But not quite over, even then. When I have gone at last to
bed, and lie there half-asleep, thinking about the day and the
rockets in the park, kids who have a few firecrackers left are
still setting them off, finishing the long day. I can hear them
through my open windows, far off across the flat dark town:
pop-pop, pop-pop-pop.

Pop.

JO ANN BEARD

BEHIND THE SCREEN

'm looking at the backs of all their heads. They're sitting on lawn chairs in the dusk and so am I, only their lawn chairs are on the lawn while mine is on the enclosed back porch. I have to look at the backs of their heads through the screen. We're waiting for the fireworks to begin.

My sister is wearing shorts, a midriff top, and all manner of jewelry—a pop-bead necklace, a Timex wristwatch, a mood ring, and a charm bracelet that makes a busy metallic rustle every time she moves her arm, which she does frequently. On the charm bracelet, between a high-stepping majorette and a sewing machine with movable parts, is a little silver book that opens like a locket to display the Teen Commandments. Engraved in infinitesimal letters: *Don't let your parents down, they brought you up; Choose a date who would make a good mate;* and the famous *At the first moment turn away from unclean thinking—at the first moment.* It has such an urgent tone it forces you to think uncleanly. Right now my sister is sitting in a lawn chair waiting for it to get dark. Every few minutes she raises and lowers her right arm so the charm bracelet, which I covet, clanks up to her elbow and then slides slowly and sensuously back down to her wrist. She doesn't bother turning around to see how I take this. She knows it's killing me.

They won't let me off the porch because I'm having an allergy attack. A low whistling sound emanates from my chest whenever I breathe. I can put a little or a lot of force behind it, depending on my mood. I'm allergic to ragweed and thistles and marigolds and dandelions and daisies, so we're all used to me being stuck on the porch while everyone else is having fun. Also grass; I'm allergic to grass. Right now one nostril is completely plugged up while the other runs in a steady drip.

My four-year-old brother is wearing cowboy boots and shorty pajamas, a gunbelt minus the guns, and a hat with earflaps. He's shooting each member of my family in turn with his crayon-size index fingers. He smiles at me, his little teeth glinting in the dusk. "You dead," he says.

I press my face up against the screen. It smells like dirt. I put my tongue out tentatively. It tastes like dirt. "Go to H," I say.

My mother turns her head halfway around and looks into my father's ear. "You're gonna get a whole lot sicker, miss," she tells me. Stars are beginning to be visible through the cloudy beehive of her teased hair. It's the Fourth of July 1962, and our city is having a fireworks display in the park. I have my own bowl of popcorn on the porch, and a glass of pop. The fireworks will be visible over the top of the dying elm tree in our backyard. It's impossible for me to eat the popcorn because I'm wearing a nose tourniquet, an invention I came up with myself: half of a twisted Kleenex, one end stuffed into one nostril, the other end in the other nostril. It has a wicking effect, and saves the effort of swabbing all the time.

"I can't even taste this pop," I say to the screen, after taking a sip. They all ignore me. The family dog, Yimmer, is sitting on my father's lap, growling quietly each time my brother shoots her.

My sister takes a loud swig out of a bottle of Pepsi, wipes her mouth elaborately, and says, "Man, was that good."

I examine a series of interesting scabs on my right knee. None of them are ready to be removed, although a couple are close. "You should see these scabs," I say to the backs of their heads.

My brother marches in place, talking to himself in a stern whisper.

My mother lights another Salem and positions a beanbag ashtray on the metal arm of her chair.

My father leans down and gives Yimmer's head a kiss.

Suddenly the scruffy edges of the elm tree are illuminated. The night sky turns pale above the garage, staccato gunfire, and a torpedo of light wiggles upward, stops, and fizzles. A long sigh is heard, from my family and the family next door.

I have my forehead against the screen, breathing in the night air and the heavy, funeral scent of roses, the only flower I'm not allergic to. A noodle skids across the sky, releasing a shower of blue spangles, jewels on a black velvet bodice. Way up there is outer space. I lean back and touch my forehead; an indented grid from the screen has been pressed into it. All these fireworks are somehow scaring me. "You should see my forehead," I say to my mother's hair.

"What's wrong with it?" she asks patiently. She doesn't turn around.

"I keep pressing it on the screen," I say.

"Don't push on that screen," my father says.

"I'm not," I say.

The sky is full of missiles. All different colors come out this time, falling in slow motion, red and blue turning to orange and green. It's so beautiful, I have to close my eyes. My family joins the neighbors in oohing. Suddenly, as the delayed booms are heard, I have to lean forward and put my head on my knees, inhaling the scent of Bactine and dirt. Everything is falling away from me. I open my eyes.

Black sky, dissipating puffs of gray smoke, the barely visible edges of the elm tree. My father's hand is dark against the white of the dog's fur. My brother is aiming both forefingers at the sky. A match flares suddenly; my mother touches it to her cigarette and inhales.

I am stuck somewhere between the Fourth of July and the rest of time, the usual chaos inside my head distilled down into nothing. I put my cheek against the screen, feeling the grid. There is an uproar, gunfire, sounds from the crowd.

Shooting stars in the cold of outer space; one after another the missiles are launched until the sky is brilliant with activity and smoke. Huge arcs of pink and yellow. Orange things that fizzle for an instant and then send out sonic booms. Long terrible waterfalls of yellow and blue. In the brightness, the backs of all their heads look rapt. My brother has his hands over his ears. My sister's mouth is open. The dog has her head in my father's armpit. It goes on for minutes, the booming sounds and the brilliant light. Closing my eyes doesn't work, it makes me feel like I'm falling backward. Instead I watch their hair, all the different styles right in my own backyard, and say the Teen Commandments quietly to myself: *Avoid following the crowd; be an engine, not a caboose. Stop and think before you drink.* Gunfire, one last wild spiraling of colors, and it's over.

"I'm not going to bed," my brother says resolutely.

The dog jumps down and stretches.

I remain in my lawn chair as they all troop into their house. One of my sister's better personalities comes out and she stops to comb her fingers through my hair and carries my full popcorn bowl into the house.

"She can't eat a thing," she tells my mother piously.

"Bath," my mother says to her. I hear my sister stomp up the stairs and then I hear my brother stomp up behind her, two feet on each stair.

"I saw a goddamned mosquito in here," my mother says. There's some flailing around, the whap of the flyswatter, and then my dad says, "Ick." The freezer opens, a bowl is clattered out of the cupboard. Ice cream. There's the unscrewing sound of a jar opening. Marshmallow stuff. My head hurts. I remove my spent nose tourniquet and start twisting a new one. Before I can get it in place there is a damp trickle on my lip.

"You guys?" I say. Any minute now they're going to send me upstairs.

There's an expectant pause in the kitchen.

"This lawn chair is stuck to my legs," I tell them.

A bottle is opened and an audible swig is taken. The lighter snaps and there's silence while she exhales.

Uh-oh.

"Bath," she says.

EMILY HIESTAND

HOSE

Circa 1953, the fattest woman in the world lived on my street, Gordon Road, in the small Tennessee town where I grew up near the purple-gray Cumberland Mountains. The fattest woman in the world had a daughter named Alice, who was nine, three years older than me, and one day I asked Alice why her mother was so fat. "She is *not* fat," Alice replied indignantly. "She is pregnant."

I could tell from Alice's tone that this *was* an explanation, but it was the first time the word "pregnant" had ever been used in my presence, and it failed to signify, it failed to mean anything to me, a complete blank of understanding that was the product of an old Southern tradition, among both men and women, of using euphemistic terms such as "She's in a family way" or "She's far along," or best of all, simply not mentioning it.

Alice and her family, about whom I have no further memory, lived next door to Mrs. Bayliss, an elderly lady whose
house sat on the crest of a hill and at the extreme edge of what
my brothers and I considered known territory. We had the
impression that Mrs. Bayliss lived on a cliff, although looked
at in later years and strictly topographically, the land only
sloped rather gently at Mrs. Bayliss's yard, descending into a
thicket of pungent persimmon trees.

Our house stood on flat, sunny ground, about nine houses
away from Mrs. Bayliss and the cliff. One very hot August
afternoon, as Kevin Hennessey and I were playing with the
garden hose in my front yard, Mrs. Bayliss appeared, walking
alongside the low hedge of privet that demarcated our yard
from the sidewalk. She was wearing a silk print dress and a
close-fitting hat. She wore white gloves, and carried a patent
leather purse over a crooked arm, exactly as the Queen of
England always did. This was Mrs. Bayliss's formal market-
ing outfit, which she wore whenever she walked the half-mile
from our street down the hill to the A&P grocery store in
Jackson Square.

I had the garden hose in my hand as Mrs. Bayliss passed
in front of our yard, and when the thought came into my
mind to point the hose at Mrs. Bayliss and soak her—nothing
intervened.

I did know, of course, that it was considered wicked to
squirt a jet of water at a grownup—most especially a frail, old
widow grownup, but that day something strong and ancient
rose up in me to override this feeble teaching. The sensation
of joy—the abandoned, transcendent joy that now came to

me, as the water arched toward Mrs. Bayliss and landed in a great whoosh directly in her middle regions—was unparalleled. I had crossed a line, and known the ecstasy of dissolving an absolute rule, in this case, Decency.

By great good fortune, silk turns very dark when it is wet, and Mrs. Bayliss not only was wet, she looked wet. For a moment, all three of us stood frozen, staring at one another, unsure if we actually believed what had happened. Mrs. Bayliss's dress was sopping wet and water ran down her face and plopped onto her shiny black purse. She must have said something to us at this juncture, but from my daze I cannot remember any words, only watching her come slowly to her senses, turn herself around, and go home. Kevin and I played now in the yard in the same frame of mind that bank robbers must experience after they have pulled off the heist, and are back safely in the compound running their hands through piles of gold, but listening to the radio for police reports.

In about twenty minutes Mrs. Bayliss reappeared, again walking along the well-trimmed hedge in front of our house. She had put on a fresh silk dress, and had dried off her hat and purse and face. When she came into range, I squirted her again, same as before. The inward, guiding voice had spoken afresh, suggesting that once over the line you might as well linger there a while.

I remember that Mrs. Bayliss did speak to us this time, in sharp, high sounds. Then she turned around, went home, changed her clothes, came back a third time in a different silk dress, and—Yes. Three times she appeared before us, trusting in our basic goodness; three times she tempted us; and three times we soaked her to the skin. Times two and three, Kevin and I fought over who would get to do it. But it had been my brilliant idea, and when the blade came down, Kevin was the one who had been "led on" and I was the ghastly child.

The fourth time that she set out for the grocery, Mrs. Bayliss turned *left* at the fork in Gordon Road, rather than right towards our yard (where we were waiting, poised), and went the long way down Georgia Avenue to Jackson Square to shop.

She called my mother the next day. After replacing the receiver in its cradle, my mother used my full name, and told me to come into her room. Language is greatly a tonal affair, and no one could have failed to tremble at the eschatological, end-of-the-world timbre now flowing in my mother's voice. She directed me to sit down on the ottoman by the window. During the "very serious talk, young lady" that ensued, my mother's own sunny nature was replaced by the scorches of Presbyterian Hell. Afterwards my mother helped me into one of my fancy outfits, a dress with dozens of dainty buttons down the front. We practiced my apology several times, and then my mother walked me up the road to Mrs. Bayliss's house on the edge of the cliff, and knocked on the door.

Mrs. Bayliss had always been kind, in a syrupy way, to all the children in the neighborhood, including me. Now, as we waited at the door, I felt not precisely remorse—the feeling my mother had done her level best to arouse—but rather a dim sense that Nature had chosen me to redress this goo of kindness. But this was a far too subtle and dangerous idea of Justice to explore in the moment. I knew that, so I only hung my head in Mrs. Bayliss's foyer, offered my whispered apology, and then sat in her living room and ate butter cookies. Mrs. Bayliss forgave me, and continued being sugary and frail. The only lesson that I learned at the time (if you can call it a lesson) was that for an exquisite joy, for the ineffable feeling of surety, of being perfectly in tune with nature and the gods, there will be a price to pay—and it will be worth it.

Recently I asked my mother, now eighty-three, about this long-ago event and what her point of view was at the time. "My point of view," she replied, the incident coming rather easily to mind, "was the point of view of a mother who wants to crawl under the foundation of the house and never show her face again." My mother also claims that Mrs. Bayliss was neither old nor frail at the time of her soaking. In fact she was not much older than my mother herself, which would have put Mrs. Bayliss in her early forties, younger than I am now. Nor was she a widow—there was a *Mr.* Bayliss! "And, Dear," my mother continues, "the dress" (she means *dresses* plural) "could *not* have been silk. In summer, Mrs. Bayliss would have been wearing *voile.*"

About these variances: I doubt neither my mother's memory nor her greater perception of the victim and her character. I can only say that the person she describes is simply not the person I hosed, although I grant that the dresses were very likely voile.

The savage glee of that afternoon has lodged itself firmly in my mind and body, where it seems to contrast completely with my present moral life. I am often these days trusted—not only with hoses but with several hearts, with civic causes, sharp knives, and jumper cables. Recently I traveled from my home in New England to the Tennessee town of my childhood, and the woman who answered the door of our family's old house on Gordon Road let me wander for a while in a yard where the hemlock, planted for my birth, has now grown taller than her house. I stood under the maple tree where Kevin and I liked to open the wing-like seeds, arrange the cases over our noses and walk around like that. Mrs. Bayliss, I was sorry to learn, had died, only the year before.

How I would like to have visited her once more, or to have taken our chances on a walk together down the hill to Jackson Square. Could I have found a way to thank her? It would have been a delicate undertaking, involving the risk of appearing completely unreconstructed. But I might have tried, for by her person, by her profoundly misplaced trust, the lady, Mrs. Bayliss, provided me a singular and pristine happiness—undimmed across five long decades.

JOSEPH EPSTEIN

TAKE ME OUT TO THE BALLGAME

My Cubs tickets have arrived. Seven sets of two tickets each. And what seats: eight rows off the field, on the first-base side, right at the visiting team's on-deck circle. I buy them from a friend who has held Cubs season tickets through three marriages. He could get more for my seats by selling them to an agent, but he generously sells them to me. He told me that he was reserving a seat to one of last year's Cubs World Series games for me. But, as every baseball fan knows, for the Cubs it didn't happen.

It's supposed to happen this year, though one would have to be Dr. Pangloss's even dreamier brother not to have the most strenuous doubts. Most Cubs fans, if they are anything like me, are working out scenarios of disaster for the team this year: Two pitchers from the starting rotation go down with shoulder and elbow problems in August; a $10 million-a-year outfielder loses his concentration afield because he is contemplating a same-sex marriage; the team's manager is accused of having al Qaeda connections. Many are the roads to failure, of which the Cubs have traveled most, few those to success, of which the Cubs have found none.

I don't have the Cubs sickness at the fatal or even chronic stage. I'm pleased when the team wins, slightly down when they lose, but thoughts of suicide do not play in my head. The larger fact is that I enjoy baseball, and seem to enjoy it even more as I grow older. I continue to discover details of deeper intricacy about this ostensibly simple game: such as the complaint that the greatest catcher Ivan Rodriguez, to protect his percentage of throwing out base runners, calls for too many fastballs with men on base. But I find no subtle metaphors in the game, seek no secret geometries as I gaze out at the diamond. I merely enjoy watching the players do the remarkable but insignificant things they do for the astonishing sums they are paid to do them.

As with all baseball fans, I have also had to apply at a high power what, in a very different context, Coleridge called "a willing suspension of disbelief." I have to put out of my mind that those players feel less loyalty to the teams for which they play than does the normal fan. Let their agents arrange another million dollars or so for them and—later, alligator— they are gone. Ballplayers on steroids is another matter that must be put out of mind, as home runs go crashing out of parks and asterisks are one day likely to come flying back, noting that certain records were established with chemical support. About player salaries, best not to speak.

The greater part of the attraction to the Cubs for me is what old-timers call the ballyard, the team's splendid old stadium, Wrigley Field. Anyone who has been there knows the charm of the place. Wrigley Field has serious advantages over more modern baseball parks. Fans are closer to the playing field than in most other parks; no signs advertising products are allowed to deface the field, though I did note last year that the Cubs ownership, the Chicago Tribune Company, permitted Sears to attach its name, in fairly subdued yellow neon, to a sign that registers the speed of pitches. The team still plays the preponderant number of its games during the day; this, too, is slowly changing, and the number of night games— which was originally supposed to be no more than eighteen—is scheduled to increase in coming years.

But the greatest advantage of all in Wrigley Field is that it does not have a scoreboard on which televised images are shown. This means that one doesn't have to endure the sound of trumpets drawing one's attention to an immense television screen where a race of M&M's is under way.

Nor is any but organ music played at Wrigley Field, and this, happily, only intermittently, which gives one a chance to talk to friends between innings. Unlike NBA games, where no time without entertainment is allowed—bring on the dancing girls, clowns, small blimps—at Wrigley Field one feels the sweet slow leisure of a summer afternoon, given over to the fine but trivial pursuit of watching men do superbly what as a boy one did merely enthusiastically.

My Cubs tickets are always for midweek day games. Going to a baseball game during the day in the middle of the week, when everyone else is working, lends the outing the small but genuine piquancy of vice. I usually leave home a full hour before the game so that I can find a free parking space and thus save the twenty-dollar fee. (This, along with being one of those selective cheapnesses that I believe we all have, gives me a precise valuation of my hourly worth: twenty bucks.) I buy my peanuts and hot dog outside before going into the park. Eight rows off the field, I sit in the sun, watch the game, and, my mind floating pleasantly, wonder why it was that I ever thought life was complicated.

PETER BALAKIAN

THE OLD COUNTRY

My grandmother and I followed the Yankees together, and by the time I was ten it had become an ongoing conversation between us. Box scores, averages, pitching rotations, prognosis for the World Series—because there was almost never a series without the Yankees. In August of '59, my grandmother walked around our backyard in Teaneck muttering, "The damn Chicago," because by the end of the month it was clear the White Sox and not the Yankees were headed for the series, which would mark the second time in my short life that the Yankees would not be playing in October. In April of '60, she said about the Yankees' acquisition of Roger Maris from the Kansas City A's, "We say in Armenian, one man's luck is another's stupidity."

The Yankees of the 1950s and early '60s were more than a team, they were a mood, an image, a feeling. They were thin blue stripes and elegant numbers on a white uniform. They were a Y spliced into an N on a blue cap. Power and muscle and confidence, and they did what great teams do, they won in ways that seemed inevitable yet magical. Even now when I see the Yankees logo—a red, white, and blue Uncle Sam hat topping a bat inside the white circle of a baseball with the Yankees script across the center, I feel not just nostalgia but a thrill, and I think, too, of my grandmother's quiet, intense passion for her team.

After we had moved to our new house in Tenafly, my grandmother began to appear at the door after dinner when the Yankees were on channel 11—now that she and my aunts lived a five-minute bus ride away in Englewood. In our new, paneled TV room, the two of us sat on a black leather couch beneath big framed posters of the Côte d'Azur and Monaco, while upstairs my mother put my brother and sisters to bed. As the light coming through the sliding glass doors turned purple and then black, the blue-gray of the TV lit the room.

By the early sixties, my grandmother had come around on Mickey Mantle. Perhaps because of his bad knees, his constant struggle to stay healthy enough to play, and maybe because there was something pathetic about this man who undermined his brilliant talent by his own foolish behavior off the field. He was, she said, a *tutoum kulukh*, in Armenian, a pumpkin head, a dumbbell. But by the end of the 1961 Mantle-Maris duel for the Babe's season home-run record, my grandmother came to see Mantle as a tragic figure who endured his own frailties with grace and courage and who was forced to watch from the sidelines in the second half of September as Roger Maris hit sixty-one to break the record.

So as the camera caught Mantle's boyish blond face and zoomed in on his wondrous 17½-inch neck while he took his warm-up swings in the on-deck circle, my grandmother and I grew silent. "His swing is like a great wind," she. said, "sheeewwww." And when he sent one out of the park, my grandmother would say "Outta here," and dish into the crystal bowl of pistachio nuts on the coffee table. Splitting the shells with her thumbnails, she would pass me the salty green nuts so that we could celebrate with our teeth.

I remember my grandmother during the '62 Series between the Yankees and the Giants, because that October she decided to watch all the Series games in our new TV room. "It's a bigger screen," she said to my mother about our new RCA, "and I can see better," and although she didn't say so, I think she wanted to watch the games with me. But that fall I disappointed her by listening to every game on the radio with my friends behind the chain-link backstop of our sandlot diamond. We scurried between the field and transistor radio and sometimes stopped our play as we did for the final half-inning of Game 7. I remember how Yankee fans stood on one side of the backstop and Giants fans on the other as Ralph Terry faced Willie McCovey while Willie Mays and Felipe Alou stood on second and third waiting to break the Yankees' 1–0 lead, and how the loud crack of the bat came over the radio as McCovey smacked a line drive that seemed destined for right field and a 2–1 Giant victory to win it all when Bobby Richardson leapt to his left and snatched the ball to give the

Yankees another World Series. When I returned home, my grandmother was waiting in the driveway for me, dressed in a beige linen suit and a choker of pearls, with a quiet smile on her face. "Good ole Richardson" was all she said.

About two weeks after the Series had ended, the Cuban Missile Crisis took over our lives, and my grandmother began showing up after dinner to watch the news with us. Walter Cronkite's face, slightly worried and avuncular on the big black-and-white screen, followed by aerial footage of aircraft carriers and the shoreline of Cuba. My father mocking Kennedy's Boston accent, saying, "Cuber's just a stone's throw from Florida." My mother passing a tray of dried fruits and nuts that my aunt Alice had just sent from Fresno. In my sixth-grade class everyone was talking about the bomb and the end of the world. Meredith Gutman, sensing my inclination toward morbidity and terror, stared at me one morning and said, "This whole world will go up in smoke," as she wiggled her fingers and raised her arms like a conductor.

That week I had found on my parents' night table a small pamphlet called "A Citizen's Handbook on Nuclear Attack and Natural Disasters," published by the United States Department of Defense. It was written for barely literate people and illustrated with cartoons. Aimed at assuring Americans that no harm would come from nuclear war, it read:

> *If an enemy should threaten to attack the United States you would not be alone.*

If a person receives a large dose of radiation, he will die. But if he receives only a small or medium dose, his body will repair itself and he will get well. Most of the nation's food supplies would be usable after an attack.

. . . Also, to avoid injuring your eyes, never look at the flash of an explosion of the nuclear fireball.

Even to a sixth grader this seemed ridiculous; it was clear from the media that nuclear war meant death and destruction. The pamphlet, which went on to instruct families on how to make a bomb shelter, must have been geared for suburbia, for who else but suburbanites would have basements large and fine enough to be converted into bomb shelters? And we were to stock our new shelters: 6 months of evaporated milk, 18 months of canned poultry, 12 months of ready-to-eat cereals in metal containers, 18 months of hard candy and gum, 24 months of flavored beverage powders, jugs labeled "water," pills labeled "medicine."

I was sure my mother would prefer the end of the world to this menu. Disgusted and secretly terrified by the whole Cuba business, I went home each day in late October after playing football, ate dinner, and opened the door for my grandmother and followed her into the TV room to watch the images of aircraft carriers and Cuba on the screen.

I lay in bed one night sweating, filled with images of bomb shelters and cereal in metal containers, and decided to go downstairs for a bowl of Frosted Flakes. As I passed the partly opened door of the TV room, I noticed that my grandmother was watching the late night news. Just as I was about to fling the door open, she took a long ivory pipe out of her purse, filled it with tobacco, and lit up. I was so startled that I stood frozen in the dark hallway, watching her through the two-inch crack between the door and the doorjamb.

I could hear Kennedy, Khrushchev, Castro, Cuba from the newscaster's voice. My grandmother drew long puffs on the pipe and put it down on the coffee table, then made the sign of the cross and said some Armenian words: *Der Voghormya, Der Voghormya, Der Voghormya* (Lord Have Mercy, Lord Have Mercy, Lord Have Mercy). Then she crossed herself again, took a puff on her pipe, and said *Sourp Asdvadz, Sourp Asdvadz, Sourp Asdvadz* (Holy God, Holy God, Holy God). She stood up, crossed herself, sat down, and pulled from her purse a dazzling blue and ivory and apricot striped cloth. She placed it on her lap like a napkin and then opened up a big fat biography of Mary Todd Lincoln, in which a '57 baseball card of Hank Aaron was tucked as a bookmark.

For days afterward, I thought of my grandmother's strange ritual in the TV room. Because I felt guilty for spying on her while everyone else slept peacefully upstairs, I couldn't mention it to anyone in my family. Weeks later, after the Cuban Missile Crisis was settled and enough time had passed so that what I had seen seemed like fiction, I told my mother that one night in the summer I had seen Gran take a smoke on a pipe. Seeing on my face that this amazed and somewhat frightened me, she said, "Oh, in the old country, at a certain age, women smoke pipes once in a while. It's a sign of wisdom."

If I was relieved that my mother had given me an answer, I was unsettled that the answer had unfurled more questions.

The old country. That phrase that came up now and then. A phrase that seemed to have a lock on it. I knew it meant Armenia, but it made me uneasy. If I asked about the old country, the adults would change the subject. Once my mother said, "It's an ancient place, it's not really around anymore." Where had it gone? I asked myself.

If I lived in a house where the old country still had a presence, why wasn't there a map, or photograph, or beautiful drawing of it somewhere, like the one the Zandonellas had of Milan in their TV room? Since there was no picture of the old country in our house and since I didn't have one etched in my mind, the old country came to mean my grandmother. Whatever it was, she was. Whatever she was, it was.

HAYDEN CARRUTH

HUMAN CRUELTY

Human cruelty made Carruth ill.

Once in the 1920s or early thirties a radio program called *Major Bowes' Amateur Hour* brought his family, like many others, together around the Atwater Kent in the parlor. It was a contest for amateur performers. The major presided. Winning performances were determined by the applause of the audience. But the major had a little gong, and if someone was performing badly and had no chance of winning, he would bang the gong, interrupting the presentation, sending the person—singer, impersonator, monologist—into embarrassment and withdrawal. At that time a World's Fair was in progress in New York—was it 1932?—in which case Carruth would have been about eleven years old, and the producers of the amateur hour thought they could spice up their program by importing a tribal drummer from one of the

African exhibitions at the fair. He understood no English; he was bewildered to find himself so far from home and in such an unlikely predicament. He was no doubt a fine drummer, someone to whom Louis Belson, for instance, would have listened with fascination, but his drumming was meaningless to the audience and to the major. Booing broke out, the major banged his gong repeatedly, relentlessly, but the drummer had no idea what this meant. He kept on drumming until he was forcibly removed from the stage by the major's attendants. And Carruth burst into tears and ran from the room, gasping and retching.

In the whole history this was a minor episode, of course. But Carruth gave his heart to that drummer from Africa once and for all.

The images persist, even now that he is old. Polish farmers, for instance, who are dancing in a field beside the railroad tracks, laughing and making the throat-slitting gesture, as trainloads of Jews pass by on the way to Treblinka. He could understand more easily the existence of individual pathological monsters, twisted and sick, serial killers, organizers of political genocide, the Khans and Hitlers of this world, than he could understand the existence of such brutality in the general population. Hence much of his life was spent in gasping and retching. Call him lily-livered. He captured the moths and wasps that came into his house and released them outdoors. Call him womanish. In the hypothesis of conventional masculine culture, he was indeed more a woman than a man, although he himself gave no credence to such distinctions of gender and had proven his manhood many times over in other ways. He was *glad* to be a woman.

And if his revulsion from cruelty was an effect of his lifelong unfitness and his consequent suffering, so be it. He would not exchange the suffering for admittance to barbarism.

LUC SANTE

THE UNKNOWN SOLDIER

The last thing I saw was a hallway ceiling, four feet wide, finished along its edges with a plaster molding that looked like a long row of small fish each trying to swallow the one ahead of it. The last thing I saw was a crack of yellow sky between buildings, partly obscured by a line of washing. The last thing I saw was the parapet, and beyond it the trees. The last thing I saw was his badge, but I couldn't tell you the number. The last thing I saw was a full shot glass, slid along by somebody who clapped me on the back. The last thing I saw was the sedan that came barreling straight at me while I thought, It's okay, I'm safely behind the window of the doughnut shop. The last thing I saw was a boot, right foot, with nails protruding from the instep. The last thing I saw was a turd. The last thing I saw was a cobble. The last thing I saw was night.

I lost my balance crossing Broadway and was trampled by a team of brewery horses. I was winching myself up the side of a six-story corner house on a board platform with a load of nails for the cornice when the weak part of the rope hit the pulley sideways and got sheared. I lost my way in snowdrifts half a block from my flat. I drank a bottle of carbolic acid not really knowing whether I meant to or not. I got very cold, and coughed, and forgot things. I went out to a yard to try and give birth in secret, but something happened. I met a policeman who mistook me for somebody else. I was drunk on my birthday and I fell off the dock trying to grab a gold piece that looked like it was floating. I was hanged in the courtyard of the Tombs before a cheering crowd and people clogging the rooftops of the buildings all around, but I still say that rascal had it coming to him. I stole a loaf of bread and started eating it as I ran down the street, but there was a wad of raw dough in the middle that got caught in my throat. I was supposed to get up early that morning but I couldn't move. I heard a sort of whistling noise above my head as I was passing by the post office and that's all I know. I was hustling a customer who looked like a real swell but when we got upstairs he pulled out a razor. I owed a lot of rent and got put out and that night curled up in somebody else's doorway and he came home in a bad mood. I was bitten by that black dog that used to hang around and I forgot all about it for six months or so. I ate some oysters I dug up myself. I took a shot at the big guy but the hammer got stuck. I felt very hot and shaky and strange and everybody in the shop was looking at me and I kept trying to tell them that I'd be all right in a minute but I just couldn't get it out.

I never woke up as the fumes snaked into my room. I stood yelling as he stabbed me again and again. I picked up a passenger who braced me in the middle of Broadway and made me turn off. I shot up the bag as soon as I got home but I think it smelled funny when I cooked it. I was asleep in the park when these kids came by. I crawled out the window and felt sick looking down, so I just threw myself out and looked up as I fell. I thought I could get warm by burning some newspaper in a soup pot. I went to pieces very slowly, and was happy when it finally stopped. I thought the train was going way too fast but I kept on reading. I let this guy pick me up at the party and sometime later we went off in his car. I felt real sick but the nurse thought I was kidding. I jumped over to the other fire escape but my foot slipped. I thought I had time to cross the street. I thought the floor would support my weight. I thought nobody could touch me. I never knew what hit me.

They put me in a bag. They nailed me up in a box. They walked me down Mulberry Street followed by altar boys and four priests under a canopy and everybody in the neighborhood singing the *Libera Me Domine*. They collected me in pieces all through the park. They laid me in state under the rotunda for three days. They engraved my name on the pediment. They drew my collar up to my chin to hide the hole in my neck. They laughed about me over the baked meats and rye whiskey. They didn't know who I was when they fished me out, and still didn't know six months later. They held my body for ransom and collected, but by that time they had burned it. They never found me. They threw me in the cement mixer. They heaped all of us into a trench and stuck a monument on top. They cut me up at the medical school. They weighed down my ankles and tossed me in the drink. They gave speeches claiming I was some kind of tin saint. They hauled me away in the ashman's cart. They put me on a boat and took me to an island. They tried to keep my mother from throwing herself in after me. They bought me my first suit and dressed me up in it. They marched to City Hall holding candles and shouting my name. They forgot all about me and took down my picture.

So give my eyes to the eye bank, give my blood to the blood bank. Make my hair into switches, put my teeth into rattles, sell my heart to the junkman. Give my spleen to the mayor. Hook my lungs to an engine. Stretch my guts down the avenue. Stick my head on a pike, plug my spine to the third rail, throw my liver and lights to the winner. Grind my nails up with sage and camphor and sell it under the counter. Set my hands in the window as a reminder. Take my name from me and make it a verb. Think of me when you run out of money. Remember me when you fall on the sidewalk. Mention me when they ask you what happened. I am everywhere under your feet.

STUART DYBEK

CONFESSION

ather Boguslaw was the priest I waited for, the one whose breath through the thin partition of the confessional reminded me of the ventilator behind Vic's Tap. He huffed and smacked as if in response to my dull litany of sins, and I pictured him slouched in his cubicle, draped in vestments, the way he sat slumped in the back entrance to the sacristy before saying morning mass—hung over, sucking an unlit Pall Mall, exhaling smoke.

Once, his head thudded against the wooden box.

"Father," I whispered, "Father," but he was out, snoring. I knelt wondering what to do, until he finally groaned and hacked himself awake.

As usual, I'd saved the deadly sins for last: the lies and copied homework, snitching drinks, ditching school, hitchhiking, which I'd been convinced was an offense against the

Fifth Commandment, which prohibited suicide. Before I reached the dirty snapshots of Korean girls, stolen from the dresser of my war hero uncle, Uncle Al, and still unrepentantly cached behind the oil shed, he knocked and said I was forgiven.

As for Penance: "Go in peace, my son, I'm suffering enough today for both of us."

SEBASTIAN MATTHEWS

KIND OF BLUE

ad's out behind the house with Underdog. *Finally*, he tells himself, *the place to myself*. Marie and the kids will be back Thursday night. This gives him an extra day to straighten things up, maybe get to his work. Or maybe he'll pack his things and leave.

He's already into the second bottle of cabernet, and ideas for poetry slogans are zooming down into his head like asteroids. *There's new hope for the dead.* That's what the magazine advertisement would say: *New Hope for the Dead.* One-liners. There's the one about spiritual life, as an antidote to all the innocuous messages on church bulletin boards. This one would read: *To be warm, build an igloo.* Or how about the one on the imaginary safe-sex pamphlet handed out to poets on the eve of their first major publication? It's on premature ejaculation: *I'm sorry this poem's already finished.*

He is trying them out on the dog, his test audience, but the loyal shepherd keeps giving him the same *Aren't you coming?* look that this wandering out behind the house warrants. He tries one out on the blue jay dangling from the branch of the holly, not getting more than a few words out before the jay darts for the wire overhead.

"You good-for-nothin' jaybird."

The stereo is still on in the house, turned up high on his coveted Advent speakers. He can hear the flowing undercurrent of a jazz bass, which, by passing through the windowpanes, has taken on a silvery, humming edge. It's one of the cuts of *Kind of Blue*. He listens carefully, proud of his ear. "Flamenco Sketches," for sure.

With the sun caught behind a cloud, it all of a sudden turns cold. He's only wearing light pants, a cotton short-sleeve. Noticing how thin his arms look, he wonders when the winter will finally seep out of the spring days. It's about time for a bit of color, he thinks. About time for some warmth.

The thought of simply packing up and leaving has awakened something in him. Normally, a guilty conscience smothers the thrill. He can't (won't let himself) leave the boys. But today the feeling stands before him like an open road. *Why the fuck not?* With his book published, he can get a teaching gig just about anywhere. It's not like there's much left between them. Marie has already told him to take his women and go.

Underdog has unearthed something behind the shed. His narrow hindquarters wiggle eagerly, tail wagging, as he digs his front paws and snout into the ground. The music has stopped momentarily. My father waits for the next cut. It takes so long to come on that he thinks maybe he got the other tune wrong: that the album is now over and the needle is treading water at the center of the rotating disc. But then it comes. Like a heartbeat it comes (*dum . . . dum dum . . . dum dum . . . dum dum . . .*): its "All blues" pulse strutting confidently, slowly, forward with the inevitable momentum of the blues. His body rattling vibrantly in the day.

The sun's come out. He is past the yard now, out beyond the two old shaggy willows. It feels good to be ambulating. He can still hear the music. Miles has moved into his opening chords, as though dressing for the show, fixing his tie in the mirror. And if the rest of the band is the song's mise-en-scène, then the bass is the slanting sun, thrumming through his veins like aged Scotch.

Now Underdog has rejoined him under the trees, a wet smear of dirt on his snout. Standing at the edge of the field, hand up to his drunken hair, my father looks out at the old apple trees. He's not sure if he's going to cry, scream, or pull down armfuls of crab apples and chuck them (*Thwap!*) at the barn door like a boy (*Thwap!*) practicing to be a great pitcher. *Thwap.*

He decides to keep moving, to walk out into the woods. "No one here but us chickens," he tells the dog. And then a few steps later: "No one knows the trouble we've seen." And though with each step the pulse of the song gets fainter, he keeps heading out into the field. He knows the land, knows the song. Knows when it's time to come in, when Trane will step into the current of his solo. He's got the bass in his blood now. He knows what to do. He'll just keep walking the dog.

DINTY W. MOORE

SON OF MR. GREEN JEANS

An Essay on Fatherhood, Alphabetically Arranged

Allen, Tim

Best known as the father on ABC's *Home Improvement* (1991–99), the popular comedian was born Timothy Allen Dick on June 13, 1953. When Allen was eleven years old, his father, Gerald Dick, was killed by a drunk driver while driving home from a University of Colorado football game.

Bees

"A man, after impregnating the woman, could drop dead," critic Camille Paglia suggested to Tim Allen in a 1995 *Esquire* interview. "That is how peripheral he is to the whole thing."

"I'm a drone," Allen responded. "Like those bees."

"You are a drone," Paglia agreed. "That's exactly right."

Carp

After the female Japanese carp gives birth to hundreds of tiny babies, the father carp remains nearby. When he senses approaching danger, he sucks the helpless babies into his mouth, and holds them there until the coast is clear.

Divorce

University of Arizona psychologist Sanford Braver tells the story of a woman who felt threatened by her husband's close bond with their young son. The husband had a flexible work schedule but the wife did not, so the boy spent the bulk of his time with the father. The mother became so jealous of the tight father-son relationship that she filed for divorce, and success-fully fought for sole custody. The result was that instead of being in the care of his father while the mother worked, the boy was now left in daycare.

Emperor Penguins

Once an emperor penguin male has completed mating, he remains by the female's side for the next month to determine if the act has been successful. When he sees a single greenish-white egg emerge from his mate's egg pouch, he begins to sing. Scientists have characterized his song as "ecstatic."

Father Knows Best

In 1949, Robert Young began *Father Knows Best* as a radio show. Young played Jim Anderson, an average father in an average family. The show later moved to television, where it was a major hit, but Young's successful life was troubled by alcohol and depression.

In January 1991, at age eighty-three, Young attempted suicide by running a hose from his car's exhaust pipe to the interior of the vehicle. The attempt failed because the battery was dead and the car wouldn't start.

Green Genes

In Dublin, Ireland, a team of geneticists is conducting a study to determine the origins of the Irish people. By analyzing segments of DNA from residents across different parts of the Irish countryside, then comparing this DNA with corresponding DNA segments from people elsewhere in Europe, the investigators hope to determine the derivation of Ireland's true forefathers.

Hugh Beaumont

The actor who portrayed the benevolent father on the popular TV show *Leave It to Beaver* was a Methodist minister. Tony Dow, who played older brother Wally, reports that Beaumont actually hated kids. "Hugh wanted out of the show after the second season," Dow told the *Toronto Sun*. "He thought he should be doing films and things."

Inheritance

My own Irish forefather was a newspaperman, owned a nightclub, ran for mayor, and smuggled rum in a speedboat during Prohibition. He smoked, drank, ate nothing but red meat, and died of a heart attack in 1938.

His one son, my father, was a teenager when my grandfather died. I never learned more than the barest details about my grandfather from my father, despite my persistent questions.

Other relatives tell me that the relationship had been strained.

My father was a skinny, eager-to-please little boy, battered by allergies, and not the tough guy his father had wanted. He lost his mother at age three, and later developed a severe stuttering problem, perhaps as a result of his father's disapproval. My father's adult vocabulary was outstanding, due to his need for alternate words when faltering over hard consonants like *b* or *d*.

The stuttering grew worse over the years, with one notable exception: after downing a few whiskeys, my father could sing like an angel. His Irish tenor became legend in local taverns, and by the time I entered the scene my father was spending every evening visiting the working-class bars. Most nights he would stumble back drunk around midnight; some nights he was so drunk he would stumble through a neighbor's back door, thinking he was home.

As a boy, I coped with the family's embarrassment by staying glued to the television—shows like *Father Knows Best* and *Leave It to Beaver* were my favorites. I desperately wanted someone like Hugh Beaumont to be my father, or maybe Robert Young.

Hugh Brannum, though, would have been my first choice. Brannum played Mr. Green Jeans on *Captain Kangaroo*, and I remember him as being kind, funny, and extremely reliable.

Jaws

My other hobby, besides television, was an aquarium. I loved watching the tropical fish give birth. Unfortunately, guppy fathers, if not moved to a separate tank, will sometimes come along and eat their young.

Kitten

Kitten, the youngest daughter on *Father Knows Best*, was played by Lauren Chapin.

Lauren Chapin

Chapin's father molested her and her mother was a severe alcoholic. After *Father Knows Best* ended in 1960, Chapin's life came apart. At age sixteen, she married an auto mechanic. At age eighteen, she became addicted to heroin and began working as a prostitute.

Male Breadwinners

Wolf fathers spend the daylight hours away from the home—hunting—but return every evening. The wolf cubs, five or six to a litter, rush out of the den when they hear their father approaching and fling themselves at their dad, leaping up to his face. The father backs up a few feet and disgorges food for them, in small, separate piles.

Natural Selection

When my wife Renita confessed to me her ambition to have children, the very first words out of my mouth were, "You must be crazy." Convinced that she had just proposed the worst imaginable idea, I stood from my chair, looked straight ahead, then marched out of the room.

Ozzie

Oswald Nelson, at thirteen, was the youngest person ever to become an Eagle Scout. Oswald went on to become Ozzie Nelson, the father in *Ozzie and Harriet*. Though the show aired years before the advent of reality television, Harriet was Ozzie's real wife, Ricky and David were his real sons, and eventually Ricky's and David's wives were played by their actual spouses. The current requirements for Eagle Scout make it impossible for anyone to ever beat Ozzie's record.

Penguins, Again

The female emperor penguin "catches the egg with her wings before it touches the ice," Jeffrey Moussaieff Masson writes in his book *The Emperor's Embrace*. She then places it on her feet, to keep it from contact with the frozen ground.

At this point, both penguins will sing in unison, staring at the egg. Eventually, the male penguin will use his beak to lift the egg onto the surface of his own feet, where it remains until hatching.

Not only does the male penguin endure the inconvenience of walking around with an egg balanced on his feet for months, but he also will not eat for the duration.

Quiz

1. What is Camille Paglia's view on the need for fathers?
2. Why did Hugh Beaumont hate kids?
3. Who played Mr. Green Jeans on *Captain Kangaroo*?
4. Who would you rather have as your father: Hugh Beaumont, Hugh Brannum, a wolf, or an emperor penguin?

Religion

In 1979, Lauren Chapin, the troubled actress who played Kitty, had a religious conversion. She credits her belief in Jesus with saving her life. After *his* television career ended, Methodist minister Hugh Beaumont became a Christmas tree farmer.

Sputnik

On October 4, 1957, *Leave It to Beaver* first aired. On that same day, the Soviet Union launched Sputnik I, the world's first artificial satellite. Sputnik I was about the size of a basketball, took roughly ninety-eight minutes to orbit the Earth, and is credited with starting the U.S.-Soviet space race. Later, long after *Leave It to Beaver* ended its network run, a rumor that Jerry Mathers, the actor who played Beaver, had died at the hands of the communists in Vietnam persisted for years. The actress Shelley Winters went so far as to announce it on the *Tonight* show. But the rumor was false.

Toilets

Leave It to Beaver was the first television program to show a toilet.

Use of Drugs

The National Center of Addiction and Substance Abuse at Columbia University claims that the presence of a supportive father is irreplaceable in helping children stay drug-free. Lauren Chapin may be a prime example here, as would Tim Allen, who was arrested for dealing drugs in 1978 and spent two years in prison.

Though I managed to avoid my father's drinking problems, I battled my own drug habit as a young man. Happily, I was never jailed.

Vasectomies

I had a vasectomy in 1994.

Ward's Father

In an episode titled "Beaver's Freckles," the Beaver says that Ward had "a hittin' father," but little else is ever revealed about Ward's fictional family. Despite Wally's constant warning—"Boy, Beav, when Dad finds out, he's gonna clobber ya!"—Ward does not follow his own father's example, and never hits his sons on the show. This is an excellent example of xenogenesis.

Xenogenesis

(zen"*u*-jen'*u*-sis), n. *Biol.* 1. heterogenesis 2. the supposed generation of offspring completely and permanently different from the parent.

Believing in xenogenesis—though at the time I couldn't define it, spell it, *or* pronounce it—I changed my mind about having children about four years after my wife's first suggestion of the idea. Luckily, this was five years before my vasectomy.

Y-Chromosomes

The Y-chromosome of the father determines a child's gender, and is unique, because its genetic code remains relatively unchanged as it passes from father to son. The DNA in other chromosomes, however, is more likely to get mixed between generations, in a process called recombination. What this means, apparently, is that boys have a higher likelihood of inheriting their ancestral traits.

My Y-chromosomes were looking the other way, so my only child is a daughter.

So far Maria has inherited many of what people say are the Moore family's better traits—humor, a facility with words, a stubborn determination. It is yet to be seen what she will do with the negative ones.

Zappa

Similar to the "Beaver died in Vietnam" rumor of the late 1960s, during the late 1990s, Internet discussion lists blasted the news that the actor who played Mr. Green Jeans, Hugh Brannum, was in fact the father of musician Frank Zappa. But Brannum had only one son, and that son was neither Frank Zappa nor this author.

Sometimes, though, I still wonder what it might have been like.

MICHAEL DATCHER

THE SPINNERS

''ve been obsessed with being a husband and father since I was seven years old. Quiet as it's kept, many young black men have the same obsession. Picket-fence dreams. A played-out metaphor in the white community but one still secretly riding the bench in black neighborhoods nationwide.

When the picket-fence motif was in vogue, only a few of us could get in the game. The swelling ranks of those who couldn't (the Perpetual Second Team) were forced to the sidelines, scowling—and pretending we didn't even want to play.

The bastard children of those Second Teamers stalk the same sidelines. We rarely sit on the bench. Too restless. We can't figure out if we want to beg to play or raise a stiff middle finger. Sometimes we do both. But usually we strike a cool pose. Hide Huxtable-family dreams in the corner: Can't let someone catch us hoping that hard.

We know few people believe in us. We struggle to believe in ourselves. So we pose. We have gotten good. We can pose and cry at the same time—no one sees. We can pose and cry out for help—no one hears. We are the urban ventriloquists.

Of the thirty families that lived in our east-side Long Beach, California, apartment building during the mid-seventies, I never saw a father living in a household. I never even saw one visit.

There were lots of boys in the neighborhood: Ricky, Dante, Pig Pen, Curt Rock. We rarely talked about our missing fathers. Instead, we poured our passion into our skateboards, our marbles, and our mothers. Yet the unspoken sparkled from our eyes whenever any neighborhood men showed us attention. Once in their gaze, we worked to outperform one another, trying our best to keep the manlight from straying.

"Watch this! I can do a back flip off the curb . . . Heh, betchu a quarter I can make a shot from the free-throw line."

It's likely one of these men laid the seed that sprouted into a back-flipper before them. Neighborhood rumors have a way of falling off grown-up kitchen tables and splattering on ghetto playgrounds.

We flipped, pop-locked, and did the Robot for them, but we were knowing: Men weren't to be trusted. Even when our mothers didn't speak these words, their tired lives whispered the message.

I knew many of these men had kids. Where were they? Why were they watching me spin instead of their own children? No, these men were not to be trusted. How could I accept their advice when their personal lives screamed, "I'm lost toooo"? There was too much fatherhood failure around. The disease seemed to be contagious given the epidemic in our neighborhood. These men could watch me spin, but I couldn't let them get close enough to breathe on me.

The ghetto irony: Many of my generation's young spinners have become the twenty- and thirty-something men who can't be trusted. Making children who will grow up to hate them.

Circumstance, suspect choices, and fear have ways of disfiguring urban hopes with surgical precision. A four-ounce bottle of baby formula becomes much heavier than a forty-ounce bottle of malt liquor. Having five women becomes easier than having one.

SONJA LIVINGSTON

THE GHETTO GIRLS' GUIDE
TO DATING AND ROMANCE

1. I know how it is. How you turn in the mirror, look here
and there for signs of change, look hard for the woman you'll
become. Well, look and turn all you want, you won't see it
happening—the bends your body will take, the pulling in of,
the swelling. You won't see, but they'll inform you. As you
walk by, they'll give an "Mm, mmmm, mmm" and "Sure
looks fine" and that's when you'll know. Just keep your eyes
down. From the time those titties erupt from your chest, point
your eyes to the ground and keep on walking. Right on by
Lynam's bar, past the fish market on Parsells and Webster
where men on break stand outside and call out to girls and
women, but mostly girls. Their voices are rainforests at night
and you don't mind being called baby all the time. But you
must. Forget the smell of them, forget their slippery skin,
ignore the slow glow of their cigarettes, the tug of August

heat. Just think of all the fish they've handled and keep walk-ing, eyes down.

2. He says come here sweet thing. He wants to talk and only for a minute. Don't be a fool. There's no such thing as a minute. He'll put his mouth on your neck, slip his hand up your skirt and press small circles into your thighs with the tips of his fingers. He'll say just a minute longer, and though you're smart in every other thing, those fingers will circle their way through your skin and you'll have no choice but to let him move up. And in. A minute becomes an hour, then a life-time. Just remember to take your watch, since he won't have his and it doesn't matter anyway, because minutes don't exist.

3. He won't be wearing a ring or maybe he will, but can explain it away. One thing's for sure, you can't count on jew-elry to tell you anything about a man. If he doesn't take you to his place, he's cheating. If he says he lives with his aunt and her sister and they go to church early in the morning and are all around quiet people so you can't go there late at night, he's lying. If he claims to have two jobs and so can't come around much, and when he does, his wallet's flat, he's lying.

4. Your mother's on the phone with the doctor on call from the Genesee Hospital, trying to get help for the pain in your lower stomach and side. The pain that won't let you sleep. Bits of you pull off and away. The bleeding is heavy. "The doctor wants to know whether you've done it." She tosses the words out like she's asking about the last time you ate, but you know

just what she means and you're scared, with your stomach tearing itself up and her sounding so casual. You'll be inclined to tell the truth, but it's much better to lie. You have no idea how disappointed mothers can be. She'll think you haven't listened to one damned thing she's ever said. Your mother won't say this, she'll just return the phone to its cradle and keep her eyes from resting on you the same way after that night.

5. You smell the perfume, find the gold hoop earring in the back seat of his orange pinto, hear from Maria Maldonado that she saw him at the mall with some other girl while she was there buying white satin baptism shoes for her baby. Don't bother asking. You don't need any evidence, because deep down you already know. If you think he is, he is.

6. When he rubs you up and whispers in your ear just how much he likes girls with a little extra flesh on their asses and says that parts of you are like hills he'd like to climb— remember that he told Wanda just last week that he likes girls with high tight asses and that hers is as high and as tight as a button. He tells you there's nothing like a white girl, then tells Stacy from down the street that mocha's his favorite flavor. And while he was talking up her tiny butt, he told small-assed Wanda that he craves the copper of island girls, said he dreamt her ass was a coin in the palm of his hand. Use your sense. He most prefers the ass nearest to his hand.

7. Stay with your girls when you walk to the store. Your mom wants a loaf of bread or a gallon of milk and you have to get

it. She can't leave and you don't want to go. You may as well be seed thrown to the birds, the way grown men on porches stare you down and call after you every time you walk to and from the store or to and from anywhere (unless you wake up early and beat them out of bed). Get your friends to walk with you. They won't want to, but they'll go because they'll need you later that same day. Two is safer than one and three is even better. Talk to each other about clothes, shoes, makeup—anything but them. Pretend they don't exist, or if you have to, lie to each other about how much you hate them. Do anything you can to keep from falling.

8. You want to so much it hurts. But don't. Don't spend money from your after-school job on gifts. He's grateful, but receiving becomes an easy habit. Don't let him use your name and phone number to buy the big black sofa from rent-a-center. He won't pay and they'll hound your mother, your sister, and everyone with your last name for payment. Don't lend money. He will not give it back. Or he'll give it back once or twice just to show he can, then follow up his payment with a request for more. Then more. He can't help it, his heart is a sponge. You can't help it either—you are different sides of the same cloth. Your heart is liquid—it would fall through your fingers if you ever tried to touch it. It's better to say you have nothing to give, then hide the bags of stuff you buy at Midtown Plaza at your best friend's mother's house, so he doesn't ask how you paid.

9. The one who gives you roses. The one who says your eyes are better than the stained glass at church, that your skin is like milk. He's the one for you. He wants you to meet his mother, his brother, his Titi Eva in from New York. But it feels all wrong so you push him away. He keeps at you, until you can't take it any longer and give him one last slam. He sees something you don't see and to be wanted like that is a spice you've never tasted. So you spit him out and long for something regular, some taste you recognize. He cries and writes long sad letters. You fold your arms over your chest and laugh. Crow of a girl. You'll never have him, but he's the one for you.

10. He will not take care of you. Even if he wants to, even if he cries in your ear and looks into your eyes while you fuck. He's good deep down, but then so is everyone. He'll walk to your job and meet you there for three days straight, though you look away and pretend to be alone. Though he's five or maybe ten years older and you tell him not to, he's there after work, grabbing at your hand. These are his lies: *She doesn't mean anything. You can drop out of school, quit this job. I'll take care of you.* Listen closely. This is the prettiest of poisons. He's talking crazy, and if you believe him, you're living in la-la land. To be taken care of is not an option. It is for girls on TV and people inside borrowed library books. But for you, it's not an option. It never was.

11. Fool of a girl. You believe he'll meet you on the corner at eleven like he said. Though he did not show last night and was

an hour late the night before, you rub oil onto your legs, push yourself into your new white sweater, and wait. He won't show, and even if he does, he'll do nothing but stain up your sweater—but hope is worse than a pebble in the shoe, so you wait and watch, make up counting games with passing cars, and an hour later, walk back home and fold the sweater away for some other night.

12. Avoid boys with warm hands on Halloween night. They smell like falling leaves and overripe cologne and even though they can't dance, one touch on your arm and they melt you. They push you against the fence and groan their way into your long white gown and it's so cold, you don't mind the fog of their breath, the pink of their fingers. The party's over, your friends have all gone home, and his mouth is wet and hard and knows you better than you do. You've been an Egyptian princess all night, snake coiled on your arm, eyes lined in black. Now you're caught between him and a chain-link fence and there's nowhere to go but down.

13. When his woman calls and tells you stay the hell away from her man, you should. You'll be tempted not to—she sounds so broken and he'll explain about how crazy she is, how she won't let go, has their child spy on him during visits, found your number and is making up lies. She'll tell you how it really is. But you won't believe something as ragged as her voice could ever touch those big green eyes or the mouth whose inside tastes of warm beer and coconut. You won't lis-

ten, but when his woman calls and tells you to stay the hell away, you should.

14. Run in place. Do jumping jacks. Jog around the park at the end of the street five times. Then five times more. Your period's late and there's only one thing to do. Walk and pray. Jog and pray. Squish your body into sit-ups, push-ups, knee bends. Pray. You hardly believe in God, but this is not the time for questioning. Just pray. When it finally comes, you are happy and grateful and fresh and clean. You help your mother scrub the walls and gather lilacs into jelly jar vases. You'll never take that risk again. Ever.

Until the next time he calls.

15. The health teacher, the parish priest, the public service announcement don't mean to suggest that nothing good can come from you. They don't mean to talk like you're some Humane Society stray. It's just that they know things. Pregnancy equals failure. You see it too. The way your friends drop off one at a time. They let someone into their pants, their bellies swell, then they fade into the gray. They might go to the Young Mothers' Program for a month or two, until the baby comes. Then it's as if they never existed. So be strong, say the health teacher, the priest, the message on TV. Keep your legs safely fastened, or if you absolutely must, be sure to roll the latex on like so. It's the truth and you know it, so don't think so much. Don't be so sensitive. They don't mean to imply that there's something wrong with having more around like you.

ANNE PANNING

THE MOTHER

After I give birth to my son, I reach for my eyeglasses so I can see him. There's a photograph of me crying immediately post-birth, and I'm wearing nothing but a blue and white hospital gown and my tiny brown glasses that people—total strangers—used to always compliment me on back when they were still in style.

But life with baby wears on me. Nursing in the middle of the night in the near-dark, glasses off, all is a blur. In fact, day and night bleed into one cloudy gray. I lose the baby weight but also lose all energy or insight. I simply want to eat potato chips and watch reruns of *Providence* and cry.

When the baby is almost a year old, I fly to California for a friend's wedding. I'm so unused to a lack of responsibility for others that I'm giddy just to ride solo on the airplane. I fall asleep before we're even out of my time zone. When I wake up, mountains and buttery sunshine fill the window. In the taxi, I sit back and imagine staying here forever. I will live in a bungalow, wear linen pants, and eat salad every day.

I stay in a hotel with fresh cedar shingles that's located next to a mall. This is Marin County, which I've heard about and have associations: wealth, convertibles with their tops down, women wearing white, fancy sunglasses, health food stores. I am not incorrect. But it is also sunny and warm and invigorating. Somehow living in the grim gray cold of New York State seems to be the reason for much of my exhaustion. I have been missing simple sunshine.

The day before the ceremony, I walk over to the mall and pass a vitamin shop. What catches my eye is the display case of eyeglass frames advertised for twenty-five dollars. "Latest styles from Italy," a sign says, and I am perplexed. Thinking they must be drugstore magnifying lenses, I almost pass, but hesitate. The frames are so stylish, so rich in color, so differently shaped that I want to own a pair and start over and not look like a "mom."

Inside, the clerk explains that the owner takes a yearly vacation to Italy and brings back last year's models at deep discounts. There's no catch, she says. It's just something he does. I pore over the black velvet tray of frames, finally deciding on an elongated rectangular pair in a color much like toffee with a tiny tiny hint of orange blended in. When I try them on, even without my prescription lenses, I think I look European.

On the plane ride home, I keep the red velvet glasses' case in my carry-on. I am torn: a deep, almost primal urge to get back to my child, smell him, hold him, feel his small soft hands, and another competing urge to live in California in a light and airy house with eucalyptus trees and an open porch and childless friends who mix sangrías on Saturday afternoons and eat tapas.

Back home, my husband and I both teach and tag-team with our child. When the winter gets particularly unbearable, I take my son to the community toddler gym to let him blow off steam. Before we are allowed entrance into the stark, padded room, we must pose for photo ID cards. When mine is handed back to me, I'm flummoxed, out of focus, and feel I'm looking at a stranger. I've got my "pimp" coat on, a black Persian lamb's wool with shiny buttons, which is really an old-lady Presbyterian church sale coat I got for three dollars. My bangs are cut very short and my California eyeglasses look almost bright orange, too European, too West Coast, too something. Holding a toddler in flannel shirt and overalls in my arms, I am completely mismatched with my life—an impostor, a stand-in, a woman I barely recognize.

※

CLEAN SLATE

In the photo my parents nestle on a square blue couch that looks about as comfortable as plywood. They are not yet who they will be. There are no rings on fingers, no wedding cake, no kids, no mess.

In a few months my father will be the valedictorian of their high school class, and, by the looks of him, belongs in the cast of *Revenge of the Nerds*. His glasses are mason jars with thick black frames and his hair is parted halfway down the side of his head, by his ear. Luckily his sideburns give him a dorky kind of charm. He wears a light blue shirt with a black necktie, vest and jacket. His brown glasses' case is tucked into the jacket pocket. He is tall and extremely thin, with a long face, a crooked nose, and later in life his kids' dentist will compare his chin to Jay Leno's.

But not yet.

My mother is far too beautiful for him and they both know it. She wears a short black skirt. Short enough to reveal the nude pantyhose lining on her thigh. But like a good Catholic girl her arms are folded over each other and resting on her lap. Her brown hair is parted smack down the middle, so long it covers both her breasts. Her legs are crossed and she smiles, facing in the direction of my father.

This is before anything crazy happens.

He doesn't look capable of getting as angry as he will. But he will. And my mother. My mother is very beautiful, but her dark brown eyes conceal a deep sadness. Her father has just died and her smile is flawless. It doesn't seem as if she would spend her life passively smiling like that. But even when things get bad, she will.

VALERIE MINER

RITUAL MEALS

1977

Mom and I are eating lunch in my cute new Berkeley apartment. Finally, things between us feel almost balanced. We are developing a friendship. I am mature enough now to admire my mother. She is beginning to understand me, or at least beginning to relinquish some expectations. Shopping, of course, is a major bond. I visit her in San Francisco, where we scout out sales at the big stores; she takes the bus to Berkeley to hunt with me through the quirky boutiques. Today we have been talking about our jobs, her customers at the Yum Yum Room and my students at U.C. Berkeley.

The perfect setting for a good talk: sun pouring through the big living room window, comfortable chairs. Heaped in a basket on the table are French rolls, her favorite bread. I have prepared Salade Niçoise, something simple, healthy, elegant. For dessert, I've bought chocolate truffles.

"You seem a little nervous," she says.

"Oh, no," I answer, spearing a piece of tomato and putting it in my mouth. But I *am* nervous, because this is the day I have planned, with excruciating care, to tell Mom about Pat, my lover, to tell her I am a lesbian. I want an honest relationship, a solid friendship with this wonderfully brave and witty and vulnerable mother. Months have gone into the planning of this lunch: the salad, the rolls, the truffles, the gentle conversation.

I breathe deeply, reminding myself that I have done everything right, for once. Finally, at age thirty, I am living back home. I am publishing stories and essays, working on a novel. She still urges me, every three or four months, to consider a more secure job at the telephone company, holding up cousin Billy as a model. Yet she likes the idea of her daughter teaching university, even if only as a lecturer.

"It really is a lovely apartment," she says, looking around, happily, from her perch on the chair, "and so convenient to the buses."

"Yes," I smile. I am renting my own apartment, after years of what were to her morally dubious housing collectives. This year I have had my ears pierced, learned to drive, and even bought a secondhand car. I should know that for her this is enough. She doesn't need any more news.

She picks around the funny little olives, but is enjoying the rest of her salad.

I take another breath, look out the window for courage. We need to talk.

"That was delicious," she says, filling the silence, putting down her fork.

Serving tea in the flowery china cups I have bought second—or sixth—hand at the Leeds Market and Covent Garden Market in my adventurous youth, I begin tactfully. "I
have something to tell you."

She sips the tea.

"I want us to be friends, to share our lives. But, well, this
is something that might upset you."

"Then don't tell me," she suggests, shrugging her small,
sturdy shoulders.

But I have spent so much time shopping, cleaning, practicing my disclosure, getting advice from friends, I have spent all
of my life preparing. I hate her denial, can't see it as just a different approach to truth.

"Where are we shopping this afternoon?" she asks.

I roll my eyes at her deflection, feeling both guilty and angry.
I don't yet understand that one difference between us is that
while Mom negotiates difficulties, I believe in conquering them.

Suddenly the chocolate truffles feel like a stupid, gross idea.

I sit back on the couch, inherited from Mom's recently dead
friend, Mrs. Decoto. Honesty, I remind myself, is the only
passage to trust. Then I reveal yet another thing she does not
want to hear about my life. When I come out to her, do you
know what she says?

My mother, cashier at the Yum Yum Room, looks at the
ceiling and says, "There are more things in heaven and earth,
Horatio, than are dreamt of in your philosophy."

Then Mom puts her head back against the chair and asks,
"Is it my fault? Is this because of something I did wrong when
you were growing up?"

1989

We're having a drink at the Claremont. One of her favorite things to do on a Saturday night is to take BART from her stop in San Francisco to my stop in Oakland, go out to a cocktail lounge overlooking the City, her city, have a meal at Norman's (taking half of it home in a doggie bag), and watch *Golden Girls* and *Empty Nest* on TV before going to sleep in my spare bed.

I like the view of San Francisco Bay from the Claremont Bar. I love watching the sun set over the ocean and witnessing my mother loosening up over a margarita. I don't like the smoke or the executives visiting from Los Angeles. Or the jars of tasty, fattening pretzels-seaweed-nuts marinated in soy sauce. We both enjoy the broad-hipped, no-nonsense waitresses and like to think that Martha and Monique and Molly—are they hired for their names?—remember us, although it's such a busy place, they probably don't.

On this hectic, crowded night, I curse myself for not planning better. We're too late for our usual window table. I'm not sure which of us is more disappointed, but Mother will never show it, will never indicate directly that I have failed. *Mom*, she prefers me to call her Mom and I try to remember. Here in the middle of the bar, we can look past the two thin young men sipping Heinekens, out to the butterscotch ball dipping slowly, irrevocably, toward the Pacific. What is it like for her to watch the sun set over an ocean she could only imagine as a Scottish child? I was shocked to learn that she never saw the Atlantic Ocean, either, never knew waves larger than those of the Firth of Forth, until she was already on the ship from

Glasgow. She had read about waves, of course, she thought she had read about everything.

Now I want to ask if she finds this confusing, distressing, magical, the idea of day dropping into Asia. But she will look disturbed or impatient at yet another oddball query. Lately she has given me to understand that there isn't time for silly questions. She's not interested in "theorizing," prefers to spend her time remembering our life: family Christmases; the delinquent dog, Friskie; fabulous sales at Magnarama. Or recalling provocatively disjoined fragments of *her* life—those first thirty-seven years before I was born.

Abruptly, the sun disappears, leaving a yellow haze over the water, just below the slate sky. Off to the south, a jet streaks its white trail of possibility, contradicting the day's surrender. I imagine myself on that plane now, heading away.

"Days like this remind me of Peggy," she muses.

"Who?" I ask.

"Peggy," she repeats impatiently.

"Who's Peggy?"

"My sister," she answers, sipping the margarita pensively. Then a strange expression crosses her face, a new look that has come to Mother in her late seventies, a face of shame and relief that another secret has slipped from the war chest.

"Who is she?" I am alarmed, excited. "Whose side of the family—your mother's or your father's?"

"Peggy, my sister." She is annoyed with me, with herself, with the whole unwieldy experience of family. Making herself even smaller, she pulls in her elbows tightly. "No *side*. She was born between Colin and me."

As she explains, I wonder if it is impertinent to believe these stories are mine as well. How can it be that I am forty-two years old and have never heard about my aunt, who is not even a half-aunt like Bella and Chrissie, but an aunt who was born of both my grandparents, who lived in the same apartment with Mom for ten years?

"You never mentioned her. Ever."

Mom pauses to fish for a cashew from the jar of marinated goodies. "Oh, you've just forgotten. Remember the family who wanted to adopt me?"

"Yes."

"Well, Peggy went instead," she says matter-of-factly.

I watch this small woman picking the cuticle on the side of her corrugated thumbnail and I wonder how many other secrets she has. When she dies, will I discover answers in the bureau drawer, or carefully slipped into that cardboard box between old bills and Christmas cards? Whom has she been protecting with this silence? Perhaps for years she did manage to forget her sister Peggy, her closest sibling. Mom's secret making has shaped and fortified her optimistic keep-on-keeping-on-with-the-world view. She has constructed a story of the cosmos as intricate as Milton's theology, a universe in which she is both innocent and sinner, a life in which what you don't remember can't hurt you.

"But, well, did you stay in touch?" I finally ask.

"No." She stares at the last yellow shimmering. "I never saw her again."

A familiar, awe-filled sadness silences me.

She barely knew her mother; her father would "always be with her," and her sister had just disappeared for sixty-eight years. Mother is losing a grip on her imagined life. The characters are beginning to seep back. So much for the power of fiction. The family history is deep in her body.

"Enough of that." She wipes her hands on the small magenta paper napkin. "I'm getting hungry. And I don't want to fill up on these silly nuts."

I am tempted to explore this new opening, press another margarita on her, but I can tell she will admit no more questions.

"Dinner, Madame?"

She looks out at the dimming sky, then smiles coquettishly, takes my arm.

No more reminiscing.

I leave a big tip for Martha.

And we hurry out the door, because Mom is right, we don't have much time left. We might miss our reservation.

JOYCE THOMPSON

GETTING RID OF THE GUN

ords did my mother's bidding, but things defeated her. She could not throw them away. Much of her house in Seattle's Seward Park neighborhood was furnished from her family's home at Maple Valley. The workshop where no one worked and the space under the staircase were filled with boxes that hadn't been opened for twenty-five years. After my father died, my mother gave in to her own peculiar combination of mourning and inertia, simply, mostly silently, coexisting with her things. Every week, I offered to help her excavate the premises. For months on end, she refused me. Finally, one late-fall day she nodded yes, and the work began.

In the most unlikely places, we found empty bourbon bottles my dad had drained and neglected to throw away, and full ones he'd cached against times of drought and forgotten all about. Hidden among rusty, old-fashioned tools in the workshop, we found my father's service revolver, a sleek, mean-looking metal sculpture reposing on blue satin in a wooden case. My mother had always taken a nonnegotiable position: no handguns in the house. When we found the revolver, she was beside herself.

"He swore he got rid of it," she said.

"We'll get rid of it now," I said.

"How?" she said.

"Sell it."

"We can't sell it. It's unlicensed."

"We'll say we found it."

"I can't let people know the gun-control judge kept an unlicensed handgun."

"Let's throw it away, then."

"Teenagers would find it in the dump. They'd rob a convenience store."

"I'll hide it inside something else," I said, remembering finding this same gun or another in the back of my mother's closet when I was little, tucked inside one of a pair of riding boots she never wore, remembering how illicit, how dangerous it felt to come upon it there.

My mom was still heavy enough then that her jowls jiggled a bit when she shook her head. "Absolutely not. What are we going to do?"

I volunteered to call the police station and ask how to dispose of an unwanted firearm.

"No names," my mother said. "Promise me you'll never give your name or his."

I made up a story. My uncle had just died. I was his heir. Cleaning out his things, I'd happened on the gun. Because I had two children, I didn't want to keep it in my house. Please, Mister Officer, what should I do?

Just bring it on in to the station, Little Lady. Glad to oblige.

When I did, the enthusiasm of the sergeant on duty for the revolver was almost sexual. He lifted it reverently from the case, sighted along its barrel, ran his hands over it, opened the chamber, clicked it shut, all the while making little sounds of hardware appreciation deep in his throat. "A mighty fine piece," he told me. "How about you sell it to me instead of turning it in?"

"Well, I—"

"How much you want for it?"

I was torn between saying I'd pay him to take it off my hands and wanting to see what he'd offer.

"How about, say, two hundred?" he said.

The desk cop, hairy and middle-aged, with a hanuman monkey face, spoke up. "He's trying to take advantage of you, Miss. That's a nice gun. Don't sell it cheap."

"Oh, all right," the sergeant said, pulling out a wad of money so big in diameter I couldn't imagine where in his pants he could conceal it. The bills he peeled off were fifties. "Five hundred."

"He'll pay more," the desk man said, but I'd already chirped, "Sold." I handed over the revolver in its fancy box and left the station grinning, with ten bills still warm from the cop's body in the pocket of my jeans.

When I handed over the wad of cash and told the tale, I

expected my mother to be amused, but she wasn't, really. The next labor of her widowhood had already commenced—how to sneak a probate file back into the county clerk's office without alerting anyone to its long absence. My father was, evidently, a couple of decades derelict in his responsibilities as the court-appointed trustee of the estate. To my mother, so long used to sweeping up behind him, neither mailing the file back nor tossing it in the trash was an option. She was already seeking a third, more complicated way.

"How come Dad was so determined to hang on to that gun, anyway?" I asked her.

Her answer was a long time coming. "His friend Andy called him henpecked when your father told him I wanted him to get rid of it. Only I'm sure he used a different expression."

"Like what?" I asked.

"Pussy-whipped," my mother said.

"Machismo," I said.

"There are some things about your father you don't know," my mother said. She pushed the stack of fifty-dollar bills across the table at me. "You can keep the money," she said. "I don't want it."

I was a single mother with two kids to feed. I folded the five hundred back up again and put it in my jeans.

GERALD STERN

BULLET IN MY NECK

am so used to having a bullet in my neck that I never think
of it, only when the subject comes up and someone—full of
doubt or amazement—gingerly reaches a hand out to feel it.
It is a memento of the shooting on an empty road on the edge
of Newark, New Jersey, when Rosalind Pace and I got lost on
the way from Newark Airport to a conference of poets in
Bethlehem, Pennsylvania. We made the mistake of stopping at
a red light and were cornered immediately by two boys, sixteen or so, dressed in starched jeans and jackets and sporting
zip guns. Before we could reason with them, or submit, or try
to escape, they began shooting through the open windows.
The boy on Rosalind's side pointed his gun, a .22, directly in
her face, a foot away, but it misfired. The boy on my side emptied his gun, hitting the steering wheel, the window, and the
dashboard. One bullet grazed my right shoulder, and one hit

my chin, then buried itself in the left side of my neck, less than a half inch from the carotid artery.

Everything in such a situation takes on a life of its own, and the few seconds it took me to realize I wasn't going to die seemed like a much longer stretch of time, and though my neck swelled up and blood was pouring out, my only thought was to get out of there as quickly as possible. My memory was that I fell to the floor, pushed the gas pedal down with one hand, and with the other put the gear into drive till Rosalind took over and drove us out of there. All the time I was screaming at her not to lose control, that she had to save our lives. It was Friday night and we were someplace in downtown Newark, and it was 1986 or 1987. No one would give us directions to the hospital; it seemed as if everyone was drunk or high. I kept jumping out of the car to stop cabs, but when they saw the blood they rushed off. Then, by some fluke, we found ourselves driving up a lawn to the back entrance of Beth Israel where, after a crazy altercation with a ten-dollar-a-day rent-a-cop with a noisy beeper, we drove over another lawn to the emergency entrance where, thanks to the fake cop, two doctors were waiting to rip my clothes off and save my life. I'd told the fake cop that if there wasn't someone waiting I would crawl back and kill him, even if it was the last thing I did in this life—I think I said "with my bare hands" for, after all, I was in the midst of a great drama—and that may have awakened him.

The one thing the doctors, the nurses, and the police lieutenant, who came later, said over and over was that it was a mistake to stop at the red light. "Why did you stop at the red light?" I was asked. "No one stops at that light!" I felt guilty, as if I myself were the perpetrator. It was as if Newark lived by a different set of rules. Certainly it was a battle zone and probably more intensely so in the mid-eighties than it is now in the twenty-first century, at least at this point. There is rebuilding and there is talk about rebirth. But the burning and the racial wars and the final flight may have been too much, and New Jersey may have lost its only true city.

Rosalind has written an essay about the event. Some of the differences in our memory are striking, particularly in details, but what interests me is the emotional difference, what we make—or made—of the shooting. She remembered the boys as eleven or twelve years old—I thought they were a little older; both in freshly ironed matching jacket and jeans, almost like uniforms; she remembers us going up a drive, at the hospital, into an entrance—I remember us driving across the lawn. We could either be right, or neither, and it makes little difference—it is how we received the event in our lives, how we absorbed it and located it. For her the initial emotional response was a mixture of shock, disbelief, and fear. Later, it was more anger, mixed with guilt, sadness, and frustration. My initial response was also disbelief and fear, though later it was mostly grief—and almost no anger. I don't mean to make an odious comparison; if anything, I am perplexed at my lack of anger, and if I comment on my own feelings it is not by way of either denigrating or elevating Rosalind's. I may have been only concealing or converting my anger; furthermore it is a quite decent and quite useful emotion—anger—one which I make use of all the time, and I get furious at soft-spoken cheek-turners who smile lovingly at the slaps, however their eyes are wet with pain, rage, and disappointment. It just didn't happen for me here. Also, Rosalind's experience was different from mine in two ways: she was driving and therefore felt responsible, and she wasn't shot, and I was. It was more than guilt, her pain; it was agony.

I know that I was more "accepting" of the event than she was. I never argued with the circumstances or raged against the gods. Nor, for a second, did I blame her. We did make a wrong turn off the highway, we did stop at the red light, we didn't leave ten minutes earlier—or later. That's that! If anything, I felt lucky. The bullet didn't kill me, the gun on her side misfired. There were angels watching over us and they had a hell of a time leaping from side to side of the car, deflecting and stopping the shots as well as they could, keeping enough blood in my body, helping us out of there, guiding us to the hospital. If anything, I am grateful, and I love and kiss everyone and everything involved. I regret Rosalind had to go through this. I'm sorry for her suffering. But I don't hate the boys and I'm not angry with them and I don't hold it against Newark. In a way, once it happened I was glad it did, which doesn't mean I wouldn't prefer that it hadn't. I suffered a few months from a stiff jaw and swollen neck, but there's no permanent damage except for the bullet that lodged in my neck and was never removed and, as I say, I forget it's there unless I'm telling the story to someone and press his or her amazed finger to the center of my neck, a little to the left of the windpipe.

MICHAEL PERRY

THE BIG NAP

Sometimes I go to the forest and prepare to die. So far, I've simply fallen asleep, but it strikes me that sleeping directly on the dirt is good practice for the Big Nap. I usually conduct these rehearsals while hunting. I'll put my rifle down and curl up on a patch of leaves, or settle against the base of a solid white pine—if the air is crisp and I can cop a patch of sun, *c'est magnifique.* Jack, my brother's beefy, half-Labrador mongrel dog, often tags along on these walkabouts, and if I stop to sleep, he drops to his haunches at my side, bull-chested and alert, sniffing and cocking his ears, seated but still on the hunt. As I drift off, I can feel him glancing down, impatient to move on. Eventually, he slides to the ground, drapes his jowls across his forepaws, heaves a deep sigh, and settles to his own rabbity dreams.

I've had the bug to sleep in the woods ever since I was a

child. My brothers and sisters and I—five of us—rarely slept in the house during the summer. We would gather at bedtime and traipse off to the woods, trailing our sleeping bags and dragging our pillows in the dirt. Out beneath the trees in the Breeds Woods forty, we'd lie on our backs and pick out stars, and speculate on the nature of the satellites that moved through the branches on their slow, straight line. I don't remember ever being caught in the rain, or worrying about bears or hydrophobic skunks. I also don't recall the mornings . . . whether or not we trooped home *en masse*, or just straggled home as we woke. We didn't always sleep in the forest. I can remember sleeping in the yard, although not often, because in the morning everything would be chilled and soggy with dew. I recall sleeping in the smooth concrete mangers of the cow barn, and we spent many nights atop the haystacks of the pole barn, burrowed into the bales twenty feet off the ground. Our sleeping bags were lousy with chaff.

But back to the woods. To sleep in the presence of trees and in the proximity of the earth is to get a sense of what it is to be holy. They say when Christ needed to get his head together, he did forty days in the wilderness. I stop at forty winks, but I believe I get a taste of what he was after. When I sleep on the forest floor, I never feel as if I'm simply taking a nap. I feel as if I'm performing some sort of embryonic ritual. When I awaken, I feel as if some important work has been done. This is not rest—this is ablution. By placing myself on the altar of the earth and retiring all my defenses, I am receding within myself, plucking a little transcendence from the perpetually gnashing jaws of time.

I am on the verge of rhapsodizing, so let me reframe: I'm no tree-hugger. I'm a tree-leaner, and a tree-sitter, and a tree-seeker, but I also have the ability to appreciate a tree in the form of a straight set of two-by-fours. I do not believe the trees are sentient beings, nor do I believe they have a spirit of their own. The trees do not speak to me. But I am pleased to take their shelter, pleased when they reinforce my smallness, pleased when they give me separation from the everyday static jamming my head. There is a big old white pine I like, deep within the same forty where we slept when we were kids. It is ringed with a blanket of shed needles, rusty orange and springy. They make a fine mat, and while the tree towers above me, I am equally humbled by the idea of the tremendous roots threading the soil beneath me, knitted to the earth, clasping the soil in a way we surface-running humans never do. Such gravity. I rest above them, and they feed me as surely as if they were joined to my own veins. I absorb their ballast, re-setting my keel for the journey back into a spinning world.

You have to get right down there. Don't mind the dirt—we need more of that anyway. Our society has gone bonkers for clean, but I fear—and research biologists are beginning to confirm—that all of this compulsive disinfecting will ultimately leave us vulnerable. I'm all for a little dirt in the gut, if only to hatch some resistance to a broad spectrum of microbaddies. So. Catch the scent of the earth. Smell that vital decay. Put your cheek to the rough skin of the planet. What you feel is time settling constantly into itself, and this is deeply reassuring. You belong here, you see. This is where your cells, your minerals, all the microscopic bits of you can best blend

into the cosmos. To seep gently through the leaves in a graceful descent back to the beginning of things. I have come to
think of my forest sleeps as a rehearsal for burial, and I have
come to wonder why anyone would sequester themselves in a
casket, sealing themselves away from the embrace of all this
peaceful dirt.

The earth is a fine cradle. We are all bound to sleep there.

As an EMT, you are at war with death. Collateral damage is
inevitable. And sometimes, in the middle of the battle, you
wonder why we fight at all. On a sweet spring morning, I am
struggling to push a Combitube down the throat of an elderly
woman when I glance up to see her husband, silent and teary-
eyed in the corner, and I wish we hadn't been called at all. I
wish he had simply put the phone down and held her hand as
she died. Instead we push back the little wooden table where
their coffee cups still rest, and we tear at her clothes, poke and
prod her, shock her weary heart, strap her to a plastic board
and scream away, and she will die anyway. The first time you
press on the chest of an elderly person, the ribs separate from
the sternum, popping like a string of soggy firecrackers. There
are times when rescue is nothing more than organized physical assault. Sometimes I wish we would just leave people be,
let them slip quietly over the vale. Sometimes life is not ours
to save. Driving east one day, I passed an abandoned farmstead glittering in the winter sun, and thinking of the hands
that built the tumbled wooden buildings, I suddenly saw
death as a peaceful thing, an opportunity to check out of the

game, to dispense with toil and trouble, an inky comfort in the unknown. No more appointments, no more petty recriminations, no phones, no more hurry or worry. Gonna be easy from now on, as the song goes.

When my brother died, we had a parade. First came the hearse, Eric's little casket curtained within, then a heat-skewed line of cars that stretched the length of Main Street, headlights switched on and sapped by the midday sun. We drove from the city of Bloomer—population 987, Rope Jump Capital of the World—and rolled slow and easy up and over the middling hills of County Highway F, northbound.

It was July. Hot, and the corn was coming on. Twin Lakes Cemetery lay fourteen miles upcountry, notched from a farmer's field half a forty shy of the Rusk County Line. Ten miles into the trip, we banked through the cambered sweep of Morley's Corner and strung out along the straight stretch running past the old Alan North place. The North place, with its patchwork pines and long dirt drive, was long ago flattened by a turkey farming conglomerate. My brothers and I always resented the giant irrigation circles that had replaced the tuckaway meadows, and by virtue of association, the men in the behemoth articulated tractors churning to and fro across the fertile dirt. Omnivorous dusty green bullies, they didn't so much till the land as rough it up and leave it humbled. But today, as we filed down the two-lane beside the factory fields, the man in the monstrous John Deere, its eight-row cultivator tailed by a scudding dust bank, drew his rig to a stop smack in the middle of the field. The dust bank converged on the cab and rolled beyond, and still he held his place, the tractor idling, until the whole quarter-mile-long run of cars passed. I thought of the missing man formation, in which a squadron of fighter planes performs a flyover and one craft separates, veering to the heavens. Howling ballet, starring killing machines. But it tightens my throat every time. The figure in the air-conditioned tractor cab was indistinct, but I wondered who he was and what was in his heart as he held the clutch down, his steady foot restraining the diesel while it knocked and grumbled, raring to plow to the end of the row.

All around these townships, I see the dead. It is landscape as sepulcher. There's the school sign erected in memory of Tummer Olson; there's the ski hill where Lisa Stansky died; in that house we found an old woman gone in her bed; here is where Harry lay; there is the house from which they ran with the Jensen baby, too late. Bill shot himself in that cabin, the train hit Jake right at that bend. How important this is, this constant remembering, these unremarkable memorials. Every death is a memory that ends *here*. These are stakes to peg your history on. Be grateful for death, the one great certainty in an uncertain world. Be thankful for the spirit smoke that lingers for every candle gone out.

BILL CAPOSSERE

THE MUSEUM OF OBSOLETE COLORS

From the outside, the Museum of Obsolete Colors looks like a giant open box of crayons. A long rectangular structure, its upper third, through some clever stonework, is seemingly hinged and pulled back so as to reveal tiered rows of larger-than-life faux crayons. The crayons originally covered the full spectrum of colors, but the wearing of time and weather have produced in most a sort of uniform pastel, so it is often difficult to distinguish, say, between indigo and sky or magenta and maroon. Many of the crayons as well have become the favorite perch of the city's pigeon population, whose leavings have over the years produced the effect that the dominant color is not even a color, but simply a dull shade of white. Still, here and there, a few have stead-fastly resisted the depredations of time and nature, and in those moments when a shaft of sunlight breaks through the

usual cloud cover even longtime natives of the city will slow
their strolls along the street to look up at the sudden raft of
color unfurling in the air above.

Walking back through unfamiliar streets, less familiar even
than yesterday's as you seemed to have somehow gotten off
course from the path back to the hotel, your attention had
been immediately captured by the building, and despite that
it was already late and you were if not lost at least momentarily mislaid, you stopped and turned to face it more fully
from across the street. Just to look, but that was enough for
your youngest to glance up from the ice cream he had extorted
from you on the previous street corner which had proven yet
again to not be the one around which the hotel lay and it was
his sudden movement to cross the road, you tell your wife as
you dress for bed, that drove you off the curb and somehow,
minutes later, inside.

"Flesh," she sleepily guesses. "And Indian Red." And you
wish she would stop because though she is right it was so
much more than that and though the words form pale and
waxen in your mouth you know you could if you had a
chance explain to her how it was more than just kids and
Crayolas. How it was about birds that no longer fly and
apples that no longer propagate. About reflections off surfaces that no longer exist and robes that no longer clothe.
How it was even, at the end, about the way the light seems to
fall on the small exposed place on her neck where her hair and
the sheet almost but do not quite meet, the way the skin softly,

pinkly bridges the contrast between the stiff bristly black of her hair and the starched white of the fabric. You would tell her all this and maybe even more. But then she reaches for the lamp and the cover slips farther down her back and in the sudden colorless dark what now could there be to say. So yes, you say, Flesh and Indian Red.

And Prussian Blue, though she does not recall that one. And telling her you picture the row of animatronic soldiers in their dark blue uniforms marching off toward a horizon of the same color though now it is called Midnight Blue. Over the crack of rifles and the larger boom of cannon a voice-over repeated in dull metallic tones the rise and fall of the Prussian nation. The whole thing a bit corny you say and even a little sad—the soldiers stiffly outdated, flecks of silver metal showing like the pox under their face paint, their uniforms frayed and forgotten much like their history, and your youngest, you tell her, watched for only a bored moment or two before moving off to the next exhibit.

Despite its failed attempt at spectacle, however, or perhaps because of it, part of you enjoyed the show and by the time you turned away your son was standing at a low counter, carefully dipping his hands in and out of shallow depressions filled with warm colored wax to determine which best matched his skin. Behind the counter, an ethnically ambiguous guide tested the heat of the waxes, handed out warm towels, helped people pluck at wax that had cooled and stuck to their skin.

So yes, Flesh, bleached now of possible offense. And later of course Indian Red. But before that you will confess to your wife how you left your son there at that second exhibit, peeling strips of colored skin from his hands and arms, shedding flesh by the foot and leaving behind shrunken husks of himself. You could not stomach the way they piled up around him like so many discarded selves, flesh of your flesh going formless and cold, so you told him you were just going to wander about, then stole away softly, folding cowardly into the jostling crowd.

And how in the dark will you describe out loud the strange chambers, the colors that you found? The Emperor's Room and its grand parade of stern-faced mannequins, each clad in a blue-red so rare it was forbidden to the masses to wear on pain of death. Tyrian Purple—created from the crushed pulp of forty thousand saltwater snails gathered by hand from the now-submerged sands of Phoenicia. The Garden Wing: whole orchards formed indoors of archaic trees, color pooling in their branches like drips of paint: forgotten fruit, their taste and skin shade long faded away—Yellow Transparents, Rabun Golds, Red Detroits, Stroat apples hanging a more yellow-green against darker leaves.

One room seemed rather a courtyard open to a wide blue sky, but not, it turned out, because the sky was in fact visible, but because at just that moment over just that spot millions of passenger pigeons chose to take flight, and while parts of them—their bellies, their beaks, their folded legs—were some pink and some white and some pale or bright red, the shoulders and heads and wing tips were an unnamed blue, not indigo blue or midnight blue or Prussian Blue. Paler than those, paler even than the sky blue you had first thought it was; almost gray, blue-gray, and when they took off it must have looked, you thought, to those with the survivor's eyes to remember like the whole of Lee's army at Gettysburg had taken sudden timorous wing, leaving the earth and its muddy, bloody ground behind before it pulled them under forever.

And it was here, you say, between Passenger Pigeon Blue and Absinthe Green that your son, pink-skinned and sore, finally found you. But by then she is asleep and so will not hear as you try to figure out what it all means. And you are left blind to trace in the night with your eyes closed tight all the variegated paths that have led you here to catalog alone in the dark the lost hues and shades by a slumbering wife whose hair once black as a starless sky is like her eyes as well as all the world turning surely if slowly to gray.

MARVIN BELL

FOUR

The Cosmosphere

At the Cosmosphere in Hutchinson, Kansas, you can touch capsules that went into space. Many of the vehicles look like Frank Gehry designs after a night of Guinness. Giant tinker toy constructions, their Mylar sleeves looking like cheap red and gold tinfoil, sprouting antennas that seem to have been bent into shape by the local mechanic. The Americans and Russians linked up in space through an accordion. The astronauts relieved themselves into tubes and pouches stuck to their private parts. Complex machines sent to explore the universe look like a gathering of lobsters. You see it all and come away thinking your old piezo-electric crystal-controlled oscillator, the twenty-watt transmitter you built as a teen, could have been a rocket ship. All museums are like that. It's the humanness of history that lingers. The brilliance, obsessions, and rage of mankind. Tour the Holocaust Museum in D.C. and you know again the banality of evil. The piles of shoes, the sick logic, the obsessive record-keeping. At the Museum of Natural History, it's the dinosaurs that bring in the children. They like seeing something that isn't us. Uncle Nat took me to the Museum of Natural History while my parents visited my grandmother in the Bronx. He told me he was an FBI agent on a day off, his gun and badge at home in a drawer, but he was actually a janitor at the New York offices of Warner Brothers. We knew he entertained at hospitals, but not what he did. Then he appeared on the Ted Mack Amateur Hour—playing kazoos. My mother felt embarrassed before her mah-jong pals. But Uncle Nat, lacking a drum machine, did what he could do, as Wernher von Braun did what he could do, and others did what they could do or were put up to. Everyone and everything imitates someone or something else. Space travel imitates falling. On the blackboard of outer space, we draw pointed stars, round suns, and aviators slowly tumbling while they labor to make things go down.

A Brief History of the Time

I don't believe in time. I believe in entropy, but not time. Once I knew why, but when it came to me why I didn't believe in time, I neglected to write it down. So I can't tell you why I don't believe in time, but I don't. I feel funny saying so and thus I rarely do. But I did speak up one evening at dinner with friends. Then I sat back, expecting funny looks. Instead, someone said, "Stephen Hawking doesn't believe in time either." "No kidding," I said, pleased that a notable physicist thought so too. "I didn't know that," I said, at which Dorothy looked at me with what Hawaiians call the "stink-eye" and said, "I GAVE you the book."

On Language

A kiss is just a kiss, but a sneeze is a small heart attack. That sound of a sudden sneeze is part of everyone's second language along with ow's, ouch's, ach's, arghh's, the throat-clearing Yiddish *ch* when it goes on and on, orgasmic cries, and a lexicon of sounds that don't make the dictionary. Sylvester Quinitchet made a bee sound in the back of the classroom whenever he did the dance of the zipper on the fly of his pants. While he ran his zipper up and down, Sylvester hummed like Leroy "Slam" Stewart, the great jazz stand-up bass player, though I'm pretty sure Sylvester had never heard of Slam Stewart. Sylvester made another contribution to the language, too. He'd say, "Well, tickle my wig." Was it funny, defiant, sexual? One never knew which aspect was dominant. He said it in amazement or dismissal, he said it to friends and teachers, he said it when he had nothing else to say. I heard that Sylvester died when a dump truck backed over him. I imagine him saying, "Well, tickle my wig," before the other things he said, all of them heartfelt, none of them in the dictionary, every one of them spoken daily all over the planet.

Echoes

As students, my friends and I decided to establish Meat Loaf University, the motto of which would be "Man does not live by bread alone." Professors were to be paid for their vigor, which meant they would be hired at top salaries and their pay reduced each year. One of us made a Meatloaf U breadboard, its cutting surface encircled by decals of dancers. Another made the crucial item, the Meat Loaf Flag, which proclaimed in words and images, moons and stars, the subjects we would offer: wizardry, juggling, and so forth. Our muse was a naked cherub. No one passed a law saying we couldn't burn our flag. No one was required to salute it, or fold it just so, or display it. It could stay up in the rain. It wasn't "loaded," it was a symbol of promise, imagination, and freedom. Well, I know about flags. Flags of surrender, semaphores, checkered flags, the Jolly Roger . . . Each July 4th, I was assigned to play taps at the cemetery. It was adorned with small flags at grave sites, and larger ones near the folding chairs, and of course the military marched in with the largest flags. At first I was given the role of echo. I preferred being the echo because I could walk away from the crowd and go linger among the dead. My echo was enlarged and sweetened by the tombstones around me. I imagined the audience hearing it and realizing that it meant distance. The dead were not sleeping, they were gone. Later, I had to stay with the crowd and play the first taps, not its echo. It sounded brassy to me, not sweet like the echo. Not bitter-sweet like the meaning of the echo. The imagination is a survival skill. After a while, an echo is enough.

S. L. WISENBERG

MARGOT'S DIARY

Photos: Anne, 1941; Margot, 1941

They both part their hair on the left side, wear a watch on the same wrist, have the same eyebrows, same open-mouthed smile. Their noses and eyes are different, the shape of their faces, the cut of their hair, the fall of it. Books are open in front of each of them. One photo we glance past. Because she is unknown. We don't care what she looks like—she's vaguely familiar. Not the real one. She is the sister of. The shadow. The first child who made way for the second, the important one. Who is more alive. Whose photo is crisp in contrasts, not blurry.

The Diaries:

Margot kept one, you know. She was the daughter known to be smart, studious, reflective. Hers was lost. Among the many items lost in the war, among millions. Perhaps her diary was darker—she was older, quieter, frailer. More naturally introspective. Perhaps she did not write that she believed that people were good at heart. (Which is something Anne believed only some of the time, anyway.) Perhaps Margot did not rejoice in nature. Perhaps she wrote: "There must be something wrong with us or else they would not be after us. We are cooped up here like mice. Anne is the only one who seems not to know we are doomed but she may be the bravest of all. We learn our French for what. In order to learn our French. We will be so warped upon our exit here that if we ever do escape, if there ever is freedom, we will not be able to live among the others. We shall be marked more than by the outline of the yellow badges."

Why We Like Them:

They were suburban and then urban. They had bicycles and birthday parties. We know how to put both of those things together. Or whom to call to arrange them. The girls were just like us—the thrill of the avalanche missed.

Not that we would ever sacrifice someone else—

In the Anne Frank *Huis*, Amsterdam:

Which was not a house, but an apartment over the office where her father had been in business selling pectin for making jellies, and spices for making sausages. In July 1992 a young girl on a tour smiles in recognition of Anne's familiar

face in a photo. On the wall are French vocabulary words
Anne copied out:

la poudre à canon	[gunpowder
le voleur	thief
la maison de commerce	business firm?
le conseil	advice
de retour	returning back
le gluie (het glure)	glue?
le musée	museum
la cause	cause
le bouquet	bouquet
l'éducation	education
envie	desire
après-demain	the day after tomorrow
avant-hier	the day before yesterday
le sang	blood]

Five thousand visitors a year stream into the old narrow
house. Often, there are lines.

In Frankfurt:

There's a plaque on the door of the duplex that was the first
Anne Frank house, which the family left the year of Hitler's
election. They went west, to Aachen, then Amsterdam, for
safety. Someone lives in the house still; it's private, not open
to the public. The neighborhood is outside the center city, an
area where young families set up hopeful households in the

late 1920s and early 1930s. Streets named for poets, three-story stucco buildings. Cars are parked all along both sides of the street. You can hear TVs, dogs, birds, children playing. Occasionally a bike rider glides past. I wonder if it was as leafy sixty years ago. There should be plaques on houses throughout Europe: a Jew lived here and was taken away.

Anne was four when they left in 1933; Margot was six.

Perhaps Margot remembered:

"Frankfurt, the house, the neighborhood, the protected feeling of it, safe, bright, like in the country, but the excitement, too, the newness of it. The best of everything, said my mother: Brand-new sturdy outside, delicate antiques inside. In Amsterdam, we learned to see vertically, to look up and down. All is narrow and the streets are crooked and thin. Contained. I was sorry to move away from everything familiar. From my native language. Everything in Amsterdam is approximate. And old. Compare the contrast. In Amsterdam we find what is already here. Someone else has already named everything. Anne, I don't think, really understands what is happening. We brought our old grandfather clock with us here, because it too is tall and thin. Ticks like a soft heartbeat, brooding over us."

Perhaps Margot grieved:

"July 1942. To leave yet again another house, in Amsterdam. They have named me. The Nazis have found me. They know I am here. A postcard ordering me to pack my winter clothes and appear for a transport to Germany. Instead I left the house, rode my bicycle with Miep to what became the Annex. Rain protected us; no one stopped us. And we arrived. I was the first one in the family to enter it that day. The boxes were already there. Night fell.

"July 1943. Over time I grew quieter and quieter, they said. My thoughts raged inside, then slowed. Everything slowed. I followed the course for French, for shorthand. At night we went downstairs to file and alphabetize for the company—for its benefit, for ours, a slender thread connecting us to the real world, commerce.

"We could not get away from the chime of the Westertoren clock, every quarter hour. It surprised me each time; nothing seemed predictable about it. I missed the steady ticking of our clock at home, imagined it slowing down to match the winding down of my thoughts. My stomach throbbed, my head. My heartbeat pounded in code. It is time to die. That's why I was so quiet, in order to hear the heart's message. I couldn't tolerate Anne's chatter. I abhorred singing."

Margot also didn't write:

"Of the day they came for us, August 4, 1944. It was late morning, happened fast. I gathered some bread, a Bible, a threadbare sweater—buttons missing. We tramped out, like machines set in motion. The sun hit us for a moment before we were herded into the car. Silent, of course, on the way to the station. Anne couldn't bear to look out the window. I did. Hungry for the familiar but impersonal landmarks. Signs in

Dutch and German. German, the language we no longer memorized. Everyone was thin. But their hair shone. Wind riffled through skirts. That's what we'd been missing: the benign unpredictability of the breeze.

"You can imagine the rest."

At Bergen-Belsen, Winter 1945:

Margot ran out of language. Everything seeped from her. She was barely eighteen. Her name appeared on lists of people who didn't come back. The day of death unmarked. She left no papers behind that were gathered up and stored in a file drawer in a *maison de commerce* in Amsterdam, then translated, published. Of her family, only her father came *de retour*. The Annex is now a *musée*. It is a center for *l'éducation*, to search for *la cause*. Margot has lost her *envie*. It no longer matters if it is *après-demain* or *avant-hier*, she has lost today, the glue that binds one minute to the next, as once marked by the German-made grandfather clock. Her *sang* is as dry as *poudre à canon*. Time is the *voleur*. She offers no *conseil*. This is not her *bouquet*.

JANE BROX

SALT HAY

FROM "GRANGE"

Perhaps it's only that my father had no time for the sea and my mother was always dreaming of it, but sometimes I say *salt hay* to myself again and again for nothing beyond the pleasure of the slight discord I feel between the two words, discord of both sound and sense. *Salt:* the one curt syllable glints sharp and stinging. To stand at the headlands and smell it, however much you love the ocean, is to know there's no sheltered world. Steadily roaring breakers are constant in your ears, you gaze into infinity, whatever weather moves out over the water and curls back contains a fierce and renewed strength. But *hay*, with its open *a*, is assuaging, and suggests an infinite calm: it belongs to an inland world, and lies at the heart of agriculture, for hay must always be made, and does not exist without human effort. Cultivation itself is a dream of shelter against the unpredictable, and essential to our dream of it is the sweet and redolent smell of cut grasses blooming and deepening on the air, then diminishing as the harvest dries and burnishes. In those marshes alone, on the margin between land and sea, salt and hay shoal one into the other, each word claiming the shifting boundaries of both worlds. A scythe sweeps the grass, somewhere out beyond the surf a buoy bell clangs. *Have salt in yourselves*, says Mark, *and have peace one with another.*

TERRY TEMPEST WILLIAMS

REVISION

When I was young, I fell in love with a fly fisherman. His preference was always toward small streams, tributaries to the Missouri. He dreamed of retiring in Montana.

He would walk the creek's willowed edges, halfway hidden, his fly rod in hand with an eye upstream and down for trout. And when he saw the sweet risings of lips to water, he entered the current.

This fly fisherman would stand thigh-high in the Madison with rod in hand and make the most beautiful undulations, waving with his right arm, pulling line with his left. Back and forth, the bamboo extension of himself would arc above his head seconds before he cast his line of light.

"It is an art that is performed on a four-count rhythm between ten and two o'clock," Norman Maclean writes in

A River Runs Through It. This I saw on the river and recognized as the hours we secretly inhabited. Ten at night until two o'clock in the morning. We were awake while others slept.

Letting the line gracefully slip through his fingers, he placed the dry fly (I believe it was a Royal Wulf) perfectly inside the eddy where he imagined the cutthroat to linger. The ritual of the cast like a tease was repeated again and again between the man's daydreams. The trout would strike. The man would smile with a quick flick of the wrist to plant the hook and then slowly reel the creature toward him until it was time to land the fish. Out of the water, the man would kneel on the bank with the rod between his legs, steady the trout (native trout), unhook the fly from its white upper lip (she feels no pain, he assured me), then return the fish cradled in both hands to the river (let her adjust and get her bearings), face the trout downstream, tickle her belly, and let her go.

Cutthroat.

Catch and release.

Our friendship was no different. It wasn't until he slipped with his tongue and said, "I made love to you because it was the only way I knew how to reel you in. I was afraid of losing you."

Catch and release.

To fish is to flirt. To flirt is to fish. Is this the sporting nature of love? Lips to water. We kiss. We bite the hidden barb. We are pulled out of the river and brought to shore barely breathing. Through the lens of a cutthroat's eye, we look up to see who has desired us.

That night, I pulled the hook of the dry fly out of my own lip and swam downriver.

Catch and release.

JOHN McPHEE

THEY'RE IN THE RIVER

FROM THE FOUNDING FISH

American shad are schooling ocean fish, and when they come in to make their run up the river they follow the deep channels. In the estuary toward the end of winter, they mill around in tremendous numbers, waiting for the temperature in the cold river current to rise. When it warms past forty Fahrenheit, they begin their migration, in pulses, pods—males (for the most part) first. Soon, a single sentence moves northward with them—in e-mails, on telephones, down hallways, up streets—sending amps and volts through the likes of me. The phone rings, and someone says: "They're in the river."

No two shad fishermen agree on much of anything, but I would say that if a female takes your lure, you know it from the first moments, or think you do, and you're not often wrong. If you have a male on, you may be at first uncertain, but then he displays his character and you know it's a buck shad. The roe shad is often twice the size of the buck shad. She may weigh five to six pounds, while he weighs two or three. Shad don't exactly strike. First there's a fixed moment—a second or two in which you feel what appears to be a snag (and might be); then the bottom of the river seems to move, as if you are tied to a working trampoline; and you start thinking five, six pounds, big fillets in the broiler, the grained savor of lemoned roe; but now this little buck shad—two and a half pounds—takes off across the river, flies into the air, and struts around on his tail. He leaps again. He leaps once more and does a complete somersault. He can't be said to be cocky, of course, but he suggests cockiness and pretension. He's all show and no roe. She doesn't move. Her size and weight are not at first especially employed. Yet here is the message she sends up the line: If this isn't bedrock you'd be better off if it were; if you're in a hurry, get out your scissors. She stays low, and holds; and soon you are sure about the weight and the sex. Now, straight across the river and away, deep, she strips line, your reel drag clicking. She turns and moves back, an arcuate run. You're supposed to keep things taut but often she'll do it for you. When, rising, she rolls near the surface, she looks even larger than she is. She, too, can leap, can do a front flip, but she obviously knows that her shrewdest position is broadside to full current. It's as difficult to move her as it would be to reel in a boat sideways.

Like salmon, shad return to their natal rivers and eat nothing on the spawning run. Like salmon swimming two thousand miles up the Yukon River, migrating shad exist on their

own fat. So why do shad and salmon respond to lures? Up
and down the river, almost everybody has an answer to that
fundamental question, but no one—bartender or biologist—
really knows. A plurality will tell you that the fish are
expressing irritation. Flutter something colorful in their faces
and shad will either ignore it completely or snap at it like pit
bulls. More precisely, they'll swing their heads, as swordfish
do, to bat an irritant aside. They don't swallow, since they're
not eating. Essentially never does a hook reach the gills or
even much inside the mouth. You hook them in the mouth's
outer rim—in the premaxillary and maxillary bones and
sometimes in the ethmoid region at the tip of the snout, all of
which are segments of the large open scoop that plows
through plankton at sea.

Three of us were in the boat, close and tandem. I was in the
middle, fishing over the shoulder of the skipper, Ed Cervone.
Fishing over my shoulder was Ed's son, Edmund Cervone. Each
of them had caught several shad, varying in sex, notable in size.
I had caught two roe shad. The sun was setting. It was seven-
thirty. Quitting time was upon us, but the rod in my hand was
suddenly pulled by a great deal more than the current. The Cer-
vones reeled in their darts and stowed their rods. They would
wait and watch, as people do when someone else in a boat has
a fish on the line.

It felt heavy. It maintained for some time a severe tug without much lateral movement. "Female," I said. "Six pounds."
Cervone the Elder, who has a doctorate in psychology, seemed

unimpressed—seemed to be suggesting, through a light shrug, that he knew bullshit by its cover. He knew he wasn't fishing with Buddy Grucela. He knew he wasn't fishing with Erwin Dietz or Gerald Hartzel—living figures in the Cooperstown of shad. He knew that in my seven years as a shad fisherman I had risen steadily into a zone of terminal mediocrity. And he was well equipped to empathize. Ours was one of twelve boats below and around the western bridge piers. Nearly all the others had been doing well, too. When that fish of mine came on the line toward the end of the day, a guy in the boat next to us looked over and said, "It doesn't get any better than this, does it?" At that moment, thirty feet of line came off the reel against the drag. I thought the line would snap.

You can learn a lot about shad just from their appearance. Their bodies predict what they can do. Nowhere is this as emphatic as in the deeply forked tail—the caudal fin—which is tall, and, as seen from the side, narrow. It is not as tall, narrow, and deeply forked as a tuna's tail, but it's getting there. Like the wings of a U-2, it has the high aspect ration (span versus width) that you associate with extreme high speed. The dorsal fin, like a sail rising up from the shad's back, is centered—midway from nose to tail. Dorsal fins in various fishes can be forward, or aft, or anywhere along the back. The centered ones speak of an ability to swim steadily, sustaining high speed. The range of the American shad is from northern Florida to the Labrador Sea, and within the range a typical individual will swim twenty-five hundred miles in a year. They return to their home rivers after four or five years. One look at that forked tail and you know that the fish is active in the middle of the water column and not sitting around on the bottom like a bullhead catfish, whose tail is so rounded it looks like a coin. A trout has a rounded tail as well, and, as a swimmer, is one notch up from a catfish.

When the fish had been on my line forty minutes, dusk had begun to gather. Forty minutes was twice as long as any shad had been on my line anywhere before. The bridge above, with its open-grate steel roadway, was humming with tires—cars in rhythm like breaking surf. On the bridge walkway were prams, strollers, couples on their way to dinner. In the festival ambience of New Hope and Lambertville, babies never sleep. People stopped to lean over and watch. They shouted encouragement. They hung around to see the fish. No fish. Just a taut line, a rod-tip high, an occasional plunge or lateral dash, a stripping run downriver. This was a scene from the nineteenth century below the old green bridge over the wide river between the two steepled towns, with narrow streets among riverine houses. Downriver past rapids was a stone tower—Bowman's Tower—rising from the top of a hill. And just above the bridge, off Lewis Island, Lambertville, a crew rowing a small boat was hauling a nine-hundred-foot seine in a great circle in the river, making—as the Lewis family has done since 1888—a commercial catch of shad.

More time went by. I'd had the fish on the line for an hour, and then an hour and a half. The guys in the boat next to us—now the only other boat—finally pulled anchor and left, mentioning something about their wives. There were people on the bridge who had been watching earlier, and had gone off to dinner, and now had come back from dinner and were watching again. One of them shouted, "Are you still catching that same fish?"

The free-flowing Delaware is the only main-stem major river in the forty-eight contiguous American states that is not blocked by a dam. A large proportion of the spring migration seems to prefer to spawn between the Delaware Water Gap and Minisink Island—a piece of river two hundred and ten to two hundred and forty-five miles from the sea buoy. Considerable numbers, though, continue. Those that reach the head of the river at Hancock, New York, have ascended three hundred and thirty miles, yet many of them keep on going. They go up the Delaware's tributary branches and swim on into a dendritic shrine—the streams of sacred origin of American fly fishing. They go up the Beaver Kill to the Willowemoc and sail through the trout at Junction Pool. What an experience it must be for a trout to see these argent zeppelins go by. Shad have been known to go on up the Willowemoc to the Little Beaver Kill, passing the Catskill Fly Fishing Center and Museum at Livingston Manor . . . Shad have been seen a mile up the Little Beaver Kill, four hundred miles from the ocean, where they were stopped by a ten-foot waterfall.

Shad vary, right enough. I thought of my own Olympic fish— two and a half hours on the line at Lambertville. Had I not interfered, she would have gone up to the Little Beaver Kill, jumped that waterfall, jumped the Catskill divide, swum up the Hudson to Lake Champlain and down the Richelieu River to Montreal, gone up the Ottawa to Lake Nipissing and down the French River into Lake Huron and on across Superior and up the Pigeon River to the Lake of the Woods and on to Lake Winnipeg and Reindeer Lake and Lake Athabasca and the Great Slave Lake (doing the Methye Portage in a heavy rain) and down the Mackenzie to the Rat, and up the Rat to the Porcupine, and down the Porcupine to the Yukon River, and down the Yukon River to the Bering Sea. It's a shame I ate her.

SANDRA SWINBURNE

ESSAY, DRESSES, AND FISH

For decades I believed that being ordinary precludes good writing, so I refrained. All the while, there was essay, modest and dignified and waiting to be noticed. Essay welcomes the ordinary, knowing that there are big things— true things—nestled within the small and familiar. Essay counts on the notion that good writing comes from good thinking from ordinary people on ordinary subjects. In some ways, it seems a simple thing.

In some ways, a fish seems a simple thing. I don't like eating fish—except for broiled salmon. I don't like catching fish—ever. Yet I love reading *The Founding Fish* because John McPhee reveals the American shad as a thing of wonder and there is pride in his voice as he proclaims: "I'm a shad fisherman." Of course, it's true that a fish is just a fish—except when it's not. And McPhee's fish is just a fish except when knowing, catching, and eating the American shad becomes a quest for truth about the at once fragile and sinewy threads of *being*.

What sort of life form is this fish that returns to its home river from the sea to give its offspring optimal chance for survival? Can this determination be distantly akin to parental love? Can courage be used to describe the behavior of a fish? What splendid signals instruct an American shad in the rhythm and purpose of its existence? What sort of life form is a man that he has the capacity to seek, see, research, reflect, describe, and devour the fish? I wonder.

McPhee reflects on the experiences of living as a fish and as a man and shows that their meeting in nature confronts ancient rules about what each fundamentally is. He knows that man has dominion over the fish, but he also knows that this role should be exercised with humility as well as pride. Yet doesn't it seem like the fish sometimes outsmarts the man? The pursuit of the shad becomes a tableau in which man can honor the essence of the fish as he honors his own stewardship as he honors the mysteries of life.

There are human constructs and choices that are against the natural rules of fair cohabitation—like dams and hydroelectric turbines—and they should be repudiated. Ideally, man *should* respect the fish—even while catching it and eating it. McPhee's good thinking about fish emerges as a blend of scientific information, quest psychology, ethical contemplation, ordinary observation, and a reverie on the intricacies of life. He is both witness and participant in a drama that is at once great and small.

In late April I drove from Rochester, New York, to Boston. From reading McPhee, I knew that it was time for shad to be swimming toward Holyoke to spawn, and I could hardly wait to cross the Connecticut River—to scan the shores for shad fishermen. I looked down from the bridge on the Mass Turnpike for a glimpse of an American shad on a line, I wanted vivification of McPhee's image: "little buck shad—two and a half pounds—takes off across the river, flies into the air, and struts around on his tail." It was raining hard, the car shimmied a bit on the slick surface and there were no fishermen in sight.

In Boston I spent a morning at the JFK Museum, then took to the city streets on foot. I examined the gravestones in the Old Granary Burying Ground. I brooded over the recurrent image of the lightbulb-shaped skull on many of the old tablets, some with crossed bones above. Forget the subtle urn and willow symbols of passing. Death is represented as *death* in this seventeenth- and eighteenth-century funerary art. I continued on to Faneuil Hall and bought a vegetarian wrap and iced tea to have while watching the street performers. It was nearly eighty degrees, the sky was perfectly blue and the sun was perfectly bright. A blindfolded young man walked skillfully across a makeshift tightrope and juggled while his lovely assistant fluttered near the collection bucket. My feet hurt from walking unskillfully on solid ground.

I wandered past the shops, resisting Boston tea towels and Irish knit sweaters. But the warmth and the blue and the bright of the day nudged me into an expensive-looking shop because its windows were full of flower-print springtime dresses and its sign read "April Cornell." Cautious about prices, I pretended casualness as I gravitated to the clearance rack. Yes, I did want a new dress for sixteen dollars and I was willing to brave the disappointments that lurk behind dressing room mirrors to get it. But sure enough, each chosen and tried dress was too small, too long, too flowered.

The nice, not pushy, manager must have noticed the "I'd love to have a sixteen-dollar dress" look in my eyes, or spotted my swollen tourist feet that had slipped the confines of their shoes. She appeared at the curtained cubicle with a dress of a larger size and a different style saying, "I know it's brown but trust me. It's good on." She was right, and limping but smiling, I went to pay for my new brown with banana swirl print dress.

At the register I thanked the manager for her visionary assistance and she offered to put me on their mailing list. My response of "No, I'm from Rochester, New York" led to conversation with another customer whom I discovered lives in Holyoke, Massachusetts. Feeling the tug of an idea that I hoped would take off, fly, and strut, I repeated, "Holyoke?" and she nodded. Anyone could see that John McPhee ought to be there, so I went ahead and dragged him out from under a rack full of yellow and pink voile dresses that were giggling over their own profusion of blossoms.

I told my fellow shopper—as if she didn't already live there and know—that there's a dam in Holyoke. She told me—because I don't live there and probably didn't know—that there were once mills there. She looked a little confused by my interest in the town dam, so I (informed by John) eagerly explained that American shad are spawning this time of year and there is some serious fishing near her hometown dam. "Not that I fish," I explained, "but I've been reading a book about it." She doesn't fish either and didn't seem to want to talk about spawning, so with my dress paid for, it was time for me and John McPhee to go.

I am left wondering why I wanted to talk about dams and fishing in that nice dress shop. What I know for sure is that John McPhee's good thinking and good writing made me want to think hard about the messy business of living. Could it possibly be that what we call courage makes a fish fight the hook and the fisherman for two and a half hours?

McPhee takes an ordinary thing and makes it so compelling that I earnestly took up his thinking, baited my hook with it, and tried casting my line in a spot where there was virtually no chance of a bite. In that dress shop, I seemed odd even to me, but I was hoping for an eyewitness report from Holyoke of what it's like to see shad seeking their place of origin year after year. I wanted another witness to give me another detail about what the living do to ensure life.

ALBERT GOLDBARTH

SOME CLOTHS

1.

The color wrung out of a wrung-out cloth, a flock of city pigeons on the roof is no one's notion of exalting. Lumped like wads of used-up hankie tissue, littered on prodigiously beshitted tiles . . . who could work up interest in their lax—their close to coma'd—doze in the vitiating late-afternoon Wichita sun?

But then a cue—invisible to me, and silent—clicks them into shared awareness . . . and, as one, they lift in the single undulant length of some Baghdadian flying carpet: keeping that roughly oblong shape, they sleek their aerial way throughout the maze that city skyline spires, antennae, and towers are to a flight of birds. They're one communal motion now, all zip and grace and speedy slink.

Invisible to me, and silent. . . . Not a sign: there wasn't any slam I heard, there wasn't any sudden, overlooming dangershadow, nor could I detect their alpha-pigeon shrugging subtle coded orders backward down his shabby ranks. Whatever it was, it passed for spontaneity. However it worked, its nanoincremental links engaged themselves somewhere below my threshold of perceptions . . . the same unknowable level where magic cooks, before the allakazzam of its being served well-done on stage; the place where quantum physics zizzles with its here-then-not-here, if-and-almost, sub- and anti-particles.

Amitov Ghosh: "For about five hundred years Aidhab functioned as one of the most important halts on the route between the Indian Ocean and the Mediterranean. Then, suddenly, in the middle of the fifteenth century, its life came to an end: it simply ceased to be, as though it had been erased from the map. The precise cause of its demise is uncertain." *That's* the level I'm talking about!—where cities-sundering vectors of climate/high priests/economic curves/political alliances . . . exercise themselves, like fault lines, miles under our ability to notice . . . except, of course, for the effects of those accumulated movements, finally immanent in the terms of our daily world. A city: vanished. A city: lost to sight as easily as a hen's egg up a magician's sleeve.

And in fact the magician reminds us that my reverie on Aidhab is misleading in scale. Every second, every inch, it happens; every time the atoms of a solid, any solid, decide—if "decide" is the word—to remain inside the field of the molecules of that solid, it happens. Under our notice: it happens. Here, in the world of our notice: we have "stone"/have "cloth"/have "flesh." A rush of pigeons: "rush" as a singular noun.

Below the table, inside the dark, the dozen unremarkable, preparatory steps get made. What we see is the bird in its astonishing arc from below the conjuror's hat, flapping in the air like a jellabeya snagged on a summer day's wind.

2.

One dandy understanding the politicians are pleased to have (and put to use) is that they *don't* have to lie: if only two half-truths are placed in a smartly artful proximity, *we'll* fill in the blank between them. What the brain has been evolved to do: make wholeness. It's how movies work: the brain makes continuity out of two distinctly separate visual units. "Life" and "afterlife": the mind imagines a link called "the soul," and moves it (often with a rich religious drama) across a ligature of its own devising. Give us point A-1 and point A-2, and we'll elide, we couldn't *not*.

It may be thirty-seven pigeon-language signifiers that ultimately get those birds airborne; and it may be a process that, to the view of a god or a hawk or a moon rock, is a staggered and gradual thing; no doubt, the orchestration of optic nerve and hormone-trigger and muscle-contracting across the population of a rooftop flock is multi- and omni- and pan-. And yet for us it's one gray tablecloth pulled off the roof: a *snap*.

And what of the fires that were burning up my Auntie Hannah, eighty-nine?—alone in the world (except for myself and my sister) and alone in its representative space for her: a Medicare hospital bed. "It's burning me up alive," she'd tell us seven, eight times in an hour; we could see the surface of her shrivel and blotch, her tongue crack in the act of speech. But no one—and here I'm including the corps of indifferent medical specialists—could see inside remedially to the cause. Those fires licking her clean were each just the size of one cell in her body. Every nucleus in her had its own inferno, somewhere underneath the line that separates the unknown from the comprehended. Calling this by a latinate name, a textbook designation weighty in syllables, didn't *explain* it at all.

And what of the dinosaurs? Something gigantic, naturally, it would have to be: the impact of a comet, at least, a crash the size of an ocean. Although the lesson of *The War of the Worlds* is that the monstrous military might of Mars is vanquished by a sneeze. It seems ridiculous to say it, it's so obvious: an invisible comet is equally unseeable as an invisible microbe.

Macrobe: why isn't *that* a word? Thóse ancient Mayan cities that were emptied of their populations seemingly overnight, the way a chrysalis is left behind, or the jettisoned flesh of the Rapture . . . these are terraces, though, and altars and avenues . . . monuments and granaries and hallways of empiric power . . . those cities with names that sound so exotically floral to our ears, that hint at such exotic appetites: emptied of their people in the blink of a Mayan eye, abandoned and left behind like sloughed stone skins . . . with no clue of invasion, revolt, or rampaging disease. Whatever rock it was that toppled this Goliath of an ancient urban network, it's as deep beneath our notice as the algae in the bodies of the polyps that, by thousands, make a branch of coral we hold as if it's a single and uniform thing.

It's what I do with these two photographs—eighty-five years apart—of Auntie Hannah. She's four in the first, a wide-eyed child stiffly standing in a checked dress (with a matching bow in her hair of such enormity it looks like a lavish Amazonian jungle moth that's preening on a tiny cake-top figurine). In the second—only a month ago—she's eighty-nine, and already almost smudgily translucent in her illness; there are patches of tarnish under her eyes and, under her skin, the look of heavy webbing. What I do in my mind is fill in the blank between. I reminisce—invent, extrapolate, and reminisce—and make, between those poles, the bridging arc we call "biography." "A life."

"Knock on wood for me, kiddo." Right: "wood"; "diamond"; "brick"—as if in these we'll come upon a final, an unparsable, solidity to count on. Sure: as if that hard, impervious shape way off in the sky—that thick dark bolus—doesn't settle down somewhere on a rooftop as a scatter of birds.

3.

Amitov Ghosh: "I would go up to my room alone and listen to the call of the muezzin and try to think of how it must feel to know that on that very day, as the sun travelled around the earth, millions and millions of people in every corner of the globe had turned to face the same point, and said exactly the same words of prayer, with exactly the same prostrations as oneself."

The phototropic cells in a leaf. The gawkers at the premiere, as the sex goddess exits her limo: a star, and its magi.

On the all-nude side at Showtime Lounge, the strobes and the series of lights along the apron of the stage, and of course the poses of the dancers themselves, are all arranged to finally funnel attention to the erotico-gynelogical vee—shaved, this year, and often clit-ringed: there's no end to sexual fashion. The women are prideful, playful, paid well; and the men—whether only two or a full two hundred—are a single organism, a hive of an eye, obedient, following.

After a while, of course, the novelty wears off. And when a dancer steps offstage at the end of her three-song set, and opens the door to the wardrobe room—a sudden column of light in the relative dark, which marks the entrance to a world that's still forbidden to the audience—it's interesting to see the head of every man automatically turn to the door's six seconds of teasing promise, turn as if practiced, choreographed . . . perhaps we could say evolution *is* a million years of practice . . . as if this slice out of the darkness might reveal some amazing bodily sanctum even beyond the naked force of the official show.

On the roof of the building across from Auntie Hannah's room they land, then rise and circle like a kite, then land and individuate in the sun for a while, then rise and circle. All morning I watch them . . . when I'm not watching her, in her stuttering half-sleep. This is the time, her time, of breaking back to the body's constituent elements. This is the time of their being released.

And even so, she's alive again today. Is that good? There's some pain, but we still think it's good. My sister pats her forehead dry, then we both help Auntie Hannah sit up. "You know," she says, "I'll be with Uncle Lou soon." That's a chilling thought to me, but hey: this isn't about me. Auntie Hannah's smiling, as if she's just said a wonderful, comforting thing.

It's a morning of little miracles. For instance, the atoms inside the glass she drinks from . . . which aren't so different from the atoms in the air, or the walls, or my prickled skin . . . they *all* came from the furnace hearts of stars . . . the atoms inside the glass remain in the glass, cohere, don't effervesce away, and the glass is a glass.

The wall is the wall: a real nail could really be driven into it. My skin is my skin. The sheet on her body remains the sheet, as stable a shape as that square of birds, which rises now, a prayer shawl in the air, a wedding canopy.

BIOGRAPHICAL NOTES

Sherman Alexie grew up on the Spokane Indian Reservation in eastern Washington. Named one of *Granta*'s Best of Young American Novelists, he has published poetry, short stories, and essays as well. His honors include a PEN/Hemingway Award, a Lila Wallace-Reader's Digest Award, an NEA fellowship, and two awards at Sundance for *Smoke Signals*, a film based on his short stories.

Dorothy Allison is the author of several books, among them the best-selling novel *Bastard Out of Carolina*. *Two or Three Things I Know for Sure* was written for performance and has seen several productions. She lives in Northern California.

Susanne Antonetta is the author of *Body Toxic*, a *New York Times* Notable Book and winner of the American Book Award, and of the forthcoming study of alternative consciousness, *A Mind Apart*. She lives in Bellingham, Washington.

Peter Balakian is the author of five books of poems, the memoir *Black Dog of Fate*, winner of the PEN/Martha Albrand Prize for Memoir, and *The Burning Tigris*, a *New York Times* best-seller. He is the recipient of many awards, including Guggenheim and NEA fellowships. He teaches at Colgate University in upstate New York.

Kim Barnes is the author of two memoirs: *In the Wilderness: Coming of Age in Unknown Country*, for which she received the PEN/Jerard Fund Award, and *Hungry for the World*. Her first novel, *Finding Caruso*, was published by Marian Wood Books, Putnam, in 2003. She teaches at the University of Idaho.

Jo Ann Beard won a 1997 Whiting Foundation Award for *Boys of My Youth*. Her work has appeared in *The New Yorker* and *Story* magazine. She teaches at Sarah Lawrence College.

Marvin Bell is the author of sixteen books of poetry, including his selected poems, *Nightworks*, and most recently *Rampant*. His honors include the American Academy of Arts and Letters Award in Literature and Guggenheim and National Endowment for the Arts fellowships. He divides his time between Iowa City and Port Townsend, Washington.

Charles Bergman has written and photographed extensively on nature, and his latest book, *Red Delta*, won the Benjamin Franklin Award for Best Book in Science and the Environment in 2003. His work has appeared in such journals as *Smithsonian, Audubon*, and *National Geographic*. He teaches at Pacific Lutheran University in Tacoma, Washington.

Sven Birkerts is the author of five books of essays and a memoir, *My Sky Blue Trades*. He teaches in the Bennington Writing Seminars and edits the journal *Agni*.

Mary Clearman Blew grew up on a small cattle ranch in Montana. Her books include *All but the Waltz: A Memoir of Five Generations in the Life of a Montana Family*; *Balsamroot: A Memoir*; *Bone Deep in Landscape: Writing, Reading, and Place*. Currently she is Professor of English at the University of Idaho.

Jane Brox's most recent book is *Clearing Land: Legacies of the American Farm*, published in September 2004. Her other books are *Here and Nowhere Else* and *Five Thousand Days Like This One*, a finalist for the National Book Critics Circle Award. She lives near Brunswick, Maine.

Bill Capossere lives in Rochester, New York, with his wife and two-year-old son Kaidan. When he isn't home full-time with his son, he teaches high school English and continues to work on finding more museums to visit.

Ron Carlson is the author of five books of fiction, including *The Hotel Eden*, named a *New York Times* Notable Book and *Los Angeles Times* Best Book of the Year. His stories have appeared in *The New Yorker, Esquire, Harper's, Tin House*, and elsewhere. He lives in Scottsdale, Arizona.

Hayden Carruth has published thirty-one books, chiefly of poetry, but including also a novel, four books of criticism, and two anthologies. He has been editor of *Poetry*, poetry editor of *Harper's*, and has received fellowships from the Bollingen, Guggenheim, and Lannan

Foundations. He taught at Syracuse University and currently lives in upstate New York.

Kelly Cherry's most recent books are *We Can Still Be Friends*, a novel, *History, Passion, Freedom, Death, and Hope: Prose about Poetry*, and *Rising Venus*, poems. Her story collection *The Society of Friends* received the Dictionary of Literary Biography Award in 2000. She lives in Virginia.

Stephen Corey's essays have appeared in a number of periodicals, including *Poets & Writers*, *The Laurel Review*, and *Connecticut Review*. His tenth poetry collection, *There is No Finished World*, was published by White Pine Press in 2003. He has been on the editorial staff of *The Georgia Review* since 1983.

Michael Datcher is a journalist and spoken-word poet. His work has appeared in the *Los Angeles Times, The Washington Post,* the *Baltimore Sun,* and in *Testimony: Young African Americans on Self-discovery and Black Identity* and *Soulfires: Young Black Men on Love and Violence*. He lives in Los Angeles.

Ann Daum writes and breeds sport horses from her family's ranch, located in the White River Valley of south-central South Dakota. She winters in Budapest. In 1999 she received a Bush Artist Fellowship.

Stephen Dunn is the author of fourteen books, including *Different Hours*, winner of the 2001 Pulitzer Prize for poetry. A new book, *The Insistence of Beauty*, was published by W. W. Norton in 2004.

Stuart Dybek's most recent work includes *I Sailed with Magellan*, a novel-in-stories, and *Streets in Their Own Ink*, a collection of poems, both published in 2004 by Farrar, Straus and Giroux. He lives and teaches in Kalamazoo, Michigan.

Scott Ely's latest book is *Pulpwood*, a collection of stories, from Livingston Press at the University of West Alabama. He teaches at Winthrop University in South Carolina and spends as much time as possible in the Languedoc in southwest France.

Joseph Epstein is the author of *The American Versions, Fabulous Small Jews* (a collection of short stories), and *Envy*. He is currently at work on a book about contemporary friendship.

James Galvin is the author of five books of poetry, a novel, and the critically acclaimed prose book *The Meadow*. His honors include a Lannan Literary Award and NEA, Guggenheim, and Ingram Merrill Foundation fellowships. He teaches at the Iowa Writers' Workshop and divides his time between Iowa and Wyoming.

Albert Goldbarth is the author of four collections of essays and a novel. He has also been publishing poetry for over thirty years; two collections have received the National Book Critics Circle Award. His most recent collection is *Budget Travel Through Space and Time*. He lives in Wichita, Kansas.

Emily Hiestand is the author of three books, including *The Very Rich Hours* and *Angela the Upside-Down Girl*. Hiestand's writing has appeared in such places as *The Atlantic Monthly* and *The New Yorker*. Her honors include the Whiting Award, the National Poetry Series Award, and the National Magazine Award. She lives in Cambridge, Massachusetts, where she is also a visual artist.

David Huddle is the author of two novels, a novella, five collections of short fiction, five poetry collections, and a book of essays about writing. He teaches at the University of Vermont, the Bread Loaf School of English, and the Rainier Writing Workshop.

Barbara Hurd is the author of four books, among them *Entering the Stone: On Caves and Feeling Through the Dark* and *Stirring the Mud: On Swamps, Bogs, and Human Imagination*, a *Los Angeles Times* Best Book of 2001. She teaches creative writing at Frostburg State University in Maryland.

Samuel Hynes taught at Princeton University and is the author of several works of literary criticism. His memoir, *Flights of Passage: The Soldiers' Tale*, won a Robert F. Kennedy Award. He is also a fellow of the Royal Society of Literature.

M. J. Iuppa lives on a small farm near the shores of Lake Ontario. Her creative nonfiction has appeared in *Chelsea* and *Tiny Lights*. She has published three poetry chapbooks and a full-length collection, *Night Traveler*. Currently she is the Writer-in-Residence at St. John Fisher College in Rochester, New York.

Pico Iyer is the author of several books about cultures converging, including *Videonight in Kathmandu* and *The Global Soul*. His articles appear often in *Time, Harper's*, and *The New York Review of Books*. He lives in Nara, Japan.

Mary Paumier Jones's essays have appeared in *The Georgia Review* and *Creative Nonfiction*. She works as a public librarian in Colorado, and consulted on this volume. With Judith Kitchen, she coedited *In Short: A Collection of Brief Creative Nonfiction* and *In Brief: Short Takes on the Personal*.

Judith Kitchen is the author of two collections of essays, most recently *Distance and Direction*, and a novel, *The House on Eccles Road*, winner of the S. Mariella Gable Award. She lives in Port Townsend, Washington, and teaches in the Rainier Writing Workshop, an M.F.A. program at Pacific Lutheran University. With Mary Paumier Jones, she coedited two other anthologies of nonfiction (see above).

Verlyn Klinkenborg is the author of *Making Hay, The Last Fine Time,* and *The Rural Life.* He is a member of the editorial board of the *New York Times*, and his essays on rural life are a regular feature of that newspaper. He lives on a small farm in upstate New York.

Ted Kooser was named Poet Laureate of the United States in 2004. His prose memoir of place, *Local Wonders*, received a Barnes & Noble Discover Award. His most recent book, a collection of poems, *Delights & Shadows*, Copper Canyon Press, was awarded the 2005 Pulitzer Prize for Poetry. The University of Nebraska Press is publishing *The Poetry Home Repair Manual*, a book on poetry writing for beginners.

Stephen Kuusisto is the author of *Planet of the Blind*, named a *New York Times* Notable Book of the Year and *Only Bread, Only Light*, poems. He is a spokesperson for Guiding Eyes for the Blind and teaches at Ohio State University. "Night Song" is from *The Art of Listening* (forthcoming, W. W. Norton).

Paul Lisicky is the author of *Lawnboy* (Turtle Point, 1999) and *Famous Builder* (Graywolf, 2002). He lives in New York City and Provincetown, Massachusetts, and teaches at Sarah Lawrence College.

Sonja Livingston's nonfiction has won an Iowa Award and an AWP Intro Award, and has appeared in *Alaska Quarterly Review, Gulf*

Coast, Puerto del Sol, The Iowa Review, Brevity, and other literary magazines. She has just completed an essay collection, *White Girl: And Other Girls I've Been.*

Joe Mackall is the cofounder and editor of *River Teeth: A Journal of Nonfiction Narrative.* He has written essays and articles for *The Washington Post* and NPR's *Morning Edition.* He teaches at Ashland University in Ohio, and is working on a memoir titled *The Last Street Before Cleveland: A Blue-Collar Pilgrimage.*

Barbara C. Mallonee, a native of Wisconsin, teaches writing at Loyola College in Maryland. She has published fifty short essays in the *Baltimore Sun* and longer essays in *The Georgia Review.* "The American Essay: Where Spirit and Silence Meet" appears in *Minding the Light*, a collection of pieces on Quaker pedagogy.

Michael Martone by **Michael Martone** is Michael Martone's newest book. The book is made up of fifty Contributor's Notes, many of which were published in the contributors' notes sections of magazines.

Sebastian Matthews, the author of the memoir *In My Father's Footsteps* and coeditor (along with Stanley Plumly) of *Search Party: Collected Poems of William Matthews*, lives with his wife and child in Asheville, North Carolina. He teaches at Warren Wilson College and edits the journal *Rivendell.*

Rebecca McClanahan's most recent book is *The Riddle Song and Other Rememberings* (essays). She has also published four volumes of poetry and three books about writing. She lives in New York City and teaches in the M.F.A. Program at Queens University in Charlotte, North Carolina. www.mcclanmuse.com

Anne McDuffie lives in Seattle, Washington, where she divides her time between raising children and writing. She is currently working on an M.F.A. in the Rainier Writing Workshop. "Winter Wheat" is her first major publication.

Joanna McNaney recently completed an M.A. in English and is now teaching as an adjunct faculty member at Monroe Community College in Rochester, New York.

John McPhee is a staff writer for *The New Yorker*. He is the author of over thirty books of nonfiction, among them *Annals of the Former World*, which was awarded the Pulitzer Prize for general nonfiction in 1999.

Kent Meyers is the author of four books: *The Witness of Combines* (essays); *Light in the Crossing* (short stories); *The River Warren* (a novel); and *The Work of Wolves* (a novel). He lives in Spearfish, South Dakota, where he teaches at Black Hills State University.

Pamela Michael is a freelance writer and radio producer. She is cofounder and director of the River of Words Project, an international children's environmental poetry and art contest. She is an editor of *Travelers' Tales: Rivers* and *Travelers' Tales: A Mother's World*.

Brenda Miller is the author of *Season of the Body*, which was a finalist for the PEN American Center Book Award in Creative Nonfiction. She has received four Pushcart Prizes for her essays, and she coauthored, with Suzanne Paola, the text *Tell It Slant: Writing and Shaping Creative Nonfiction*.

Lawrence Millman has written for *Smithsonian, National Geographic, Sports Illustrated*, and other magazines. His books include *Our Like Will Not Be There Again, Hero Jesse, A Kayak Full of Ghosts*, and *Last Places*. When not on the road, he lives in Cambridge, Massachusetts.

Valerie Miner is the author of twelve books, including *Abundant Light, A Walking Fire*, and *Blood Sisters*. Her work has appeared in *The Georgia Review, Salmagundi, Prairie Schooner*, and elsewhere. She has had Fulbright fellowships to India and Tunisia and divides her time between Minnesota and California.

Dinty W. Moore is the author of numerous books, including *The Accidental Buddhist* and a forthcoming creative nonfiction textbook, *The Truth of the Matter*. He has published essays and stories in such journals as *Harper's*, the *New York Times Magazine*, and the *Utne Reader*, and teaches writing at Penn State Altoona.

Kathleen Dean Moore is chair of the Department of Philosophy at Oregon State University. She is the author of *Riverwalking*, winner of the Pacific Northwest Booksellers Award, and *Holdfast*. Her essays have appeared in *Discover, Audubon*, and *Orion*.

Naomi Shihab Nye's most recent books are *Is This Forever, or What?: Poems & Paintings from Texas* and *Baby Radar*. In addition to a book of essays, *Never in a Hurry*, she has also published a collection of very short nonfiction pieces, *Mint Snowball*. She lives in San Antonio, Texas.

Ann Pancake has been the recipient of an NEA grant, the Glasgow Prize, a Pushcart Prize, and a 2003 Whiting Fellowship. Her collection of short stories, *Given Ground*, won the 2000 Bakeless Prize. She lives in Seattle, Washington.

Anne Panning has published a book of short stories, *The Price of Eggs*, and has published fiction and nonfiction in places such as *Prairie Schooner, Black Warrior Review, The Florida Review, Bellingham Review, New Letters*, and others. Originally from Minnesota, she lives and teaches in Brockport, New York.

Lucia Perillo's fourth book of poetry, *Luck Is Luck*, will be published by Random House in 2005. In 2000 she was awarded a MacArthur Foundation fellowship. She is now at work on a collection of essays, *The Calling of the Loon*.

Michael Perry lives and writes in northwest Wisconsin, where he serves as a volunteer firefighter and EMT. His essays have appeared in *Esquire, Men's Health, Outside*, and *Road King* trucking magazine. His live humor recording, *Never Stand Behind a Sneezing Cow*, remains popular at seed corn conventions. www.sneezingcow.com

Lia Purpura is Writer-in-Residence at Loyola College in Baltimore, Maryland. She is the author of *The Brighter the Veil* (poems), *Stone Sky Lifting* (winner of the OSU Press Award in Poetry), and *Increase* (winner of the AWP Award in Creative Nonfiction). Her awards include a National Endowment for the Arts fellowship and a Fulbright Fellowship.

Katrina Roberts lives amid vineyards in Walla Walla, Washington, and teaches at Whitman College. Her books include *How Late Desire Looks* (winner of the Peregrine Smith Prize for poetry) and *The Quick* (selected by Linda Bierds for the Pacific Northwest

Poetry Series). Her work has appeared in *Best American Poetry* and the *Pushcart Prize Anthology*.

Richard Rodriguez, a journalist and an essayist, has written three collections of autobiographical essays—*Hunger of Memory, Days of Obligation*, and *Brown*—a trilogy describing the intersection of his personal life with America's public life. He appears regularly as an essayist on the *NewsHour with Jim Lehrer* on PBS.

Salman Rushdie is the author of eight novels, including *Midnight's Children,* which was awarded the Booker Prize, and *The Satanic Verses*, winner of the Whitbread Prize. His books have been translated into thirty-seven languages.

Longtime Coloradan **Reg Saner** has published four collections of poetry, three of which won national prizes. His essays appear in *The Four-Cornered Falcon* (Johns Hopkins) and *Reaching Keet Seel* (University of Utah Press). The selection here is included in his latest, *The Dawn Collector* (Center for American Places).

Luc Sante was born in Verviers, Belgium and immigrated to the United States in 1963. He is a book critic for *New York* magazine and has written about books, films, art, photography, and cultural phenomena. He has received a Whiting Writer's Award and a Guggenheim Fellowship. He lives in New York City.

David Sedaris is the author of *Barrel Fever, Holidays on Ice, Naked*, and *Me Talk Pretty One Day*. His essays appear regularly in *Esquire* and *The New Yorker*. His original radio pieces can be heard on *This American Life*. He has received a Thurber Prize for American Humor and was named Humorist of the Year by *Time* magazine in 2001.

Peggy Shumaker's most recent books are *Underground Rivers* and *Wings Moist from the Other World*. She is at work on *Blaze*, a collaboration with the Alaskan painter Kesler Woodward as well as a nonfiction manuscript entitled *Just Breathe Normally*. She lives in Fairbanks, Alaska, and travels widely.

Mark Spragg is the author of the memoir *Where Rivers Change Direction*, and the novels *The Fruit of Stone* and *An Unfinished Life*. He lives with his wife, Virginia, in Wyoming.

Gerald Stern is the author of thirteen books of poetry, including *This Time*, which won the National Book Award in 1998. His collection of personal essays, *What I Can't Bear Losing: Notes from a Life*, was issued in 2003, and a new book of poetry, *Everything Is Burning*, was recently published by W. W. Norton. He was the first Poet Laureate of New Jersey.

Lawrence Sutin is the author of *A Postcard Memoir, Do What Thou Wilt: A Life of Aleister Crowley, Divine Invasions: A Life of Philip K. Dick*, and the author/editor of *Jack and Rochelle: A Holocaust Story of Love and Resistance*. He has won a Loft-McKnight Writing Award and a Minnesota Book Award. He teaches at Hamline University and the Vermont College low-residency M.F.A. program.

Sandra Swinburne lives in Rochester, New York, where she raised four children. She recently completed an M.A. in English at SUNY Brockport. This is her first publication.

Amy Tan is the author of several novels, including *The Joy Luck Club* (for which she also wrote the screenplay), *The Kitchen God's Wife*, and *The Bonesetter's Daughter*. Her essay is taken from her first work of nonfiction, *The Opposite of Fate*, where she explores some of fate's opposites—lucky accidents, choice, and memory.

Joyce Thompson is the author of a memoir in essays as well as five novels, including *Bones, Merry-Go-Round*, and *Conscience Place*. She grew up in Seattle and environs and has been a writing teacher and an editor. She recently moved to Oakland, California.

Wang Ping came to the United States in 1985. She has published books of nonfiction, short stories, poetry, and a novel. She is the recipient of an NEA fellowship, a New York Foundation for the Arts fellowship, and a Bush Foundation fellowship. She teaches at Macalester College in St. Paul, Minnesota.

Terry Tempest Williams, an ardent environmentalist and naturalist, is a native of Utah. Best known for her book *Refuge: An Unnatural History of Family and Place*, she has also written *Red: Patience and Passion in the Desert, An Unspoken Hunger, Leap, Coyote's Canyon, Pieces of White Shell*, and two children's books.

S. L. Wisenberg is the author of a creative nonfiction collection, *Holocaust Girls: History, Memory & Other Obsessions*, and a short story collection, *The Sweetheart Is In*. She teaches in the Master of Arts in Creative Writing Program at Northwestern University.

Larry Woiwode's fiction has appeared in *The Atlantic Monthly, Harper's, The New Yorker*, and other publications. His novels include *Beyond the Bedroom Wall, Born Brothers*, and *Indian Affairs*. He lives on an isolated farmstead in southwestern North Dakota where he raises registered quarterhorses.

Janet Wondra's prose has appeared in *Denver Quarterly,* the *Christian Science Monitor,* and *In the Middle of the Middle West.* Also a poet and filmmaker, she has screened her work at art museums and film festivals across the United States and Europe. She heads Creative Writing and Film Studies at Roosevelt University in Chicago.

Paul Zimmer is the author of twelve books of poems, including *Crossing to Sunlight: Selected Poems.* His memoirs and essays include *After the Fire: A Writer Finds His Place* and *Trains in the Distance.* He worked as a scholarly publisher for thirty years and now lives on a farm in southwestern Wisconsin.

ALPHABETICAL CONTENTS

LIST OF THEMES

NOTE: Writers do not have "themes"—they have concerns. Readers find themes. At the risk of being reductive, I've listed several of the dominant ideas or images that I noticed while compiling these shorts, along with essays in which those concerns are evident.

America/Immigration/Settlers: Alexie, 133; Balakian, 264; Barnes, 97; Bell, 333; Birkerts, 128; Blew, 44; Galvin, 110; Hynes, 244; Kooser, 122; McPhee, 347; Miner, 307; D. Moore, 283; Pancake, 219; Rodriguez, 41; Sutin, 75; Tan, 88
Animals: Antonetta, 213; Bergman, 208; Goldbarth, 359; Hurd, 196; Kitchen, 152; Klinkenborg, 112; Kuusisto, 28; Matthews, 280; McPhee, 347; Meyers, 124; D. Moore, 283; Purpura, 81; Roberts, 107; Saner, 200; Swinburne, 354
Art/Beauty/Literature: Antonetta, 213; Birkerts, 128; Carlson, 173; Corey, 192; Dunn, 137; Ely, 147; Goldbarth, 359; Hurd, 196;

PERMISSIONS